Bunnyman

BUNNYMAN

Post-War Kid to Post-Punk Guitarist
of Echo and the Bunnymen

Will Sergeant

THIRD MAN BOOKS

https://www.thirdmanbooks.com/bunnymanbook
password: bunnyman

For more information:
Third Man Books, LLC, 623 7th Ave S.
Nashville, Tennessee 37203

A CIP record is on file with the Library of Congress.

FIRST USA EDITION
ISBN 9781734842289

Cover design and collage by Will Sergeant
Additional layout by Jordan Williams and Maddy Underwood
Front and back cover photos by Mick Finkler

To my girls: Paula, Alice & Greta

Contents

Station Road in the 1960s.

1.

Fried Beans

'Tequila' – The Champs

I am William Alfred Sergeant aka Will Sergeant aka Sgt Fuzz. This is my story from the beginning.

The Sergeants – that is mum Olive, dad Alf, sister Carole, brother Steven and me – all lived on the council estate on Station Road in the heart of the village of Melling. The houses on Station Road were built five years after the end of the Second World War. A massive building drive was in full swing; the new government, led by the reinstated war leader Winston Churchill, was rebuilding its way to a new future, after the six years of horror the European continent had just lived and died through.

Our family moved to Station Road in 1952. I am reliably informed by my sister that we were the first family to be housed on the road. It seems my grandfather Tom Sergeant – who was a Justice of the Peace and a rural district councillor – was not averse to using his power to help his own family out. A crafty push up the council house waiting list got the Sergeants a new three-bedroom semi-detached, complete with front and back garden. They are solid houses, built of a brown brick. These bricks were used in the construction of a lot of northern council houses of this period. I'm not sure how a brand-new sturdy

1

house can become so shitty in such a short period, but by the time I was aware of these things, I knew our house was a bit of a dump. I do not think we were poor compared to others in the street. The truly poor were called 'povos', a slang word for poverty stricken or skint.

Though Melling is only eight miles from the city centre of Liverpool, it was still far enough away for us locals to be called 'woolly backs', a derogatory term connoting an intimate relationship with a farm animal. It never bothered me much; I like being a woolly back. At least it wasn't the old classic 'sheep shagger', a term generally reserved for 'real' rural folk.

I always think of Melling as the place where Liverpool's sprawl ends and the countryside begins. In Liverpool, the perception of Melling was that it was posh. Well, it might have been in some parts . . . but not Station Road. We were the scum, the ruffians from the council estate. To be fair, there was a high proportion of nutjobs, criminals, wife beaters, drunkards and thugs – and that was just in our house.

Even though Melling felt very rural, there was a great big factory right in the middle of the village: the BICC. This stood for British Insulated Callender's Cables. They made all sizes of electrical cables. Lorries – or wagons as they were called back then – would constantly be leaving the gates of the BICC transporting these massive reels of wire all over the world. It seemed that most people in the village worked at the BICC, including many of my friends' mums and dads. The factory gave the village its own distinctive smell – a heady scent best described as a cross between burning plastic and Napalm, with a hint of liquorice. Not unpleasant, and almost comforting. God knows what those noxious fumes were doing to our pristine young lungs. Probably not that much, considering everyone smoked non-stop at that time: Senior Service, Capstan Full Strength and good old Woodbines, or 'Woodies' as they were more commonly known. Ciggies would be in the gobs or sandwiched between yellow-stained fingers of just about every man, woman and child you came across. Not much time was spent worrying about what this passive smoke was doing to the kids.

The village is carved up by the Leeds and Liverpool Canal. This exciting waterway was a playground for all the local children. It was always fun messing about down there, though it was only about three to five feet deep; a death trap by today's standards, but this was a health-and-safety free time. Kids would jump off bridges into the brown water. The canal was home to discarded barbed wire, old beds, bikes and general junk. The classic shopping trolley had not turned up at this point, simply because we had no supermarkets to nick them from. It's surprising that nobody got killed or injured. We would fish for tiddlers – sticklebacks – with nets on the end of bamboo poles. We would generally muck about clambering across swing bridges or making rafts.

Among the flotsam and jetsam of the canal, the occasional dead dog would float by. Back in the 1960s, dead or even still living old dogs would be best disposed of in the canal. Alsatians mainly would appear, their backs bald and blistered by the sun. These were possibly scrapyard guard dogs, too old, arthritic and well past their growl-by date. The sad and rotting beasts, bloated with gas, floated high, bobbed in among the weeds, caught by the wind sailing alongside the towpath, flyblown ears drooping and sad. They made challenging targets for a canal-side scallywag like me, armed with a brick (you had to make your own entertainment in the olden days). Even stuffing unwanted puppies or kittens in a sack and then chucking them into the canal was normal behaviour for some of the more nasty post-war adults. I am guessing that seeing people blown up in the Liverpool Blitz, witnessing death and destruction all around Europe in the not-too-distant past, hardens you up a little.

Liverpool had the shit kicked out of it by the Germans and bore many scars of the devastation. The bombed out St Luke's Church at the top of Bold Street is a permanent reminder of those grim days, still standing roofless and pocked with bites taken out of the stone by shrapnel. The city was once an architectural jewel in the empire, but now was left as rubble, peppered with bombsites. Plenty of those wastelands were still about well into the 1980s.

My mum, Olive, in the late '40s·

My mum Olive told me of a time when, as just a teenager, she'd been caught out by a bombing raid before she could get to the air-raid shelter in Walton. Walton is pretty much next to the docks at Bootle. Bootle was and still is one of Britain's main ports, a prime target for the Luftwaffe, the German air force. Mum was rushing to get to the shelter instructed by an ARP (Air Raid Precautions) warden, on his head a shiny black helmet bearing a white 'W' painted on the front. The warden was cycling along and clearing the streets of people. A bomb fell and exploded very close, sending flames and shrapnel all over the street. My mum witnessed the warden's head getting cleanly blown off his shoulders. The black helmet with the neat 'W' stencilled on the front spun into the air and landed with a clatter on the ground. The warden's legs peddled on for one or two rotations, then the bike fell to the cobbles. Mum ran as fast as she could into the relative safety of the shelter.

The war was very fresh to all my family. The effect and the memories of events such as this were still very strong. It was all the older people ever talked about; who could blame them? We, the children of the war generation, are still trying to make some sort of meaning of it all. It's easy to forget about how hard it must have been to live through all that shit. No wonder some were left with a coldness that never warmed up. Now TV is filled with documentaries about the war such as *Hitler's Henchmen* or *World War Two in Colour*, all very popular with people my age. It's a link to our parents and the crap they had to put up with.

At the start of the war, Dad joined the King's Regiment (Liverpool) and became part of the Eighth Army. His test for being assigned to this group consisted of being stuck in a field at the wheel of a lorry and commanded to 'drive that'. Dad managed to 'drive that' in a circle around the field. 'You're in,' they said. With that, he became a driver for Royal Army Service

Corps, assigned to the famed Desert Rats commanded by General Bernard Montgomery, or Monty, as he was known. The group now had a lovely brand new rat.

My dad, Alf, at the start of the war.

After basic training, off Dad went to Greece and the deserts of North Africa. As the war wore on, he was eventually stationed in Italy, driving a lorry delivering shells for the artillery at Monte Cassino. Cassino was the location of an infamous, some say pointless, battle. The Polish had been sent in first to capture the town; the remaining Germans were holed up in a sixth-century Benedictine monastery on the top of a hill. The American Air Force were bombing the crap out of the place to get the Germans out, but it took quite some time. The battered remains of the monastery created perfect spots to hide snipers. Lots more combat followed; it is calculated five tons of bombs were dropped per German soldier. The Allies finally won; the Germans were done for and on the run. I think, after the unpleasantness at Cassino, my dad liked his time in Italy. It was pretty relaxed – for a war, that is. He was there around the time that Italy switched sides and became our friends.

A little later, in the south of Italy, Dad was wounded. He told us he'd been shot in the head, his helmet saving him. He later confessed that it was not a wound inflicted by the enemy at all; it was friendly fire (in a way). His brigade had gone out on the piss to a southern Italian town (possibly Bari), with the entire squad crammed into the back of an army truck. Driven back by the drunken captain, the truck was weaving about the road, throwing the soldiers in the back all over the place, apparently as a jolly jape. Eventually, the captain drove into a ditch and turned the lorry over, seriously injuring quite a few of the men, including Dad. He sustained a bash to the back of his head. The injury left a hole big enough for a finger. I assume that beyond the skin of his scalp, it was possible to push on his brain. This head injury could explain his black mood swings. I say swings; they never really swung back, they just held their trajectory. They would get worse, coincidentally, when Liverpool FC lost a match.

After the accident, Dad was unconscious for nineteen days. When he came to, he was taken to Palestine for recuperation where he immediately got dysentery. He later told me that nothing happened to the captain with regards to a court martial or any kind of disciplinary action. My brother Steven even says the captain was mentioned in dispatches, which was basically a pat on the back for helping with the mess he'd created. 'Give the chap a medal' – a clever way to hide any wrongdoing by the toffs.

I look at the few battered old pictures of my dad as a young man, ones taken before the war and even some snaps taken with his pals early on during the war. They show a happy young bloke, smiling and full of hope. These starkly contrast with the reality of him as a dad with zero empathy. He was always angry with all of us. I can't put the two together. The happy, smiling face looking back from the 1930s photograph and the misery guts he became. I have a theory that the knock on the head and the resulting coma altered his personality. It closed him down. This could all be a kind of wishful thinking, that he had some excuse for being so cold and uncaring, or just a load of bollocks and he might always have been this way. I want him to have a reason for basically showing no love or compassion to the extent that my brother and sister still hate his now dead guts to this day. As soon as they could, they both left to live in London, around about 1970. After their departure, my parents didn't seem to worry about them or even mention them. They were just gone, like they never existed. I also never really thought about or missed them; it's odd. That was the way of the Sergeants: everyone seemed to be on their own from day one.

My brother and sister always tell me I was my dad's favourite; all I can say is they must have had it pretty bad if I was the favourite. Like most kids back then it was normal for parents' displeasure to be followed by an odd clout or clip round the ear. Our vibe was darker than just a smack round the lughole. It was the atmosphere that Dad exuded. The fear he instilled in all of us – and most of my friends too – was real. He was incredibly unapproachable and unwelcoming. I don't think he ever really had much time for any of his children. We were all a big inconvenience that got in the way of his boozing and were a burden on his beer money. Don't get me wrong: I'm not whingeing.

I'm not after sympathy and I'm not that bothered; it was just the way it was. This was our normal. I didn't lie in bed sleeplessly worrying about it all.

Eventually, this sort of angry loveless family life just turns you cold with no real understanding of feelings, as that's what you experience day after day. I now hate confrontations and will go out of my way to avoid aggravation, even if it's to my detriment. I overcompensate and put up with a lot because I don't want to ever be as cold as my dad. I know some things don't affect me as much as they should, while others affect me more than they should. It's all a bit mixed up.

My sister recently showed me an old note from my dad to my mum. Oddly, it's written on the back of Carole's baptism certif-icate — as though it was just a worthless scrap of paper. It says:

Dear Olive
    Have gone to Horse and Jockey and keeping you a seat in
Big Room Alf X

The 'X' denotes a kiss. Pretty normal, you might think. But it's the only evidence that I've ever seen that my parents must have at some time liked each other, at least enough to sit together in a pub. Seeing this tatty note freaked me out; I am still shocked. Even the beginning, where it reads, 'Dear Olive'; I can't remember my dad ever calling my mum 'Olive', and to use the term 'Dear' . . . that's so bizarre to me. It was generally 'she', 'bitch', 'mare', 'cow'.

One of the many puzzles of my upbringing is that I can't get to grips with my conception. I know this is an odd thing to worry about and most people don't even want to think about such a gross idea as their parents on the job, but let me explain. I had never been witness to any sort of kindness, affection or contact between them. As for love, this really weirds me out even to think of the word in relation to Mum and Dad. I once saw one of my friends' dad come into his house back from work at the BICC and give his mum a peck on the cheek, and then was even pleasant to her, just like it was something off *The Mary Tyler Moore Show*, *I Love Lucy* or some other American telly thing. Nobody does that in real life, do they? At first my parents did sleep in the same bed, but in the style known as top and tail. As soon as my older sister fled the family home in 1970, Mum immediately moved into the vacant bedroom. Yet I was conceived, or I wouldn't be here. My mum always used to say I was the result of 'one Mackies too many'. 'Mackies' is short for Mackeson, a strong stout. The TV advert at the time claimed Mackeson, 'Looks good, tastes good, and, by golly, it does you good.' Well, it did its job for one night in the summer of 1957. On that occasion, all hostilities were ceased.

I'm not sure if it was an invasion or if a white flag had been raised, but I'm here now and I'm not going back. I am, in art terms, mid-century modern. I was delivered in Walton Hospital on 12 April 1958. I saw a birth certificate years ago – lost now, of course. I don't think I was adopted or found in the cabbage patch; I have the ridiculous Sergeant hooter, so that kind of proves it. At least this saves me from forking out on all that DNA malarkey.

When I was born, Conservative Prime Minister Harold Macmillan resided in number 10 Downing Street. He was old school: a stern-looking chap with pinstripe trousers and black tailcoats, all finished off with a military-style moustache perched on his very stiff upper lip. Macmillan looked like someone from another time, another century (but then again, it was another century; he looked like he was from a century before that century); a character from a Victorian story about a tax collector or petty official. Shortly before my birth, the Soviets spat the shiny, polished orb called Sputnik 1 into space. The ominous beep the satellite transmitted served its purpose: to put the shits up the West – mainly the Americans, who immediately started propelling their country into a very costly space race.

Dwight D. Eisenhower was soon to become the first US president to be broadcast in colour on TV in the States. A couple of years earlier, fuelled by the black blues music bubbling under the mainstream, Bill Haley had rocked around the clock. This in turn lit a fuse of the rocket Elvis Presley was perched on, ready to ride it straight into the world's consciousness. The resulting explosion showered the globe with brilliant sparks that floated down to Earth like dandelion seeds. They rooted themselves in the minds of anyone with enough fertile loam between their ears. This would nurture a new musical way of thinking, the resulting crop blossoming into the likes of the Rolling Stones, the Beatles, the Kinks, the Doors, the Velvet Underground and a billion other great bands.

All this is going on outside the confines of my white painted cot. I sleep obliviously as the rock 'n' roll revolution is being waged, a revolution that will still be going as I sprout into a teenager. It will change our lives forever: exciting times for the young William, fresh out of the egg.

The first thing I can remember is being in a highchair, snot clogging up my nostrils, Heinz tinned spaghetti running down my face, on to my bib, the warm squelch of shit in my nappy and an inane smile on my stupid little face. I was at Mrs Bridson's house, located a few doors up on the other side of the road from our house. This lady would look after me while my mum was at work.

I also have a misty memory of being tucked up all cosy in my pram, staring at the blue, cloudless sky. Mum and I are waiting for the number 307, a bright red bus from the local public transport operators Ribble. Our destination: the butcher's shop in Walton Vale, Liverpool. On one trip to 'the Vale', Mum recalled how she had forgotten me and went home without the pram, leaving me still farting and gurgling outside the shop. I am assuming this was an accident; I know I'm extremely annoying now, but then? I was sweet and innocent of all charges, and I'm sure a chubby joy to any mum. I was only about one year old at the time. After she realised her mistake, she got off the bus and went back. I was still in the pram where she had left me, happy as someone called Larry.

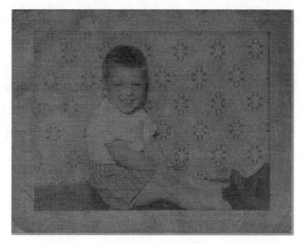

A young Will Sergeant, fresh out of the egg.

Our visit to the shop was more than likely a mission to buy chops. It was always chops back then, or lamb's liver. This was when lamb chops were the cheap option. These bony treats had a sorry destiny: a cast iron cremation. Send no flowers; just mint sauce. Other delicacies we had back then were pig heart, cow heel, oxtail, salt fish, mincemeat and black pudding. We had white sliced bread with every meal, soaking up gravy, beans or general food juice. I would mop my plate clean and never left a scrap of grub.

My favourite dish by far was the Saturday morning bacon-and-egg fry up. Most things were fried in our house back then. My mum even fried baked beans; she would put them in with the fat left in the pan by the frazzled bacon. I have to say, I liked them done this way; it took the humble bean to another level, the beans shiny and bobbing about in a lovely, lardy sea. Obviously, in these health-conscious times, I am too scared to try them now, just in case I become addicted.

The only food that escaped the frying pan was any sort of vegetable. I say any sort; in those days, it was cabbage, sprouts,

swede, carrots or peas. As far as I can remember, no other vegetables had been invented – not in Melling, at any rate. They
were boiled and boiled and then boiled some more, until they
were all squishy and just an anaemic gloop, like a smoothie –
only with all the nutritional value removed. I don't think our
family was the only one to do this. I think it was common culinary practice. The slightly crunchy legume was only to hit the
north in the late eighties.

In 1958, the Second World War had only been over for a mere
thirteen years. This sounds like a long time; it isn't. Thirteen
years are like a blink of an eye. Wartime rationing had only
stopped a couple of years before. I'm pretty sure my dad kept it
going in our house till the seventies. The war had ended in an
uneasy peace, culminating in the Cold War (my favourite war,
by the way), the victors squabbling over the spoils – the spoils
being what was left of Germany, and control of Eastern Europe.
Time trundles on. The Soviets decided to mark my third birthday, 12 April 1961, by flinging Uri Alekseyevich Gagarin into
space atop a Vostok rocket for a quick sightseeing excursion: one
complete Earth orbit. It seems like a lot of fuss; a simple card
would have sufficed. I feign gratitude and give him a little wave
from my pushchair. I could have dreamed that bit; it was a long,
long time ago.

2.

Caterpillar Rash

'Please Please Me' – The Beatles

Summer 1963. I am four years old. The Beatles are some way through their bid for world domination. On our radio, they belt out 'Please Please Me'. My sister Carole is in the house, singing along to the transistor radio, or 'tranny'. Other than nursery rhymes, this is my first memory of any sort of popular music. She sings along and I think, *Wow, my sister sounds just like that please please pleasing noise spurting out of the wireless.*

Carole would often get lumbered with the task of looking after me when it was school holidays. She wasn't happy about it but had to do it or face the wrath of the old man. It's a lovely day: sunny, warm and bright. Carole and her best friend Poppin Clarke have decided to take me on a picnic. She has made a few jam butties: thin white bread and strawberry jam. Other sandwich fillings popular at the time were Smith's crisps, brown sauce or sugar. I have never had a sugar butty and the concept of it makes me feel a little bit sick. But crisps or brown-sauce butties – they are a winner. Not both together, you understand; that would be hideous.

I'm strapped in a pushchair and we set off for a sandy footpath called 'The Pads' in the village. Its track cuts across rich agricultural land and has a dense, thorny hedge on one side and a field on the other. It creeps its sandy trail up a slight hill, leading to a more well-to-do area of Melling called the Rocks. Here sits St Thomas's Church on the highest point of the village, as do most English churches. Halfway up the Pads is a sharp right turn on to another footpath. Across a muddy field lies what will in a year's time become my junior school, Melling Church of England School.

It's nice to be out in the world. We are among the whiskered barley fields of the Matthew's farm. The warm, soft wind is swaying the golden whispering husks; they hiss and chatter in the breeze, the surface mimicking the ebb and flow of the sea. There is a smell of soon to be ripe grain. Even the slightly damp, rich dark brown soil of the path smells nice. You know the kind of thing: earthy. My little snout is cleansed of the cigarette tar and the BICC factory funk. Butterflies circle my head, and hordes of chirping sparrows tweet from the safety of the spiked hawthorn hedges.

Kicking my little legs in the air, I'm released from the pushchair. We find the driest patch and sit on a grassy tussock. Carole finds some buttercups and holds one under my chin.

'Hey, our William, let's see if you like butter,' she says.

The reflected yellow glow created by the sun's bright light hitting the little yellow flower indicates that, yes, indeed I do like butter, lovely golden, soft and slightly salted butter all the way from New Zealand.

If only I had actually ever tasted butter. Butter is a luxury that never dwells in our antique, gas-powered fridge. We have the greasy pale-yellow substitute: Echo margarine, best used for making pastry or axle grease and not much else.

As I chuckle with the buttercup tickling my chin, the hedges behind us are covered in a thick blanket of cobwebs. Inside the refuge of the silken webs is a mass of fuzzy orange and black caterpillars, thousands of the little creepy blighters, happily going about their business. Their cosy, cocooned day is about to be ruined as a grubby, inquisitive four-year-old finds poking a stick into their world just too irresistible. Soon I have them all over my arms. The tricky little critters seem to be enjoying a fun ride on a baby human. A little later, I become unbearably itchy. The larvae's microscopic hairs cause a reaction: caterpillar rash. Pink painful lumps all up my arms, very itchy and sore. The only relief is the cooling pink calamine lotion that gets freely doused all over me when we get home.

At five years old, it is my time to go to junior school. I remember the first day being taken to the Victorian sandstone building on School Lane. I am getting dragged and am screaming for my freedom. I was not at all keen to enter this scary establishment. After my mum had pried my desperate grip from her leg, I was deposited in the first year's classroom. I was begging not to be left in this dismal place. Our first-year teacher, Mrs Corsair, looked

Carole, me, Harry Corbett, Sooty and Stephen.

like a witch straight out of a story by the Brothers Grimm: tall, wiry and stern, standing up straight and occupying a grey tweed two-piece like the Gestapo occupying a town square in Belgium. On her angular face sat winged glasses popular back then, the kind that swoop up to give the wearer a cat's eye outline. These specs are considered quite sexy now, in that retro fifties pinup style; back then, to a five-year-old, terrifying. Yes, I did piss my pants; but luckily, everyone else was pissing their pants too. I think this must have been a regular event in that classroom as they had a cupboard drawer stocked to the gills with musty second-hand kids' undies. I was immediately relieved of my wet ones and inserted into a pair of formerly white but now grey, pre-war, abrasive Y-fronts.

The classroom windows are too high to see out of and too thin for much sunshine to peep into. The class smells funny, not just of the piss streaming down the legs of most of the kids in the room. It's another smell: the scent of a century of fear that has left its stink engrained in the sandstone. The room is colder than it should be. It's early September and autumn is about to sneak up on us. Outside, the pale sun is trying hard but it's a losing battle. The stone walls capture the overnight low temperature and now slowly release the dank chill like an electric storage heater in reverse, killing any warmth that the weak sun could get through the tiny windows.

Break comes at last, the first playtime on the tarmac playground and the large field at the far end of the school. This school field is enclosed by the same type of hawthorn hedge I had encountered on the picnic the year before. These hedges are also covered in the familiar silk tents, the same orange and black caterpillars writhing around in a chaotic squirm. I might be stupid, but not stupid enough to get involved with those little bastards again, although there will be many others that get the calamine lotion treatment throughout those Swinging Sixties summers. I don't see caterpillars like that any more; they must have been done for by global warming.

The kids were starting to form friendships. I already knew a couple of the kids at the school: from across the road, Billy Bessant was a new boy like me; and David Mazenko, who was a couple of years older and already a pupil. They lived next door to each other at number four and number two. Even at that young age, we were all regulars playing footie, cricket and British Bulldog on the green. Another kid I got to know that first day was Paul (Davo) Davenport. Davo wore glasses and lived on the road directly behind our house. He supported Everton while I had been indoctrinated since birth to support Liverpool. We never let this bother us; instead, we became a team and were always together right through primary school and into secondary school. I made great friends at this school; some I'm still in touch with today, including Davo, Billy Bessant, Dave Mazenko and my brother's mate, Steve Mazenko.

A little later on during the break, I saw my older brother Steven with a few of his mates. The age gap between us meant that he wanted nothing to do with me. I don't blame him for not liking me hanging about. He was not far off secondary school age and would be leaving the juniors next year. Who would want to have a snotty-nosed and piss-stained brother hanging around? His total involvement with me up to that time had been zero, unless you count the numerous times he had locked me in the spider-infested outside toilet. I would be trapped in that dark and extremely shitty place for what seemed like hours. After a few times of being incarcerated, I learned how to escape. I would stand on the toilet bowl, open the small window, grab the metal framework, then hoist myself up to the tiny opening. By squeezing through, dangling headfirst, then gripping with my legs and hands, I could get a leg out, then, getting a foothold on the narrow window ledge, manage to twist the other leg through and drop down to safety without smashing my head on the concrete flags below. Harry Houdini would have been proud.

On a plus point, I'm not scared of spiders now. Except for those great big ones you get in the desert, tarantulas. Or those nervous weird ones that can suddenly jump at you, or the fat, dark, hairy ones with big fangs, or even the type that crawl into your mouth as you are fast asleep and snoring with your gob wide open. Their mission: to set up shop in your windpipe and choke you in the middle of the night. I take it all back: I am scared of spiders. I have just made myself petrified of the evil little buggers.

As the year wore on, me and our Steven did play together on very rare occasions: piggy-back fights, Steven with me on his back against his friend Steve Mazenko with his brother David on his back, charging about the school field, pulling and shoving each other trying to topple your opponent. It was great fun.

Our headmaster was a tall, thin man called Mr Adamson, better known as Pop Addy. He was not as scary as Mrs Corsair – the fear factor was not as intense, but there was just enough level of threat that you would not mess about with him. Not that I was going to; I was only five and a quiet and distant child. Pop Addy lived right next door to the school in a detached Victorian house called The Poplars. As you would expect, his garden was surrounded by a border of tall poplar trees, all standing to attention and guarding the periphery of the house. On the school side of the property, the poplar trees plus a high wall separated his garden from the school grounds.

In history lessons, Pop Addy would transfix us with wartime tales. He had been a prisoner of the Japanese, held captive in the jungle of some godforsaken place before being put to work as slave labour constructing a railway. One such tale involved chopping the head off a snake with a spade then secretly sharing the meat out with his starving comrades.

Rather oddly, another of his stories was also spade-related and involved the nasty tale of a punishment the men suffered. The Japanese would take two long-handled spades and push them into the ground. The prisoner would be made to put a spade handle into each of his armpits, then raise his legs and swing there, the handles painfully digging into his pits. He would be left balancing on them like some sort of twisted gym equipment, legs up with feet dangling just above the ground. If his feet touched the jungle floor, the guards would thrash his ankles with bamboo canes. Eventually the punishment would become too much and the poor soul would collapse, then receive a good beating. Not many survived.

On the edge of the playground was a little brick outbuilding; this was the toilet block. It was literally built like a brick shithouse. It had no windows, as you would expect, but it did have a stone lintel supporting a horizontal slit above the urinal; it looked like the opening you might find in a wartime pill box with a heavy machine gun poking out. Our new game was 'see-who-could-pee-through-the-gap-and-douse-unsuspecting-passers-by'. I could just about get my pathetic stream of piss up to the opening and manage to get a few drops through, my sad and weak bladder just not up to the task. The undisputed champion of this game was a kid called Kevin. He could piss like a jet washer and would blast it through the little slitty opening like the legendary firefighter Red Adair putting out a raging Texan oil-refinery fire. Such talent and skill can only be dreamed of; he was our much-admired champion pisser. We would cheer him on and pat him on the back; we drew the line at shaking his hand, though.

Time creeps on. As with all new things – even the ones you hate – you eventually get used to them. Melling School became a fun time. We got older and the school got bigger as the population of the village grew. New houses were going up all around Station Road. The fields that surrounded us were now becoming private housing estates. As more and more of the countryside was eaten up, the little school responded. A large shed was erected over the summer holidays. A freshly creosote washed wooden classroom had appeared. The shed was split into two rooms with a central cloakroom, every child designated a peg to hang up the duffle coats and balaclavas that most kids had then. This hut became our form rooms and we were based there from the age of nine until the eleven-plus exam sorted the wheat from the chaff. The new classes were bright and a lot warmer than the old stone building; everything was fresh.

For some English lessons, we had a temporary student teacher named Miss Brindall. She was not at all in the stuffy Victorian teacher mould that we were used to. She was a young woman wearing the latest flowery clothes, mini dresses or brightly coloured flared trousers. This English class was great; we had no work. All we had to do was sit quiet and still while she read to us. A novel called *The Weirdstone of Brisingamen* by Alan Garner, an Arthurian legend of a wizard and goblins and sleeping knights waiting to be roused when the shit hit the fan and England needed them. All of this took place deep inside a hollow hill that could crack open when a wizard called Cadellin would pop out and be on the lookout for a magic stone – the Weirdstone. The story was based round Alderley Edge in Cheshire and we all loved it. We couldn't wait until the next lesson to find out what was going to happen. I think this was when my love for fantasy and science fiction was born: other worlds, other times and places, anything to escape the constant bad vibes in our house.

While I'm on the subject of bad vibes, opposite the school gate is a little side street, Sandy Lane. There sits a very ordinary bungalow that would become the scene of a horrific murder in 2004. The bad juju from the school walls may have seeped out across the lane and twisted a young and receptive occupant's mind. A psycho swot kid called Brian murdered his parents with the use of a claw hammer to the back of the head. To make sure they were dead, he then knifed them both a few dozen times. Once done, he took off across the world with his dad's credit card. That part of Melling used to be a very rural quiet place; the only thing to disturb the peace in my school days was a couple of hundred kids let off the leash at playtime. That sort of thing would never have happened in my day; nobody in our road had even seen or heard of a credit card.

Monday 21 July, 1969. There's a buzz going around the school – normal lessons are out today! It's a different atmosphere; something big has occurred. All the kids are gathered in the assembly hall that trebles as a gym and dining room. All of us are sitting cross legged on the floor; we are here to watch the TV coverage of Apollo 11. Buzz Aldrin and Neil Armstrong along with Michael Collins have achieved the impossible: they have piloted a sodding massive rocket into space and landed on the moon, their mission just a bit of flag planting, a small amount of soil stealing and some jumping about. The real mission is to put the shits up the East, mainly the Soviet Russians. It serves its purpose, and they continue to propel the

USSR into a very costly space race. They had landed the previous night, Sunday. We all watched the grainy black-and-white telly pictures and were awestruck. My eleven-year-old imagination is clicked wide open to all possibilities. Maybe my two favourite kids' TV sci-fi puppet shows, *Fireball XL5* and *Thunderbirds*, could be a glimpse into a real future. Surely by the 1980s we'll all have jet boots. But at this moment, these intrepid spacemen have wangled us a day free of lessons. It was worth zipping the quarter of a million miles up there for that alone in my book; never mind Velcro and the other crap NASA is supposed to have invented along the way. Our very old and very grey local vicar, Dr Hayes, even turned up to watch the lift off, so it must be important. The kind and well-loved vicar would lead assembly every morning. That would be the only time we would see him. On this day, though, he must have been rushing to get to the school, as Davo and I notice he's cut himself shaving – there is a small amount of blood on his starched white collar. But to us kids with imaginations fired, it is like someone has cut his throat. We sit inventing wild tales of ghosts or space zombies in the vicarage. He sits snoozing on a little raised stage area along with the teachers plus our new headmaster, Mr Carradine. He is a lot less scary and more approachable than the recently retired Pop Addy.

Later, at playtime, one of our classmates, Richard Brunskill, tells us that he gets paid for being in the church choir. You get a threepenny bit for rehearsals, sixpence for a Sunday morning and two and six for a wedding. This is a whopping 12½ pence in new money – life-changing cash to us. Davo and I are always skint; we are yet to make the career move to paperboy and a steady weekly wage of five bob or 25p in today's money. After school, we take the short walk to the vicarage and knock on the imposing front door. The door opens. Davo does most of the talking as we sit in the shambolic parlour of the vicarage. After a short amount of polite and nervous chat, we are in. 'Come to the church on Sunday,' the vicar says. Probably just happy to get a couple more faces in the dwindling congregation.

That Sunday we cycle up to the church on Rock Lane and get fitted with a cassock. This is a long black garment with about twenty small, cloth-covered buttons up the front. This is my first job and it's in the music industry! It's an omen, surely. My sweet pre-pubescent voice is enough to make paint peel off the walls and try and crawl back in the tin. I can't hold a tune to save my life; Davo is not much better. Yet this doesn't seem to affect our eligibility to be part of the choir. I'm just told to keep it down or, better still, just mouth the words and look holy.

After the service, we climb aboard the second-hand, cobbled-together push bikes we have christened 'Ludicrous Machines' or 'Ludes' for short. Complete with optional extras of super-wide handlebars called stags and still wearing a dusty cassock, I'm flying back from church rehearsals, a twelve-sided threepenny bit tucked in my jeans. I'm rich. I've only fastened the top couple of buttons of the cassock round my neck. As I zoom downhill from the church, it billows behind me. I am Batman.

Our time at junior school is coming to an end; we are well into the final year of Melling Church of England Primary School. We are now very well at home in the new shed classrooms. We have just taken the eleven-plus examination to determine what school we can go to. Davo and I fail the test and get sent to

Billy Bessant and me.

Deyes Lane Secondary Modern in the neighbouring town of Maghull. Billy Bessant passes and will be admitted to Maghull Grammar School. It's the end of an era. We will all still kick around together in the village on occasion, but it is never quite the same again.

Before we go for good, the school has one final cosmic trick up its sleeve, something to remember the place by. It's a breezy, warm and extremely humid summer day, close or muggy. In the sky, boiling clouds suck up moisture from the air, along with the summer heat of the sun charging up the humidity. The black clouds are churning and crashing with thunder. Negative and positive particles are building up above us and not getting on very well at all. The storm is directly above the newly constructed huts now. The class guinea pig Willie is hiding and squeaking in his little straw nest, as are most of the girls, and some boys . . . I mean squeaking, not trying to get in the little brown and white rodents' cage; let us just say a fair amount of squeaking is audible. A sudden flash and the clouds spit an unbearable ribbon of light towards the little school. We have been hit by a lightning bolt! The strike sends several balls of plasma dancing about the play-ground. There is a distinct smell of charged electricity as a cricket-ball-sized sphere of energy bounces through an open window. We watch, too freaked out to do much as the iridescent, crackling orb floats about for a few seconds, then, with a distinct pop, vanishes back into the ether. I now know this is a very rare phenomenon called ball lightning.

3.

Achtung Billy

'Telstar' – The Tornados

Because we lived in a council estate, I felt below the people in the homeowner estates that grew to the left and right of our road. Britain was and is a very class-ridden place. The posh people are seen as better than the rest. This is complete shite, of course; just look to the royal family, the poshest of the posh. They are just as big a gang of scumbags as the worst people in your town. They just do it with their pinkies sticking out. In the UK, it's seen as a major mark of success, trust and stature if you are a homeowner. I think all the kids in our road felt this slight sense of shame living in a council or 'corpy' house. Now I can see that it is a stupid way of thinking and, to my mind, the council houses were built a lot better than the other homes in the surrounding roads. Many countries around the world think it's odd to slave away all your life so you can own a place. You are only renting it until death; you are just passing through this world. This puts me in mind of when the Native Americans' land was being stolen and occasionally bought off them. These people were truly in touch with and a part of the land. They had no concept that you could own land and thought the white men fools for offering to buy their lands for whisky, guns, beads and tools, asking, 'Do you want to buy the sky as well?'

Looking at it with older, wiser eyes, Station Road is quite a nice road with a central green. The council houses ring an elongated oval of grass. When not at school, all the estate kids played on this green from dawn until dusk.

The exterior of the brown-brick houses that surround the grass was kept in good condition by the council. If any of my mates knocked round to see if I wanted to play out, however, I would keep them at the door, not wanting them to see the state of the inside of the house. A keen gardener, my dad kept our front garden nice and tidy; this belied the dismal state of the inside of number 15.

Beyond the front door was an entirely different kettle of fish: a scruffy shambles, a dump with no toilet seats and worn-out everything, an embarrassment to me and my brother and sister. We had manky old net curtains, yellow and smoke-stained. In place of toilet tissue was newspaper, usually the *Daily Mirror*, torn up into squares. Old, broken and cracked linoleum was on the floors. The only heating came from a coal fire in the front room. In the winter months, the pools of condensation on the inside of our bedroom windows were often a sheet of ice. On the beds were army blankets, rough and grey. We had a fridge, but we probably never needed one; it was always freezing in our house. Weirdly our fridge was run on gas. I still can't get my head around this. I can remember igniting the pilot light, with a flaming piece of the wax paper torn from a Wonder Loaf bread wrapper. It might have been a common type of fridge back then, although none of my friends' fridges worked on this gas-fuelled alchemy. It was usually empty anyway.

We had a tub washing machine, no spin dryer. We had a prehistoric mangle that would squeeze water out of clothes. Clothes would be slurped in by hungry, rubber roller jaws. With all the upset in the house, I peed the bed just about every night. The bed had a rubber sheet stretched across a bony mattress. I would often get out of the bed damp and smelly. I only got a bath once a week on Sunday night, so in the morning I would just get out of the pissy bed and get dressed for school. By the time it was bedtime the next night, the piss had usually dried. I hardly ever cleaned my teeth; a quick cow's lick round the face with a tatty flannel and I would be off. My feet stank and the socks were filthy. I was in a bad state of neglect. The stink must have been vile but I don't remember being bullied for smelling bad. By some good fortune, I must have always been upwind of everyone.

The one thing my dad did do in terms of home improvement was to make our living room smaller. Above the fireplace was a chimney breast. On either side of this was a floor-to-ceiling recess of about one-foot deep by four-foot wide. I had seen the same design in other houses on our street, and people had put up shelves in this handy bit of space. Instead of doing that, our dad positioned everything to make the room as tiny, cramped and dismal as possible. Dad had opted to cover up the right-hand side of this useful area with a large piece of hardboard from floor to ceiling. This ate up a fair chunk of the living area. This was doubly strange as my dad was handy at making stuff out of wood and even worked all day with it. He could have knocked up some shelves for this wasted space in no time. But no. On the left-hand side of the handy hollow, our telly sat with its arse pushed up against the wall.

He then had the genius idea of putting curtains up, not following the line of the bay window as all our neighbours had, but effectively cutting off a large piece of the front room by attaching the curtain rail to the ceiling and having the putrid, effervescent green curtains cut across in a straight line. This caused the whole of the bay window area to be separated from the rest of the room when the vomit-inducing curtains were drawn. To top this off, he then painted the textured wallpaper a depressing chocolate brown and orange. Add a shade-less forty-watt light bulb dangling forlornly and the design is complete. All this had the effect of making the already small room noticeably smaller and darker. But the design was not finished yet! Next, he got someone who was handy with a MIG welder to weld the metal window frames permanently shut. Hey presto! He had successfully turned our main living area into a very cosy cell in a Victorian psychiatric hospital.

None of the parents of my mates – even the ones on the same road with a house of similar design – ever thought, *This house is too bloody big! I've got it! Let's slice a few bits off and make it more like a hamster's cage.* They had better heating, colourful shagpile carpets, nice warm cosy lighting and comfy furniture. I can only assume that central heating was an option that the council offered to tenants at extra cash, but my dad was too miserly to pay for it. He was never in, so why would he pay to keep the wife and kids warm? He gave the impression that he hated all of us anyway. He was as tight as a gnat's chuff back then. Living in damp and cold conditions, consequently I was always snotty, with a blocked or runny nose, constantly sneezing, firing snot everywhere.

Outside, at each end of the central strip of grass, was a wooden sign attached to a very sturdy concrete post which stated 'By Order of LCC [Lancashire County Council] NO BALL GAMES'. All the kids played every ball game known to man – well, football and cricket – on the grass. Lots of other games that did not involve the use of the forbidden balls were also played endlessly, the killjoy notice ignored. We were sticking it to the man even before we knew there was a man to stick it to.

This was a time when parks had an angry 'Oi, you lot, get off the bleeding grass!' park keeper. One of their duties would be to lock up the swings in the parks on a Sunday. Pathetic! Think of it . . . some overzealous, religious nutters spoiling our weekend fun. Swings aren't even mentioned in the holy book of your choice (so many to choose from, but still no swings); I reckon Baby Jesus wouldn't be that arsed anyway. He was always messing about doing tricks and shit for his mates, some of them even better than Uri Geller, David Blaine or even the Amazing Kreskin. I don't remember having this commandment shouted at me in assembly: 'Thou shalt not piss-eth about in the park on the Sabbath.'

I was an avid reader of comics such as the *Valiant*, *Victor* or the *Hornet*. They always featured a war story or historical tale inside, something at least a bit educational. To my mind, these titles were aimed at a slightly older kid. They were the equivalent of watching the history channel or a documentary about how a can of beans is made. The more comedic comics like *Beano* and *Dandy* tended to focus on the fine art of bullying, thus the more effete or academic members of the comic universe would bear the brunt of Dennis the Menace or the Bash Street Kids. They would feature more daft adventures like hiding from the park keeper or ripping up a swot's homework. I liked both types of comic in the same way that I like a good documentary on Richard II or, when I'm in the mood, some drivel like *I'm a Celebrity . . . Get Me Out of Here!* I would say the stories about the armed forces were the inspiration for playing war, a favourite game at the time. Our imaginations conjured up all kinds of tactical scenarios; a tennis ball became a hand grenade; a stick would be a gun – all frowned on in today's politically correct climate. It is OK to play very realistic war games on a computer, though? No imagination required.

'Ginger' and my dad.

A wartime item we didn't have to imagine was a large swastika flag. During his time in Monte Cassino, Italy, my dad had a mate named Ginger (everyone in the army then seemed to have a slightly mental pal called Ginger – so why not Private Sergeant?). After the Germans had well and truly scarpered from the town, Ginger climbed up and nabbed a swastika from the post office. This battered old flag – along with another snatched trophy, a German army belt – lived hidden at the bottom of Dad's wardrobe. The belt's swastika emblem had been filed off by someone; I often wondered what the story behind that was. The tatty flag had a few holes in it and some dirty brown stains. We suspected the holes had been made by bullets and the faded brown stains had to be blood. This made it more fun to play with. Not knowing the significance of the swastika at the time, it was just a wartime flag and had no political significance to a seven-year-old.

I often played with the flag, generally taking the part of the Germans or 'Jerries'. My base was the front garden, the distinctive red, black and white flag pinned to a seven-foot pole that my mum used to prop the washing line up. Because of the use of the flag in these war games, my brother's fast-witted wag of a friend, Steve Mazenko, had given me the nickname of Wilhelm Shultz. This was an amalgamation of the two main German characters from the hit TV show *Hogan's Heroes*: the Commandant Wilhelm Klink and his Sergeant Hans Shultz. (My nickname was later shortened to just Shultz and stuck for quite a long time after these war games were well behind me.) Steve Mazenko, on the odd occasion I see him, will still call me Shultz. I like it; it's a nice link to the past me.

Somewhere I had found a large cardboard box. I cut the top and bottom flaps away. Laying the hollow box on its side, I got in and crawled forward; the box became a tank. The cardboard soon lost its stiff consistency and began rolling forward with the motion of the tracks of the formidable Tiger tank. I was crawling and making the sound of the engines, steadily advancing over the field to attack the English base behind the neatly manicured privet hedge at number four, manned by my mate Bill Bessant on the far side of the road. 'Achtung Britisher Pig Dogs, you don't stand a chance.' Tennis balls rained down as Bill made the sounds of explosions. Counterattacks followed.

After several missions of this nature, we would get bored with the bloody carnage of war and would return to playing footie. The flag was left out in front of the house for hours on end. Nobody who lived on the road gave two monkeys. They knew it was just a captured memento of the war. Alf hadn't joined some far-right movement, after all; he had recently become a Labour councillor and a big fan of the Honourable Member of Parliament for the District of Huyton, Harold Wilson, the new prime minister. It wasn't that unusual to see a gang of kids playing with a bullet-riddled Nazi flag or running around with a German helmet rattling around their tiny heads. In bottom drawers and wardrobes across the land, lots of German stuff was floating about: iron crosses, gas masks, bayonets, etc. One kid said his dad had a Luger pistol, but we never actually ever saw it; he may have been talking shite. Many soldiers had come back with plunder from their time in the war; most of it vanished now. The late, great, powerful singer and bass player Lemmy of Hawkwind and later Motörhead must have snapped them all up for his vast collection before he died.

One day in the late sixties, I was rooting about for the flag. It had vanished into thin air; it was no longer in the bottom of Dad's wardrobe or any of the other secret places I could think of. I assumed it had been chucked out. Much later, my sister Carole confessed she had burned it in the backyard, in some sort of hippie ceremony. Bummer; I could have sold that to Lemmy if our paths had ever crossed.

During this period, Mum left for the first time. All hell had been breaking out at our house. One night I was awoken by the racket. I was about seven or eight years old. I crept down the stairs and bobbed my head over the banister to look and listen to the action going on in our small front room. A full-on fight was in progress. I learned much later from my mum that, in the melee, my dad had broken her nose. The screaming intensified as she fled out of the house. She ended up back at her mum's on Lancaster Street in Walton. I was so used to the level of anger and hatred between them that this never really shocked me; if anything, it was kind of exciting. It was all I'd known, and my undeveloped mind just accepted this sort of shit as what grown-ups did.

The next day after work, my dad bundled us all into his Bedford minibus and set off to Walton. He drew up outside the house on Lancaster Street, got out and knocked on the door. My grandma answered the door, glaring at him, as you would expect. A few angry words were exchanged and they went inside, leaving me, my brother and sister in the van, noses pressed up against the window. After about twenty minutes or so, Mum and Dad emerged and silently got back into the van. Nothing was said. The next day it was as though nothing had happened.

My dad rescuing me from a holiday in hell (Rhyl).

It's November 1965. It starts snowing heavily at about 9 p.m. My dad will be at the pub until last orders, so the coast is clear for now. Mum lets me go out into the road and play with some of the other kids who have also been allowed this late-night treat. The light casts down on to the snow from the streetlamp that stands outside number 15, like a standard lamp. Up the street, the lights reflect off the snow, and the night is almost as bright as the grey winter days. Snowball fights are kicking off all over the grass, now white as milk. On my hands: socks in place of gloves. Some kids are building a snowman, starting off with a small ball of snow, then rolling it along the ground to pick up more snow. Eventually, they have a big enough ball for a rather portly snowman. We are allowed to play for an hour or so until our fingers can't take it any more and the sopping socks I have on instead of gloves have become more of a discomfort than a solution to the cold and wet. My fingers are stiff and painful pink with cold. I reluctantly go back to the house.

Station Road in the snow.

After a while and still up way past my bedtime, I hear the dreaded sound of the front-door key being inserted into the Yale lock. Shit, it's past kicking out time (only ten-thirty back then). Quick as a flash Mum says, 'Quick, Willie, turn the telly over to BBC.' I do as I am instructed, pushing the clunky buttons on the rented TV set. I can feel heat emanating from the hot tubes encased within. The channels switch. My dad flings the door open and immediately, without a word, turns the telly back to ITV, the channel my mum was watching a couple of seconds ago. He has no clue what's on or even if he's interested in watching any telly; he is too pissed to focus on anything. He's just asserting his authority in his household. He turns to me and says, 'You. Bed. Now.' Without any protest, off I scurry up to my bed, impressed by the reverse psychology that my mum had employed. Genius. This is a valuable lesson that I never forget.

The next day I'm waiting with the usual gang of village kids for the bus to take us to school. The snow is still coming down fast and it's getting towards 8.45 a.m. It looks like the bus is not going to turn up. Too scared to just go home, Davo, Bill Bessant, a few others and I decide to walk to school. We trek the mile or so up the little path of the Pads across the fields of Mathew's farm. My feet are soaking wet and freezing. I am wearing the only shoes I have at the time, brown leather sandals with socks pulled up to the knee; shorts, the standard, itchy grey, thick flannel, school uniform kind; a black duffle coat; and a knitted balaclava on my head. My little frosty face sticks out of the opening into the chilly morning. The cold grasping at my feet is nothing compared to the excitement of going to school in the snow. My mind is racing with thoughts of all the fun we can have at playtime.

The slightly higher aspect of the path gives a good view across the farm and on towards Liverpool. The whitewashed landscape is a wonder to behold. Large flakes slowly drift down, softening the scene. The huge cranes, normally standing to attention at the faraway docks in Liverpool, are now just a hint of grey, fragile twigs in the distance. I notice that the world's sound is changed; silence has replaced the background drone that generally accompanies life. The choked and belching growl of Ford Anglias, Consuls and Zodiacs, Morris Minors, Hillman Imps and Hunters, is no more; they are all asleep, tucked up in flagged driveways or outside houses on the street, still and silent under cosy snow eiderdowns; they are going nowhere today. Any sound is dampened down, becoming part of the strange stillness that accompanies heavy snowfall. The outdoor world now has the same sound as the indoor world; near sounds are intensified and distant sounds faded and muffled. The view from the Pads over the fields is like looking through a misty window, the snow silently bleaching the landscape pure white.

When we get to school, there are only a few teachers that have made it in. One is Mr Carradine, the new headmaster. He seems almost as excited as the kids and throws a snowball at us. The kids retaliate, and a full-on fight ensues. The headmaster is pelted with snow until, smiling, he holds his hands up to surrender. I have never seen a teacher display this off-duty manner before, letting slip the stern-faced mask and allowing a glimpse of a human being; teachers are to be feared at all times.

As hardly any of the staff have turned up, we are allowed to go home early. Bill Roberts from the local shop has been called up and he comes and gets us in his canvas-covered, ex-army Land Rover.

It seemed to snow a lot back then in wintertime. A couple of years earlier, in 1962 and on into 1963, Britain had one of the worst winters on record. The papers called it 'the big freeze'. The canals and rivers froze, the snow and ice sticking around from December until February. The stillness was always the thing I liked most. The snow clouds were like a ceiling above, creating the magical feeling of being indoors when outdoors. After the failure of the bus turning up, a new rule is made by the headmaster. If the bus doesn't turn up by a quarter to nine, we are permitted to go home. Every morning after that, we stand at the bus stop hoping for the bus to have broken down or be late, even by a few seconds.

4.

Kirkby Skins Rule OK

Dave Mazenko and me.

'Cloud Nine' – The Temptations

At the top of our road is a substantial metal fence, beyond which is the town of Kirkby. There are only a couple of pedestrian cut-throughs into Melling via this barrier. No road has ever been constructed to let vehicles easily access Kirkby. By car, it's about a three- or four-mile trip around the outskirts of the village to get to the other side of this fence. It's all a bit Checkpoint Charlie.

Kirkby is one of those new towns they were throwing up all over the place in the fifties and sixties. Liverpudlian families were relocated from the back-to-back terraced houses considered slums. The slums were knocked down and the occupants sent to the freshly built new towns like Kirkby or, a little further out (in every way), Skelmersdale.

My paternal grandparents Tom and Lucinda lived on the other side of the fenced borders of Kirkby, a few hundred yards towards Kirkby station. I remember being on the bridge above the track, safely with my grandad, watching the dirty black steam trains chugging past, engulfing me in the locomotive breath: plumes of smoke, soot and steam. It was fun and pretty spectacular. My grandparents had a detached house with what was to my mind a large and interesting garden with lots of apple trees and a vegetable patch at the far end. Visits to see them were few and far between; a close family we were not. Consequently, I hardly know any relatives, even though my grandfather and grandmother on my dad's side had fourteen children. Hence I have numerous cousins, nieces, nephews and aunties and uncles I have never met. The grandparents on my mum's side had thirteen kids; I know that side of the family even less. To think of meeting all those relatives is quite overwhelming and I won't be knocking on their doors anytime soon.

On one occasion when I was pretty small – five or six – I was visiting my grandparents with my dad. I got a small piece of apple from one of the trees in the garden stuck in my throat. I was choking and slowly turning blue. My dad, panicking and not knowing what to do, scooped me up and set off down the road towards the doctor's surgery, located a few doors down. Fortunately, the jogging action dislodged the fragment from my windpipe; I spat it out and started to gasp for breath. It was a close call. On that occasion, the old saying an apple a day keeps the doctor away was very nearly turned upside down. I have always been a fast eater and still struggle with trying to slow down, another consequence of being left to my own devices too much as a kid. I'm always choking on food to this day.

In my grandparents' house was a mysterious older cousin called Stella. She loved it when I visited or other young cousins played in her room. She was an odd woman and had something of the Miss Havisham vibe about her, surrounded by the ephemera and detritus of a full life lived, now sadly stagnating and confined. All these thoughts only come to me now as I look about my room and all the crap I have accumulated over forty-odd years of travel and touring. Stella was quite a bit older than me, probably in her thirties or forties. It's hard to tell when you are a kid; all grown-ups kind of look the same.

Stella had a strange faded glamour about her. We knew she had been to the USA; nobody back then went anywhere as exotic as Hollywood. The story I heard from my mum was that Stella had been working as one of Lucille Ball's assistants. She had been in a hotel with Ball in New York when another guest at the hotel was shot and killed. After this, she kind of lost the plot and had to come home. A deep depression had taken her over, nerves getting the better of her. She was always in bed. On a recent visit to the USA, I got to see Lucille Ball's dressing room on the Paramount Studios lot. It was odd to think my cousin Stella might have been in and out of that door years ago. This could all have been rubbish, of course; my mum Olive did have the trait of embellishing the truth.

When Stella returned, she had brought back various oddities from the new world. One item that sticks in my memory was a weird looking-glass contraption that hooked over the screen of a black-and-white telly to magically turn it into colour. It was a tinted glass lens – blue at the top, a kind of pink in the middle and at the lower part green. Placed over the telly, the images transformed into what looked like Technicolor to me.

To us Melling-ites, Kirkby was pretty much a no-go zone, unless you wanted to get your head kicked in. It was only a five-minute walk up through the fence if you followed a cinder path at the back of a row of houses. This brought you to the steep cutting of the Liverpool Northern trainline. This trek was seldom attempted due to the fear we all had as kids of Kirkby-ites. I did take a chance now and then, though, when all was quiet on the skinhead front.

In the late sixties and on into the seventies, Melling would be regularly invaded by Kirkby skinheads. The standard uniform of a skin back then was Dr Martens boots, black or cherry red; Ben Sherman shirts, usually a bright gingham check pattern, white or pastel-coloured Oxford style, with neat button-down collars, of course; and denim jeans. Levi's and more commonly Wrangler's were a staple. Holding their jeans up were thin, clip-on elastic braces or, as they call them in the USA, suspenders (suspenders are an entirely different item of clothing over here; Benny Hill on the telly was rather keen on those). There were also Brutus or Jaytex shirts. These smaller apparel companies were generally cheaper and poorer quality, so they had to try a little harder to get the attention of the average skin, and often used more extreme colours and bolder or crazier checked designs, plus bigger and higher collars. Other shoes favoured by the skinhead ruffians were tasselled loafers and the legendary Como. Into the seventies, Como was the shoe of choice for most lads in our school. Shiny uppers with leather soles and usually just two rows of laces. The more expensive versions had more lace rows. Nothing that special by today's standards of shoe design, when footwear looks like some sort of intergalactic star cruiser. A good basic shoe with some elegance was the criterion for the dress-smart skinhead. I have trawled the internet for Como shoes, all to no avail. There is only one video of someone wearing them outside a pub in Liverpool, so maybe they were just more of a local thing.

There were other local items from the city such as Flemings Jeans. These could be bought in all styles, mainly parallels. Parallels were jeans or trousers that sat wide at the knee then would keep this width to bottom; twenty-four-inch-wide bottoms were most popular, worn high with turn-ups to show off the heavy boot artillery. This prompted many smart-arse teachers to hilariously quip, 'Eh, Sergeant, what you wearing: short longs or long shorts?' and 'What's up with your keks [trousers]? Have they fallen out with your shoes?' At the back of these homegrown Liverpudlian jeans, sitting above the left-hand patch pocket, was stitched a little label embroidered with the words 'Flemings Supatuf Liverpool', along with crossed British and American flags, obviously signifying the special relationship and the love of denim. Flemings also sold jean jackets and even flares, some with up to thirty-two-inch bottoms. I loved that shop. It had its own scent, a slightly soapy, strange, freshly pressed denim aroma. After the jeans had been washed, I would iron them dry sometimes and the smell would emanate up in the steam. This smell only ever came from Flemings Jeans.

Over the water (the other side of the river Mersey) was another favourite: Skinners. They specialised in white denim or, as they were known, bakers. These white jeans came truly into their own after the film *A Clockwork Orange* was released in 1972, with many skins adopting the ultra-violence portrayed in the film as their philosophy. After copycat violence attributed to the movie erupted, the film was withdrawn at the request of director Stanley Kubrick. This only served to make the film more of a cult classic, with some skins even going so far as to dress in the full white boiler suit and codpiece combo topped off with an English gentleman's bowler hat, as featured in the movie.

The seventies was such an aggro-fuelled time; everyone wanted to get the boot in. Peacetime brings out the tribal nature of man. Skins and greasers aka bikers would fight each other and anyone else, even among themselves if no natural enemies could be found. Brutality often came in the form of a good kicking; weapons and knife crimes were pretty rare back then. Bicycle chains and knuckle dusters were about as far as most bovver boys went.

Skins would storm through the metal fence opening at the top of the road, looking for fish, chips and trouble. The Melling chippy had legendary status. Skins generally congregated and sat on a low wall outside our chippy, exuding an extremely menacing presence, noisily larking about, shouting football chants and being generally scary. They spraypainted on the wall of the BICC, which was located across from the chippy, 'Kirkby Skins Rule OK'. This was a common form of graffiti; back then, everything 'Ruled OK'. Simple but effective, an unruly tribe of shaven-headed Sasquatch marking their territory like a pride of scabby tomcats spraying musk all over the place. They were no Banksys, these buzzcut hooligans. The next day, someone from

Melling had countered their message with their own. It read 'Melling Hippies', accompanied by a peace sign and, for good measure, a daisy flower. That'll show 'em to not to mess with us. Peace and love shall prevail.

If I was ever in the lucky position of having any money and was hungry enough (always), I'd risk going to the chip shop to get a sixpenny bag of fried spud delights. Covert tactics had to be employed. First, a short reconnaissance mission via my bike. Second, keeping out of sight behind garden walls, observing the movements and waiting until the invaders went back whence they came: Mordor . . . I mean Kirkby. Any youth that was spotted would be chased; if caught, a good kicking would be dealt out. Luckily, they never caught me. In those days, I was as fast as a weasel and twice as tricky. After the skins had eaten their fill of chips and fishcakes or meat and potato pies (now rebranded in the interest of transparency as potato and meat pies due to the lack of meat inside the crusty shell), high on a combination of dandelion and burdock fizzy pop and Embassy No. 6 ciggies, they would often rampage up Station Road as they made their way back home through Checkpoint Charlie, nicking milk bottles off steps and hurling them and anything else they could find at the houses as they ran. Pitched battles would kick off now and then as the hard-knock families in our road would join the fray, scrapping and receiving painful visits from highly polished Dr Martens in return.

As a fully paid-up coward, I would generally keep to the rear of any aggro or hide in our entry. My auntie Jean's house, just two doors up at number 21, got a couple of windows smashed while she was happily sitting inside watching *Coronation Street*. My uncle Frank gave chase, but it was too late; the skins had already fled through the metal fence border and on to safety. The next day, a Ford Anglia cop car – a panda – turned up. (I never really understood this name as all the pandas I have seen on the telly are black and white. We did only have a black and white telly, so who knows in an alternate reality? These police cars were a rather fetching pale blue and white.) The coppers were asking questions, visiting the more, shall we say, 'well-known families'. Apparently, during this rampage one of the skins had been shot with an airgun.

The pedestrian walkway was also used by scooter boys who could squeeze through the gap. There would be a flotilla of chrome lamped and decked out scooters, whiplash aerials flexing and flicking tiger tails, Union Jacks and football insignia. Many mirrors adorned these ships of the road, creating a bedazzled moving disco light show reflecting the passing scenery, with some proclaiming proudly 'Cloud Nine Scooter Club' in bold white lettering on tinted screens. The flamboyant flotilla of about thirty or forty colourful Lambrettas and Vespas fizzed past our house in single-file formation. On they buzzed past, in a cloud of blue two-stroke fumes, using our road as a shortcut to Liverpool and some mod soul shindig. It was a great sight to see and issued little threat to a ten-year-old squirt who stopped to gaze in awe.

During the mod era, my brother briefly joined the scootering fraternity with a cheap three-button suit and button-down-collar shirt. He did not look a million miles away from Pete Townshend, the Sergeant hooter at last becoming an asset rather than a negative feature. This flirtation with scootering was short lived. His scooter seemed to require fixing more than riding, and eventually he drove it into the canal. His mate Psycho

Simpson jumped in and got a rope around it and they dragged the sorry thing out. After salvaging it, they got it dried and it was back in spluttering action as much as it had ever been (hardly ever), its chief purpose seeming to be clogging up the little alleyway that ran down the side of our house.

It was odd the way the mod scene kind of spawned a flower-power offshoot and at the same time a skinhead affiliation. Mods began to grow their hair slightly longer. Mod bands such as the Who and the Small Faces began embracing the new psychedelic scene. Meanwhile, skins began taking on the scooter as the chief form of transport. It was all very mixed up: LSD, peace, love and paisley shirts, all while putting the boot in. I liked the skinhead fashions at the time and did don the braces and turned up jeans, but flares and other hippie items would be amalgamated into the mutant hybrid look. I was still feeling my way in the world and soaking up influences from all angles.

After my sister had escaped to London in 1970, she sent me a tie-dye T-shirt from the hippie boutique, Lord Kitchener's Valet, on the King's Road in London. It was mainly purple with an ironed-on Speedy Gonzales cartoon character on the front. It arrived in a groovy bag with a picture of Kitchener doing his familiar pointing stance: Lord Kitchener wants you to go and die in a pointless war, for him and the Crown. I loved that shirt. London seemed like such a groovy place; the hippie scene was to become a fascination. The clothes were becoming a lot more flamboyant and wilder. I was starting to follow the fashions and was heading more towards the hippie world under the influence of the music that trickled into me via my brother and his mates, the Mazenkos. They had already embraced a lot of the clobber: flares, colourful cheesecloth shirts, grandad vests, Afghan coats, all accompanied by the obligatory denim. Music was edging its way in and becoming a lot more important as an escape. My sister had a Dansette record player that she had left behind. I don't remember there being many records about at the time, although my brother Steven had an LP by the Mothers of Invention, *We're Only In It For the Money*, released in 1968. Frontman Frank Zappa was pretty quick to take the piss out of the Beatles. The cover depicts a parody of the *Sgt Pepper* album cover. I'm listening to it as I type this. I've never been a huge Zappa fan, but I have to say I'm digging its experimental nature. You couldn't exactly call it easy listening. My sister's tastes were a little more mainstream: Dusty Springfield, Motown, soul, etc. So when she came in and heard this odd music wafting through the house, it's easy to explain why she threw the record down the stairs and took her Dansette record player off him.

From about 1970 onwards, I had been going to the match – Liverpool FC, of course. My dad had some sort of deal whereby he would sell raffle tickets for the club at the pubs around our area that he was never out of. Early on a Saturday morning, he would go to Liverpool FC's ground, Anfield, and hand over the money he had collected at the office. It was a small hut just beyond the gates. This act of club loyalty gave him a sort of foot in the door for a cheaper season ticket. I would go with him as a lad and often would see the legendary team manager Bill Shankly. He knew my dad's name and would say hello to him in his broad Scottish accent. It was natural that I would start going to the match. I was never really a very committed football fan; I went because a few of my mates went. We would see the same faces emanating from all parts of Liverpool and had a sort of gang mentality, a safety in numbers sort of thing. We had a regular spot by the left-hand-side wall of the Anfield Road End. These were the days when seating was only provided in the stands along the sides of the pitch. The far ends were open terraces with steel barriers to try and quell the crush.

I was an avid watcher of the crowds at the match and often missed the goals because I was scanning the stands for interesting people or trouble. Trouble or, as it was known, bovver often broke out. I think because I had been around aggro at home, it was becoming my normal and an exciting thing for me; I got more of a thrill from that than the game. At a match between Liverpool and Chelsea – famous for its Headhunters hooligan firm – about ten or so Chelsea fans had come decked out in full *Clockwork Orange* regalia: bowler hats, one false eyelash, white boiler suits, the lot. God knows what they must have been thinking. They must have thought the intimidating uniform of the Droogs – as the gang of thugs were called in the film – would give them uber-cool magic powers and protect them. The Anfield Road End was a mixture of home and away fans. They were right in the middle of an angry sea of red and getting slaughtered by the Liverpool fans. A large number of police gathered at the bottom of the terrace. They went in with truncheons drawn. In single file, the cops pushed and snaked themselves up through the packed crowd, then looped around the troop of Droogs while many a boot to the yarbles (the name given to bollocks in the film) was dealt out by the LFC fans. The cops escorted the Droogs out of the battle. It was an amazing manoeuvre that I think saved the lives of those Chelsea Headhunters (headcases more like). After the game, the crush of fans swarmed the Anfield streets. In and among the sea of red and white bobble hats, the odd battered bowler trophy sat atop Rod Stewart-style feather-cut hairdos slowly winding their way to the homes, chippies or pubs of Liverpool.

5.

Caveman Freakbeat Scene

'Resurrection Shuffle' – Ashton, Gardner & Dyke

It's 1969. The dawning of the Age of Aquarius . . . Let's all freak out! The Beatles have played live for the last time, interestingly on the roof of the Apple Corps building high above London's Savile Row, pinstripe city gents cricking necks and straining to see where that dashed awful racket is coming from. They commute home with stiff necks and even stiffer upper lips. Charlie Manson, the well-known zany hippie puppet master, is behind a daft effort to start a race war in the USA that he dubbed 'Helter Skelter' after the Beatles song from the White Album. This he hopes to achieve by sending off some of his nutty disciples to 10050 Cielo Drive, Los Angeles, the home of beautiful starlet Sharon Tate. They are on a mission of murder.

In upstate New York, the Woodstock music festival attracts around half a million music-loving dopeheads, hippies, freaks, misfits, nutjobs, runaways and flower children. They all have a jolly good time down on the Max Yasgur dairy farm. After three days of bands and brown acid, Jimi Hendrix is to close the proceedings. He manages to transform the ultra-patriotic 'Star-Spangled Banner' anthem into an anti-war song simply by the dexterous movement and nimble placement of his fingers. Stretching and hammering the metal strings of his Fender Stratocaster, the amplified vibrations are sent screeching into the stratosphere. This is magical juju few can harness.

All at Woodstock bear witness to the power of music. Music: it's the touch of the ephemeral sea in which we all swim. Whether we notice it or not, music seeps into us, creating emotions and desires that are powerful. How can it be that a couple of notes played in the right way, in the right order and making the right sound can make you laugh or cry? It can place you back into an emotional whirlpool of both good or bad or even heaven or hell. It can take your mind to other dimensions and fire ideas never before sparked in your brainbox.

These primal forces are now entering me and becoming part of me, without me even noticing. Forty-odd thousand years ago, a ragged cave dweller hit a couple of stones together to start a rhythm. Soon another cave dweller, feeling a little left out, would add bashing a couple of shells together in syncopated unison. In a neighbouring cave, a hairy troglodyte clacks a stick on a couple of skulls. The joker of the bunch blows down a hollow leg bone leftover from yesterday's lunch. Then the boffin of the tribe pricks up his ears and is intrigued by this Neolithic bozo's antics. He proceeds to carve a piece of mammoth ivory into a rudimentary flute – then guess what? The cavemen meet by the fire and the gathered ensemble have a jam; it's a prehistoric freakout. They all fall about pissing themselves laughing. It feels good, it becomes a ritual: Saturday night shindig down at their local, 'The Sabre Tooth Lion'. Just like that, they have magically formed a band, 'Uggo and the Uggymen!' Fast forward many thousands of years, what do you get? Beethoven. And by some twisted, fickle and fortunate act of fate, I am a few hundred years down the queue, waiting to join this mystic brotherhood. Hey, haters, I'm not comparing myself to Beethoven by the way; he was shite. I'm more of a Philip Glass kind of guy. Melodic drones and repetition will become the furniture of my musical landscape.

I am now eleven years old, with a solid eleven-plus fail under my striped snake belt. My mate Davo and I have now started at Maghull Deyes Lane Secondary Modern School. Yes, it's a bit of a mouthful. A few years later, the place gets renamed to the snappier Deyes Lane Comprehensive; soon 'Comprehensive' gets chopped down to just 'Comp'. Today the gaff is simply called Deyes High School. I like the secondary modern tag myself, though; good for my future punk-rock credentials and all that.

The school is comprised of a large, square, two-storey brick building facing on to the road, Deyes Lane. It is an impressive structure a few hundred yards wide. The classrooms of this structure surround a large central open area of grass, called the quadrangle or quad; I guess that sounds more scholarly than the courtyard. This is given over to the keeping of chickens. This quadrangle building is closely augmented by three 1960s utilitarian Soviet bloc . . . er . . . blocks. Not much thought to the design has been given to these classrooms: lumpy cubes of concrete, pebble dash and windows. These three-storey buildings are surrounded by several acres of muddy playing fields. The soggy grasslands are marked out as football pitches, a cricket pitch and a running track.

It's the first day of a new term at a new school. We are all pushing, shoving and shouting in an unruly manner to get off the Melling bus that has just delivered us to the gates, our school bags full of new pencils, pens, erasers and deep apprehension. The first thing we see is one of the new blocks covered in red paint; 'Fuck Off' in large letters is brightening up the dark grey pebbledash. If only we could; we would all love to fuck off, fuck off back to Melling or, better still, 1961 when school was still on the distant horizon. Below the graffiti is a raised grassy knoll. A small pond is scooped out; this water feature is polluted with the same red paint that's daubed on the wall. Among the scabby weeds, several glassy-eyed goldfish break the surface, dead and lifeless. The rumour is that the devastation was caused by a local hardcase called Nicolaides, an ex-pupil who left the school a parting gift over the summer holidays. We soon learn this lad had achieved legendary status around the older kids, almost to the point of hero-worship. He had nutted one or two of the teachers. Headbutting is very popular at the moment. It's often used as a pre-emptive strike in a scrap by ruffians not adhering to the Marquess of Queensberry rules. Bloody beastly rotters!

We are all told to line up and then we are allocated classes. Davo and I are split up and sent into different classrooms. This is where our academic abilities will be assessed over the coming term, the teachers given the job of ascertaining which stream we should be in. These streams are in alphabetical order. 'A' denotes you are clever, down to 'F' to indicate you are a thicko. Below 'F' comes 'R' for remedial, although we never knew that at the time. After a few months of this assessment stage, the class is sorted; it is good news! I'm thick but not the thickest, and it seems that Davo is just as thick as me. We are reunited in the same stream, 'E', not quite the bottom of the barrel and a couple above the really thick poor sods in the remedial class.

The days drag on with only the breaks and dinner hour having any joy in them. Not sure if it's the teachers' failure or the general mood of the youths, but we are all no hopers anyway. School leaving age is just fifteen, at which point you are expected to get a job or, if we have the practical skills, an apprenticeship. Kids in the school would dream of a job on the production line at the huge Ford car factory situated at the south end of Liverpool, right by Speke airport, now rebranded the John Lennon International Airport. I'm sure he would have loved that; a working-class hero is something to be and all that, stick your MBE, etc. If they want to name something after me when I die, that's OK. A leafy woodland, a chippy, a record-pressing plant or a weasel sanctuary – anything like that would be cool.

The days drag by; it is all very dull. The only good thing about the school is the last two lessons on a Friday, which are given over to free choice; we can choose what we want to do. Obviously maths, English or history are out, but fun things like sports, swimming, sailing and even ice skating are in. I sign up for ice skating for the first term.

Friday comes and a coach turns up, Wingate's Tours in golden lettering on its rear. We have a thirty-minute drive to the Silver

Blades Ice Rink on the far side of Liverpool. The place is rundown, but we don't care. We are provided with skates and, without any instruction, off we go on to the ice with the fearless confidence of youth and by watching some of the other kids who are regulars. I manage to be able to at least scoot in a forward motion without any injuries and spend most of the time on my feet and not my arse. The rink has a DJ booth and a bloke in a woollen Fair Isle tank top, flowery shirt and feather-cut hairdo is gyrating like a Liverpudlian Rod Stewart in heat. He's doing a good job, though, pelting out all the hits of the day: Norman Greenbaum's 'Spirit in the Sky', the Supremes' 'Baby Love' and the Ashton, Gardner and Dyke classic 'Resurrection Shuffle' – this is a favourite. The girls on the ice are flicking two-fingered peace signs like they just don't care, as instructed by the song's lyrics. The Temptations and Four Tops are in the mix. Soul music is big and the northern soul scene is building up under the radar. Whooshing along to these records fills me with a great feeling and, after a few weeks of these free-choice sessions, I am competent enough to fly around at quite a lick. The records from the Silver Blades Ice Rink days have stayed with me. All have permanent residence in the nostalgic ventricles of my heart and also on my prized 1960s greasy-spoon Wurlitzer jukebox – a bargain back in 1981 at only fifty English quid and still going strong.

As I head into my teen years, school starts to become more of a lark than a place of learning. I have become more and more interested in music. I have been infl uenced by the heavy rock bands that I am hearing at my friend Dave Mazenko's house. Dave, or Maz as he's known, left school at fifteen and is now working in Liverpool. He has a bit of cash; he and his older brother are starting to build up record collections. Bands with great guitarists are heavily featured: Taste (Rory Gallagher), Cream (Eric Clapton), Led Zeppelin (Jimmy Page) and Jimi Hendrix, naturally. Also included are an underground mob of heavy-rock, anarchist shit stirrers from London's Ladbroke Grove psychedelic scene called the Pink Fairies. All these records are emanating from the blues format. That's what's happening; these British bands are ahead of the game. I nip over and watch *Top of the Pops* at the Mazenkos' house; on Thursdays at 7.30 p.m. everything stops for *Top of the Pops*. Along with all the pop dross that we are being fed, a few bands I am now being exposed to begin to appear.

One such band is Jethro Tull. Ian Anderson, a raggedy dressed vagrant in a long checked overcoat, is the singer. Leering out of the box, in-between flute bothering and singing, he gurns at us in a piss-taking manner. Tull have long been a favourite of the Mazenko boys, so this is an event not to be missed. *What the hell are we doing on this show?* Anderson must be thinking. Also featured over these next weeks and beyond: Atomic Rooster's 'Tomorrow Night', from Germany the Rattles 'Can't You See the Witch', Black Sabbath 'Paranoid', Mungo Jerry 'In the Summertime', Canned Heat 'Let's Work Together' and Status Quo 'In My Chair'. The slightly heavier bands are having a little bit of time in the glow of the pop-chart sun. The audio from the shows is recorded by Maz on a state-of-the-art Grundig reel-to-reel tape recorder, a little plastic microphone pointing at the TV's tinny speaker. The BBC Radio 1's chart countdown is also religiously tuned into every Sunday night. This, too, is recorded and played constantly in the Mazenkos' back room. We are all moving on from the pop of *Top of the Pops* to real bands playing real music that will stand the test of time.

I am creeping up on thirteen years old and have got myself a paper round. I now work for the local newsagent and grocer, the genial Mr Arthur Atkins. Not only me, but my two good mates, BilBessantt from my 1960s war games and Davo from many adventures. All three of us have paper rounds. On payday, we are the village high rollers with five bob burning holes in our pockets, bubbles pink and sticky popping from our gobs and the latest edition of the *Beano* sticking out our Tesco tearaways jeans pockets.

Arthur is a real gent; we never hear him swear. The nearest thing to an expletive to come from his mouth is 'blimey days'; we love that. It seems to be from a time past, something you would hear in an Enid Blyton Famous Five book:

'I say, Dick, did you remember to bring the ginger ale?'

'Sorry, George, I left it on the parlour table.'

George rolls her eyes and retorts, 'Blimey days! Dick, you are such a stupid fucker.'

They all fall about laughing until they puke.

We adopt this antiquarian lingo as our own, at first as a piss take but it gets said so often it becomes part of our everyday language. A way to express shock or disdain at anything. Davo was still saying it well into his thirties: 'Blimey days.' Who'd have thunk it?

I traverse the village on my trusty bike and can make short work of the deliveries. The current trend in bikes is the extremely coveted Raleigh Chopper. I have never been in the running to get such a groovy set of wheels as a Chopper. I have a cheap, ungainly Austrian ladies' shopper bike, made by a company called Puch. It is bright orange with small wheels and has a carrier rack. Even though it's possibly the un-coolest ride in Christendom, I love this bike. As soon as I can afford it, I set to work customising her. The addition of a set of ape-hanger handlebars is a good start. I flip the rear rack on to the front and make a handy support for my heavy paper bag. A few stickers and a set of those plastic dangly streamer things that are shoved in the little hole in the handlebar grips are also added; that's about as far as it goes in the custom shop. I would have loved to have got one of the new saddles kids are fitting to bikes up and down the land, the extremely comfy but ridiculous banana seat. This would have taken my customisation of the prim ladies' shopper to the next level of chopped-hog menace. Unfortunately, I have to save as much cash as possible to feed my new addiction . . . music.

It was in the summer of my thirteenth year. One day my mum came down from the tiny boxroom where she'd been sleeping. She had a tatty suitcase in her hand; though I don't even register the scenario that is about to be played out. I'm more interested in getting round to Davo's to play Alice Cooper's album *Killer* or something. My dad is out at either the pub or betting shop. I remember it was daytime, so it might have been a Saturday because both my parents worked all week.

My mum takes me aside and drops a bomb on me. She is leaving and going back to her mother's house in Walton.

'I can't take it any more, lad,' she says.

Strangely, it's not really something that I can say bothers me at the time. I was unaware of a normal family life and stayed away from the pair of them as much as I could. The toxic atmosphere in the house was dark, to say the least.

'You can come with me, if you like?' she asks.

I'm trying to process all this: live with my grandma who just shouts at me all the time in Walton? No thanks!

I'm thinking, all my mates are here. Walton a scary place, to me anyway. I imagined it chock full of really hard kids. In a flash, I envisioned getting legged by hordes of real scousers playing a pleasant afternoon game of hunt the woolly-back and kick his head in. You have to be joking. Mum has packed up her few belongings and is ready to go right now with no hint or warning. Now with hindsight, I really don't think she wanted me to come with her anyway.

'Nah, I would rather stay here,' I say. Then I say something that has puzzled me all my life:

'I won't come and see ya, you know.'

Her reaction is lost in time. I don't remember tears or anything overemotional like that. Maybe she didn't believe me, and thought it was just a hurtful thing to say by a thirteen-year-old confronted with this odd situation.

She finally says, 'Tara, lad,' and picks up the suitcase and heads off to the bus stop and waits for the 307 to Walton.

I can't remember much else about it. I never did go and see her. As far as I'm aware, she never got in touch until I was much older. My immature mind wasn't able to deal with any of it. It just seemed like another weird thing that grown-ups did. She had escaped, at last. I'm sure deep down it affected me, but I still don't know how. At the time, I just carried on as normal.

My dad never mentioned her again. Yet one thing did change that night: I never wet the bed again. All the severe animosity between my parents was affecting me on a deeply subconscious level it seems.

After a couple of years at the school, we are allowed to roam out of the institution's boundaries during scheduled dinner breaks. I forgo the delights of school dinners and persuade my dad to give me the cash he would have spent on my dinner tickets. With cash in my pocket and records to buy, Maghull town square is the destination. We invariably head over to NEMS record store, one of our favourite dinner-time haunts. I say dinner, not lunch. In the north, it's dinner, OK? Why would the women that made the school dinner be called dinner ladies? Anyway, at dinner hour, our little gang head to the chippy or Reece's Café in Maghull town square. I can manage to save a little cash by only having a bowl of beans and a bread roll known as a barm cake: floury, soft and lovely like a baked cloud. This costs just seven new pence. I was given ten new pence, formerly called two bob, two shillings or, if you are really old, a florin. I can save a little every day for my record-buying fund.

Tucked away on the right-hand side of the square is the record store, owned by the Epstein family, the same mob whose son Brian had managed to steer the Beatles to all the early glory. I'm sorry to keep mentioning the bloody Beatles! You just can't escape them in this neck of the woods. The NEMS initials stood for North End Music Stores. I spend ages looking through albums and wishing I had the cash to buy them. I do have enough for a single though. My first seven-inch record is Jimi Hendrix's 'Voodoo Chile'. The track is taken off the 1968 album *Electric Ladyland*. What a record it is, swirling between controlled feedback and distorted riffs like a tripped-out ringmaster controlling wild beasts with a flick of a whip or a black magician summoning forth demons spitting and crackling, the air thick with other-worldly sounds. The extensive and rhythmic use of the wah-wah pedal allows Jimi to serve up sounds never before heard on planet Earth – or any other planet, for that matter. A fearless and impressive use of the Stratocaster trem bar, which if attempted by many other guitarists would sound contrived and gimmicky, add to this, and the spaced-out lyrics about chopping mountains down with the edge of his hand complete the perfection. This track is Jimi at his best and a perfect record for his fans to say goodbye to a genius we have never seen the like of since. The single was released posthumously for the bargain knockdown price of just six shillings; that's just thirty pence in the soon to be introduced decimal currency, the record label Polydor not wanting to be seen to be profiting from the recent accidental death of Hendrix. This high level of decorum will not be evident when Mr Bowie slips away. Within minutes, there are more re-releases, picture discs, old demo tapes and general shite than you could shake a stick at; most is clogging up my inbox.

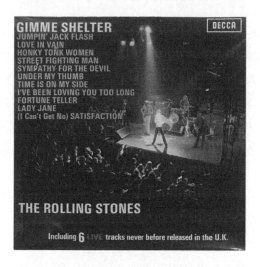

It's coming up Christmas 1971 and I have asked Santa's representative on Earth (i.e. my dad Alf) for the latest Who record, *Who's Next*. On the weekend, we head to County Road and Creasey's music shop. The Who record I am after is unfortunately sold out, so I plump for the next best thing: the recently released Rolling Stones album *Gimme Shelter*. A few days later and after much badgering, I am able to nab the record early before Santa's sooty descent of our chimney. I am allowed to take the record over to my mate Maz's house to play on their record player. It is comprised of half hits, half live album. After listening, we move on to some other record, more than likely *Stand Up* by Jethro Tull, a big favourite at the time. I foolishly leave my brand-new record on a chair and dangerously close to the Mazenkos' electric fire and the record warps in the heat. When we come to spin it again, I watch the relentless hump in the plastic disc mesmerise me and fill me with the shame of someone who can't look after his records. With the aid of a couple of pennies balanced on the cartridge head, the extra weight keeps the stylus deep in the album's groove, but it's a bitter lesson to learn.

By contrast, my next record is an EP from the foot-stomping jug-band festival favourites Mungo Jerry, *You Don't Have to Be in the Army to Fight in the War*. Like Jethro Tull, Mungo Jerry is not the name of the band's frontman. This cat is called Ray Dorset and he has the best set of mutton chops since Charles Dickens was a lad. They had recently scored a big hit with 'In the Summertime', not heard on the radio much these days, as the lyrics advocate drinking and driving plus rather unseemly behaviour towards the fairer sex, the sort of behaviour not seen since *On the Buses* was on the telly.

It is a time, after all, when the girls do domestic science lessons, the boys, woodwork or metalwork lessons. Your role is clearly defined as either male or female. Everyone hates metalwork class; it just seems to be endless filing. When the TV show *Kung Fu* aired in the UK, David Carradine's character Kwai Chang Caine is filmed deftly dodging pointed star weapons (shurikens) chucked at him by his fellow monks of the Shaolin temple. This leads to a keen upsurge of interest in metalwork classes – to the bafflement of our teacher Mr Woods. All the kids are making these deadly looking throwing stars, most for target practice – spinning them into chalk targets scrawled on a fence or garage door.

Kung Fu has a major influence on the kids in our school. Several think that, after watching a few episodes, they are immediately martial arts masters. Some even convince themselves they will fare well in a fight with the harder kids. The pre-emptive headbutt soon puts the cat among the pigeons with these misguided fools.

Our class has the distinction of having two of the hardest kids in the school in its ranks, the cock of the year Crum and another, even harder kid that could go for the cock title but is not that arsed about the glory that comes with it. He is just happy to be generally menacing and bully his regulars. I'm even still reluctant to mention his name; let us just call him Pupil X.

Davo and I are among the jokers in the class. We are dubbed Eric and Ernie after the popular light entertainers *Morecambe and Wise*, who are all over the telly. Look, don't freak out at my next statement: I don't think *Morecambe and Wise* funny. I know they are a national institution but it's all a bit cheesy, if you ask me. My sense of humour is more in tune with *Monty Python's Flying Circus*, Spike Milligan, Marty Feldman or the Bonzo Dog Doo-Dah Band – that's more my vibe. I think this leaning towards surreal humour was born from my dad being a big fan of the radio. His favourite was without doubt the forerunner to all the wacky comedy that followed, the BBC Light Programme's irreverent *Goon Show*, where Peter Sellers started his rise to worldwide stardom.

Our little gang of mates consists of me, Davo, Ian Campbell (Cam) and Simon Crumpton (Jasper Mouth-Action). This last name needs an explanation. So here goes. There is a kid in our class who is on the periphery of our little gang. His name is Phil aka Sarky Phil, due to his rather sarcastic nature. He's always first with a comment, usually very cruel and often very funny. During a PE lesson, we are sent off to run around the track on the playing field. Simon lunges into the task, his wiry frame with head back, ginger hair and freckles all over the place as he pelts along. His mouth is opening and closing in a deranged manner. Watching, transfixed by this weird display of facial acrobatics, is Sarky Phil. Well, he ain't gonna let that go, is he? He's Sarky Phil, after all; he has a reputation to protect. Out of thin air, Sarky Phil christens Simon with the name Jasper Mouth-Action, usually shortened to just 'Jasper' or, when being told to shut up by one of the many thugs at school, just 'Mouth-Action'. This is used as if it were a genuine double-barrelled name.

Other than that, we are surprisingly not picked on or bullied. We are seen as a bit odd because we like different music to the mainstream. Even though we get called 'the four freaks in the corner', we are tolerated. We get along with most of the kids at school. The trick is, don't be too good at anything and don't be crap either; average is the way forward. We get the odd wise-crack or insult, and that is about as far as it goes. We are well capable of deflecting shouts of 'Fuck off, knobheads,' with the ever-popular, 'Get stuffed, you fucking bell-ends.' Yes, it's razor-sharp wit like this that gets us through pretty much unscathed. For Davo and I, years of keeping clear of the Kirkby skinhead threat has built our defensive strategy. We have valuable skills gained in the field of conflict; day in and day out on the front-line warzone of the Melling chippy has trained us well. We can avoid most confrontations before the danger zone is entered.

We can deflect the dead-eyed gaze of the school nutjobs by acting the fool and getting them to laugh.

It turns out Sarky Phil is an expert at real explosives as well as explosive sarcasm. One summer day, he arrives with his school bag packed with enough ordnance for a small civil war. As the clock ticks round to 4 p.m., it's home time and that means freedom. We (Davo, Phil and I) leg it out of the school and gather at a little coppice of trees a couple of hundred yards from the school gate. Phil delves into his satchel and retrieves a tubular device about two inches wide and eight inches long. He sets about rigging up his handiwork. The explosive contained within is some concoction, something to do with sugar and fertiliser. It is housed in a copper pipe with the ends flattened and folded over to make a seal. Christ knows how he learned how to do this stuff – and without the internet. Nowadays every Tom, Dick and Jihadi can find out how to blow shit up, just by a small amount of sniffing around the web's smelly areas. Maybe he had relatives in the IRA or something. He straps the bomb to a low branch, lights the fuse and we leg it, all giggling with the nervous and expectant fear you get when running from someone with an air pistol that they are pointing in your general direction.

We nearly get behind a large oak tree before the thing kicks off. The bang is sensational and the limb of the tree cracks. Splinters, bark, wood chips and shrapnel are raining down on to us. We slyly escape the coppice, not wanting to attract too much attention. Having fled the scene we look as surprised as the rest of the kids at the massive boom that's still echoing. Kids running for freedom out the school's gates are stopped in their tracks;

confusion is all around. 'Wow, fucking hell, that was amazing.' Phil beams with his trademark sarcastic chuckle and grins the smile of a Cheshire Cat.

We sneak back to the bus stop and blend in with the throng. Luckily, we each still have all our four limbs in place. The poor tree doesn't; the still-fizzing stumpy limb is shattered. The power of the thing put the fear in us so much that the next time Phil asks us to join him in some explosive fun, we politely decline the offer.

6.

Look Wot You Dun

'In My Chair' – Status Quo

It's 13 May 1972. It's a very big day, for tonight we – that is, Dave Mazenko, Steve Mazenko, his very beautiful girlfriend Pauline and I – are going to watch Status Quo. Quo is the supporting act for current pop-chart favourites Slade. The gig is at Liverpool Stadium, otherwise known as the Boxing and Wrestling Stadium. Tonight, the smell of blood, sweat and pain will be replaced by the heady scent of patchouli–oil–drenched, scruffy layabouts. The exterior tiled stadium is situated in the business end of the city (what's left of it), tucked away down a little cobbled street like a dirty secret, just a weakling's stone's throw from the slow, dark brown crawl of the River Mersey's tidal ebb and flow. The polluted water flows past Liverpool's famous ferry boat landing stage known as the pier head. This area is flanked by the dirty soot encrusted 'Three Graces'; that is the Cunard Building, the Port of Liverpool Building and the Royal Liver Building.

Perched high upon the Liver Building's towers are the mythical Liver Birds, the symbol of Liverpool. If they decide to cock an ear to what's going on just a couple of streets back from the quayside, their feathery earholes will tonight be assaulted by the purity of Quo's no-nonsense, mindless boogie. On many a past night they would have heard the likes of fledgling future mega groups such as Led Zeppelin, Pink Floyd, Free, David Bowie, Roxy Music, Hawkwind, plus numerous denizens of the underground music scene.

As fully paid up members of the burgeoning hairy-hippie cult, Dave, Steve and Pauline are head to toe in cheesecloth and denim. Steve wears desert wellies (chukka boots). Dave and I have the latest trend platform boots polished and zipped; yes, these beauties are 'all the go'. The clobber we are wearing is also 'fab and indeed gear!' as they used to say in the far-flung days of the Merseybeat era, the name given to Liverpool's early sixties music scene. I am a mere hippie's apprentice and have not yet fully blossomed into a flower child. I am trying my best with my obligatory long hair, flared Wrangler jeans, grandad vest, home-made tie-dyed corduroy jean jacket – complete with sewn-on 'Ban the Bomb' patches – and even a replica German iron cross dangling from my pocket flap. As we wait for the bus, I feel excited, nervous and, above all, cool.

A little later, we pull into the darkly lit, litter-strewn and seedy Skelhorne Street bus station. We disembark the red Ribble bus and set off across to the other side of town, embarking on the ten-minute walk to the venue, first stopping for a quick pint at the Cross Keys, the nearest pub to the gig. Licensing laws are very lax; a spotty fourteen-year-old would have had no bother getting a drink. We then quickly move on and join the queue outside the gig. It's a first-in-best-seat situation. There is a lot of pushing and shoving in the queue. Suddenly the doors are flung open, the tickets are grabbed out of our mitts and we scramble into the auditorium, legging it towards the stage. The Mazenkos are well-versed in this routine. Steve, Dave and Pauline guide me through and get me to a seat; Pauline is not averse to digging the ribs of the odd hairy fucker that gets in her way. When they turn around to see her, they suddenly step aside to let her through. I'm not sure if this is because of her good looks or the hardcase look in her eye; either way, it works. We end up only a few rows back from the stage and dead centre. The place fills up quickly.

After ten minutes, some joker with lank hair and a blue grey air force trench coat starts to sing, 'Why are we waiting, ooooh why are we waiting?' to the tune of the popular Christmas carol, 'O Come All Ye Faithful'. A few scattered voices join in, but it's a poor turnout. Suddenly a painfully skinny lad is standing on the back of the seats; he must be a speed freak or something. Heroin is yet to get a hold on the city; amphetamines are the more likely culprit. He is fearlessly striding across the tatty seat backs with the confidence of a regular stadium dweller. This bony nutter is wearing a scuffed, fringed black leather biker jacket and knee-length ladies' five-inch platform boots with his black jeans neatly tucked into them. His hair is an amassed mop of Hendrix frizz. Juxtaposed to this scruffy thatch sits a battered gentleman's top hat. He is a sight to behold, very similar to the future Guns N' Roses guitarist geezer Slash, but without all the facial ironmongery and peeled of any muscle. I think it was Marc Bolan who popularised this look in England. I know hippies from the hotbed of freakiness that is San Francisco would say Jerry Garcia was the first to don the topper. Our little Liverpool chappie is a short arse but augmented with the good twelve inches of hat and massive heeled boots. This extra height gives him a gangly, stick-insect quality. He makes it to the front row and flings his arms up in the air, his twig-like digits flipping the two-fingered peace sign; the Devil's horns salute has yet to make it to Liverpool. He stares glassy-eyed deep into the heart of the crowd and begins to shout 'Sabbath! Sabbath!'

I'm thinking, *Is he so out of it, he is at the wrong gig? Shouldn't he be yelling Quo, or at a push, Slade?* Looking at the crowd with my naive eyes, most of this lot have got to be here for Quo. I can't imagine this shabby rabble being fans of the Brummie hit-parade fixtures Slade.

Then it happens; my attention is drawn from the daddy-long-legs-like presence of the kid shouting from the front. Someone from the back cries out, 'Walleeee!' It's answered by someone over to my left: 'Walleeeeee!' Then the right: 'Walleeeeeeeeee!' *What the fuck is this all about?* My mind is confused; it's like some primitive cry of anguish echoing deep into this jungle of hair and denim. They call and answer, 'Wallllleeeeee!' This goes on for quite a time. At all the subsequent shows I attend at the stadium, this anguished cry is always heard. I have asked around my mates who went to the stadium and all remember it, but nobody seems to know how it originated or who is this mythic

Wally character? Just like Bigfoot, it is mystery that will never be fully explained.

After about twenty minutes or so, the crowd starts to grow restless and a slow handclap begins. The claps are joined by a stomp. This time all are joining in – even me. It's all part of the ritual that I get to know and love. This build up is a feeling that I unfortunately no longer have at gigs. I have played too many myself, seen too many bands and met too many members of bands. All the mystery has vanished. Back then, it is a very real and pleasant feeling. It starts with butterflies in the stomach, then a deep apprehension swells up, fed by the atmospheric murmur of a full house, which is rising up to a frenzy.

The lights go down and the bass and two guitarists of Quo kick off: head down, no-nonsense mindless boogie indeed, their incredibly long hair covering their faces as they chug into the familiar riff: dan da dan da dan da dan! I've never heard volume like this before; it's incredible.

Now I know what you are thinking: *Will has lost his mind – Status Quo? Is he having a laugh?* You have to realise that Quo were then not what they were to become, sadly what the kids of today call dad rock. Status Quo at this point in time were a vital part of the underground scene, a band of misbehaving rockers loved by bikers and hippies alike.

Quo are a hardworking team and are in the middle of a UK tour supporting Slade – but they are in no way the support band to us. They are not holding back; cleared for take-off, they are launching into the current hit 'Paper Plane'. All seats are vacated from the get-go.

Rancid hair, sweat, beer, beads and earwax are sent flying all over the place. From the stage, not much is said: Quo are here to rock! They let the riffs do the talking and what great riffs they have, all gleaned from the blues, economically stripped of extraneous fripperies and as tight as Bettie Page's best Sunday corset, pared back to the bare bones of rock and served up in much the same way the Ramones will do in a few years' time, thick tones powering out of the baking hot tube amps: 'Mean Girl', 'Down the Dust Pipe' and the Doors classic 'Roadhouse Blues'. They play a selection of tunes off the LP *Dog of Two Head* and from their latest album *Piledriver*.

The skinny stick-insect kid, now devoid of the topper, is wildly flailing his hair about while standing on the seat in front of Pauline. Not a good idea. The curly mop of hair is swooshing about and hitting her in the face as he thrusts and jerks to Quo, who are now in full flow. Pauline grabs the little squirt and shouts in his battered lughole to 'Fucking stop it or else!' The steely glare gets her message home; he continues to frug out but in a slightly more amicable manner. Forty minutes later and it's all over. The sonic assault has left me dazed and confused in a good way.

It's time to get a beer from the little food and drink bar that's been set up behind the left-hand side of the stage. They sell something called Nudgers. These delights are ham and cheese rolls, so-called because they look like a nudger (penis). Serving these Nudgers is Doreen. I don't know her at this point, but in a few years she will be on the door of Eric's punk club and letting me, my mates and many regulars in for nothing. Why? Because we will then all be in freshly formed bands.

We stick around for Slade but are not that bothered. The lights go down and the singer and his boys appear on the stage. Noddy stomps over to the microphone and screams, 'Everybody alriiiiiight?' in his unmistakable Wolverhampton accent. We are still dazed from Quo's red-hot, amped up sonic assault, so you could say we are alriiiiiight. The crowd responds to the question with a less than enthusiastic, 'Yeees!' Noddy takes this as a challenge and launches into 'Get Down and Get with It'. Slade seem to be even louder than Quo. In no time at all, we do get down and are very much indeed getting with it. In fact, we are getting with it with every fibre of our being; we have little choice, finding ourselves in the epicentre of a flesh maelstrom. My initial thought that this ragged mob of ne'er-do-wells were here purely for Status Quo is immediately dispelled. We are in the midst of a rhythmic storm crashing the rocks of ancient, dandruff-dusted seating. It's a simple choice: join in or drown in the crush of bodies. Rattling through hit after hit, Slade unleash a batch of songs and I soon realise they are fucking good. They rock like bastards; the chart successes are just a by-product of being fantastic at rocking and songwriting. The set is full to the brim of oft-heard forty-fives from BBC Radio 1 and *Top of the Pops* and even includes a cover from the 1968 film *Easy Rider*, the Steppenwolf classic 'Born to Be Wild'.

Lead guitarist Dave Hill is the one with the weird fringe that sits way too high at the top of his forehead in the style of a medieval simpleton. The only difference being that a simpleton's garb would most likely be a filthy doublet, cape, tights, plus an optional codpiece. Dave is clad head to toe in a silver jumpsuit and thigh-high platform boots. The not optional codpiece is likely filled with half the contents of the dressing room's complimentary fruit bowl rattling round inside. All of this is glistening in the half-a-dozen lights that passed for a lightshow back then. As he beams with a smile that shows off his

Bugs Bunny teeth, Dave is swigging rough cider from a gallon demijohn, then spitting it at the front row like a dragon spraying fire. He passes the jug over to singer Noddy Holder. Noddy is dressed in slightly less outrageous gear than Dave, but still pretty severe: half-mast, extremely wide tartan trousers, cherry red Dr Martens AirWair boots, a tweed herringbone tailcoat. On his head sits a top hat just like our head-flailing friend's in front of us. Noddy takes a large gulp of the cloudy cider and does the same, spraying the front few rows with the cat-piss funk of the scrumpy. I'm shocked. I have never seen grown-ups behave in such a manner before. It's all very weird and makes me feel a little uneasy but adds to the rebelliousness of rock 'n' roll that I am becoming addicted to.

'Oi, Dave, I think these scousers are alriiiiiiight,' growls Noddy. Drummer Don Powell clicks his sticks to count in 'Mama Weer All Crazee Now', along with 'Coz I Luv You', 'Look Wot You Dun' and 'Take Me Bak 'Ome'. Please note: these are not spelling mistakes; this is how Slade spell.

As we leave and climb the steep steps up to the exit, I look back to see that quite a few rows of seats are trashed; the stadium is left injured. The crowd herds out of the venue with an excited feeling that we have just witnessed something really special. We cross town back to Skelhorne Street bus station, avoiding the hordes of winos that are seeking shelter for the night, and catch the last bus back to Melling.

I know I have the bug and Bowie is on in a couple of weeks, the only problem being I haven't got the few shillings it costs to get a ticket. By the time I have my paper-round wages, it has sold out. I'm still pissed off about this, but I do get to see Bowie a few years later and this eases my pain a little.

As the year goes on, the Liverpool Stadium will become a favourite haunt of mine. I get to see lots of great groups as they are climbing the greasy pole of popularity and breaking through into the sweet grasslands of stardom. For the up-and-coming bands, this is the Liverpool gig they usually play before they move up a notch to the Liverpool Empire Theatre.

Among the great bands, I see Dr Feelgood. This band's live show has a profound effect on me, mainly because of Wilko Johnson, the group's manic guitarist. Through every song, the tension is mounting; everybody is waiting for Wilko to kick off and go darting across the stage like a demented ostrich, his eyes maniacally staring into space as somehow he manages to play rhythm and lead guitar at the same time. This Thames Estuary geezer is in league with the Devil, surely. It's not a technical sequence of notes like Clapton or Hendrix is capable of, but a machine gun right into the brain. While Wilko is strafing us with rhythm and blues bullets, singer Mr Lee Brilleaux notices he is being upstaged by Wilko's antics. He takes to centre stage and drops to the floor. There's no other way of putting what happens next: he fucks the stage. I have a few of the early Dr Feelgood albums, but they never seem to be able to capture the power and glory of the live sets. I think this is often true. I'm not sure if it's the sheer volume or the atmosphere of the gig with a couple of thousand like-minded people freaking out. I think most bands are better live than on record.

The Sensational Alex Harvey Band (SAHB) are another mob of regulars at the stadium. They get let out of Scotland to come south of the border now and then to worry the English or, as the Scottish rather rudely call us, 'Sassenachs'. Davo, Maz and I are always in attendance. We love the larger-than-life, comic-book personalities of the group. SAHB shows are a theatrical treat with simple sets and choreographed interplay between Alex and the guitarist, the rather sci-fi sounding Zal Cleminson. SAHB are never given the recognition they deserve in regard to being one of the forerunners of the punk-rock scene, a bridge between glam rock and punk rock, one of the sparks that light the punk-rock fuse. Alex's attitude was every bit as unnerving as Rotten's. It seems nuts now, but to our young eyes Alex was getting on a bit when he found success, which came with a camp cover of the Tom Jones classic, 'Delilah'. It reached the charts and they got on *Top of the Pops* a few times. But to the fans that had been there from the beginning, it was seen as a bit of a joke, and soon it is all they are known for. Alex was only forty-six when he died and sadly soon forgotten. He never gets a mention on any of the endless TV rock music documentaries.

Just like David Bowie and Alice Cooper, frontmen need a character to inhabit to be able to do the things they do on stage, things they would never normally do when confronted by a shitload of hairy-arsed music fans baying for blood. Their bravery is increased, a sort of Dutch courage that builds from the feedback of the fans. This lifts them from the usually weedy persona to the level of gods. It is when singers start to believe their own hype that the trouble starts. You have to get back to reality at some point or you are lost; you will become a parody of yourself. Fans start to see though the fakery and abandon ship pretty quick. Bowie was the ultimate, of course. He would play the part; but when interviewed, he would be the same down-to-earth, slightly cockney joker he always was. During the cocaine years, he was in danger of becoming a complete knob but managed to get his shit together.

As well as attending gigs at the stadium, I see many bands at the Empire; but the Liverpool Stadium will always be the special place for me. The Empire is a much more genteel affair, with a stricter set of rules; no seats are getting trashed there. The scruffy fans' arses that get to slip into the plush velvet stalls of the Liverpool Empire generally remain there; not much in the way of seat-smashing riots takes place.

I am flirting with the hippie oeuvre, but with one eye on the fashion of the up-and-coming glam-rock scene. On the telly is a show never shown any more due to lashings of racist, homo-phobic, sexist language – yes, all the stuff that 1970s telly was best at. The show was called *Budgie* and starred none other than Adam Faith. Adam Faith was a very successful sixties teen idol and heartthrob. As time and the planet moved on, he became lost somewhere betwixt rock 'n' roll and the new psychedelic world. He had already been in the 1960 film *Beat Girl*, before turning to TV acting in the 1970s. He did a pretty good job at it. Budgie is a petty criminal often navigating his way out of trouble but usually only after a good kicking. The character inhabits the crime-sodden London underworld as minion of the character Charlie Endell, all done with a light-hearted cheeky grin, loon pants and ungainly clogs, which were pretty useless if he had to scarper from some henchmen in a hurry. I think Budgie never thought it through; a pair of Dunlop Green Flash sneakers would have been more suitable. My mum worked at the Dunlop factory at the time and could have half-inched him a pair, no bother. I was never without a pair when she worked there. The simple ploy was to walk out past the security guard's little hut with them on her feet. She even employed this tactic to get me size-eight, heavy-duty rubber wellington boots.

Budgie wore a leather two-tone zipper jacket with ornate tulip collars; these have a rounded and more flowing cut than the usual lapels, the usual sharp point. It started a trend. Soon these jackets materialised everywhere and were called – as you would guess – Budgie jackets. They were mostly made of leather in very seventies colour combinations: grey and maroon, turquoise and navy blue, orange and brown. Lovely, just like our front-room wallpaper. I managed to acquire one along with not one but two satin jackets, one in emerald green and one bright pink. These had collars wider than Concorde's wings, topped off with large extravagant buttons. Marc Bolan would have creamed his jeans in an envy overload. Unlike that dandy in the underworld, I never dared to wear them out in the street. I did wear the Budgie jacket, but sadly the shiny satin jackets hung forlornly on wire hangers in the cheapo MFI self-assembly wardrobe, never to see the light of day. Skinheads would still be on patrol in the area, and when a long-haired fourteen-year-old kid in a pink satin jacket comes into view . . . well, as they say in the good old U S of A, 'you do the math'.

I don't know why I got them. It must have just been for the glamour of it all, the glam. I'm pretty sure the pink one originated from Dave Mazenko, but I don't remember him ever wearing it much either. Maz's mum Sylvia was a lovely lady who ran a Freemans catalogue. The Mazenko lads were working and were always buying clothes from the catalogue. They would either grow out of them or become bored with the items. I was there to snap them up at bargain prices or sometimes barter with what we all used as our main currency: LPs. All I had to do was wait.

I missed the boat to be a member of the real hippie scene. The peace and free love cult was on the way out, anyway, but even today the 'hippie' has not become completely extinct; some scattered enclaves are still roaming free in the wild, clinging on to the old ways.

7.

Glam-rock Gardening

'Virginia Plain' – Roxy Music

It's good news! In a bid to massage the woeful unemployment figures, the government – led by the part-time chuckling sailor boy/ full-time dandy Edward Heath – had decided to raise the school-leaving age from fifteen to sixteen. This meant I was to stay in school for an extra year. Couldn't say I was bothered. I had no real problems at school and the idea of looking for work at fifteen filled me with dread. Who wants to enter the grown-up world? Not me.

Devoid of ambition or any skills, a dead-end job was all most in our classroom could hope for. I now know, after all the travel and the experiences I have had over the years, I am not as thick as I was deemed to be by my school. I am surprised I wasn't interested in the lessons. I am interested in all things now, except maybe mathematics, though even that comes into the making of music. I think the teaching staff in those days were pretty crappy and were adopting a completely wrong approach. They seemed to think they could scare knowledge into us. I think the lower-class kids were seen as lost causes. Easy for me to say; I wouldn't want to be a teacher for a 'big clock', as my mum always used to say.

As a kid, the cheap alternative to toys was a pencil and a drawing book. I would spend hours entertaining myself sketching . . . all rubbish, mind you. Mainly doodles of Doctor Who's salt-cellar-shaped nemeses the Daleks, space rockets or *Star Trek*-inspired fantasy worlds and creatures. I enjoyed creating drawings in the same way I enjoy creating music or art now. You would expect that art lessons would be high on my list of favourite lessons – and you would be right. They were. But they could have been so much more.

I would have loved to hear stories about artists I have learned about since leaving school, tales of the strange techniques they used. There is nothing I like to watch more on the telly than a documentary about some crazed painter lopping his ear off because he's got a cob on with his mate. Or a far-out New York geezer who was so poor, he set himself the task of making art with whatever he could find within a block of his tatty apartment. Or the one about the French performance artist and painter that loved blue so much he invented his own shade, then went on to paint many canvases entirely blue. Let's not forget the one about Piero Manzoni, the Italian artist that tinned his own shit and valued it by the weight of the price of gold. Now it's worth many times the precious metal. This was a critical statement about the value of art as a commodity.

I think of our future Bunnymen manager Bill Drummond and his bandmate Jimmy Cauty from KLF, those merry pranksters from the popular dance-band era of the raving nineties. KLF were saying the same things as Manzoni when they burned a million quid of record profits from a time when you could conceivably make a million from selling records by the shit-load. The plan, Bill told me, was to 'make a single brick with the ashes and then value the brick at a million quid'. The destruction of the cash is the art, as is the act of then selling the brick to some idiot who will get the right to brag about the purchase. Not dissimilar to the Banksy work *Girl with Balloon* that was shredded in the Sotheby's sale room in 2018, the act of destruction increasing the value of the piece. The ridiculous irony of this gesture itself is a self-fulfilling act of profitable vandalism. I get all this art fun and games, and I'm not averse to the concept myself. I would much prefer to own the Fender Stratocaster that Jimi Hendrix used and then set alight as his grand finale at the Monterey Pop Festival in 1967 than a perfectly playable guitar he used on a record. There would be no Hendrix magic entwined in the molecular structure that it could impart to me. The half-cremated guitar corpse is more a part of world history.

At fifteen, I was a blank canvas. I was watching lots of the cool films that BBC Two was showing: *Midnight Cowboy*, *The Last Picture Show*, *Dr Strangelove (or how I learned to stop worrying and love the bomb)*, *Butch Cassidy and the Sundance Kid*. I also partook of the interesting TV shows around that period: *The Stone Tapes*, *Monty Python's Flying Circus*, *Star Trek*, *Doctor Who*. I loved to scare myself shitless with Hammer Horror films. A particular one I remember from this time was 1957's *The Night of the Demon*. Screened on BBC Two quite a few times in the seventies, it is pretty tame by today's standards. The demon more closely resembles a funny dog-faced dinosaur than a being of evil. Like most kids destined to become artists or musicians, it was always the more out-there shows that attracted me. Anything to do with magical shenanigans, ghosts or science fiction, and I would be lapping it all up. I would have loved to have gone to art school or university. Those lofty ambitions were out-of-bounds to a secondary modern lower grade kid. Such notions as further education were never even talked about. It was just for the brainboxes and the posh kids. Or, at a push, the ones whose parents gave a shit.

Our art teacher also didn't give a shit. Every lesson would start with the instruction, 'OK you lot, there's some paper and there's paint in that cupboard . . . off you go.' He would then sit down and read a book while listening to the soundtrack to the hit movie *The Sting* starring Paul Newman and Robert Redford and featuring the ragtime piano of Scott Joplin. This is OK if you like that sort of thing, and I sort of did at the time. The main problem would be when he left the school record player on repeat and it became a kind of plinky-plonky torture. Now, I sort of don't like that sort of thing. I can't stand that jaunty piano shite to this day.

Back in the seventies, even the not so religious schools such as ours still had a vague Christian ethic. We had hymn singing every morning, prayers and religious education lessons given by aptly named Mr Cross. He was a very keen exponent of the threaten-the-kids-with-a-heavy-rubber-pipe method of teaching. *That'll fill 'em up with righteousness and make believers out of them,* he must have thought to himself. *I'll beat the word of the Lord into the little shits.* Sadly it never worked on this heathen. I recall him taking exception to my rather Marc Bolan-esque patent leather (in truth, plastic) wedge shoes in purple and red that were on my stinking size-eight feet, my pungent webs swathed in a pair of fluorescent orange socks. He came up behind me like a creeping Jesus and, with unnecessary force, slammed the two-foot-long rubber pipe down on my desk. No chalk and blackboard needed here; his educational weapon of choice was heavy grade rubber. Well, you need something to keep these heretic kids in order. My books and pens leaped into the air; I nearly shat myself (not literally, but you know what I mean). Apparently Jesus would never have been seen in such ungodly footwear while hiding from the Roman rozzers in the garden of Gethsemane.

Some of the lessons around this time were, even to my mind . . . well, a little odd. Fucking surreal, frightening and horrific, more like. While the girls got lessons on cookery or needlework, the lads got used as slave labour, as the lower streams were considered fodder. Our gardening teacher, Mr Sharman, had a sizeable allotment at the back of the large shed-style classroom. We were the chain gang assigned to dig trenches for spuds, weed cabbage patches and generally do all the hard labour. Dave Mazenko told me when Sharman had his class planting lettuce seedlings, Maz took great delight in pulling the roots off before planting the bloody things. No salad for Sharman that harvest. Sharman was not one of the popular teachers.

The only good thing about the gardening lessons is that you can get changed out of the uniform and into your own clothes – jeans, boots, etc. I use this opportunity to wear my latest pair of bright red bell-bottom loons, freshly delivered via an advert on the back pages of the *New Musical Express*. The ensemble is completed with a bright yellow scoop-neck shirt with flared sleeves and an impressive pair of platform clogs in maroon and navy blue.

Sharman sees me and screams, 'What the hell are you wearing, laddie? It's not a fashion show, it's a gardening lesson, you idiot!'

Everyone is laughing at me. All of the other kids are wearing Dr Martens boots and Flemings jeans. This won't be the last time I find myself in trouble for pushing the school-uniform boundaries to the limit.

Back at the classroom, after toiling on the land, Sharman spots a couple of rabbits on the freshly weeded lettuce beds. He orders everyone to be quiet, then says, 'You boy, Mathers, go to the gym and see Mr Tomlinson. Tell him Mr Sharman wants a bow and arrow from the archery equipment.'

Mathers looks confused. 'Er, what, sir?'

'Are you stupid, laddie? Go and get me a bow and arrow. Now!'

Meanwhile, the bunnies are happily hopping between the rows of salad plants like shoppers at Tesco choosing the best-quality produce. The whole class is instinctively softly chuckling and are all crowded around the classroom windows, as a rather bizarre scenario is unfolding before us. Mathers scoots off, then returns pretty fast, clutching a bow and a few arrows in his hands. The rabbits continue to nibble a radish here and a carrot there; Sharman's little gems get a right bucktoothed seeing to.

'Give them here, laddie!' Sharman grabs at the weapons. The hunter-gatherer instinct is strong in Mr Sharman. We are now pinned to the glass, silent as spiders, as Sharman creeps round the corner of the gardening shed and comes back into our view. Stifled laughs are firing up around the room; the temptation to bang on the window and warn the bunnies is somehow resisted. His arrow already in place, he creeps from behind a shrubbery, draws the bow and aims at the unsuspecting rabbits, releasing the arrow with a resounding twang! It misses all the rabbits, who vanish into secreted burrows, safe underground even as the projectile is still in flight. The arrow careers off into the potato plants and very wide of the mark. The colourful flight feathers are all that can be seen among the spud plants.

We all go wild in the class, banging on the windows and laughing at his rubbish effort, slightly relieved that the bunnies have survived to nibble another day. Sharman enters, slams the door and barks at us, 'OK, sit down and shut up. You are like a load of yapping puppy dogs.'

He would say this just about every lesson, so our little gang have nicked this rather antwacky saying. I have just thought . . . antwacky is an antwacky thing to say, too. I bet none of you has ever heard that before. Here is an explanation: antwacky is a Liverpool slang word that simply means out-of-date or old-fashioned. We use Sharman's saying to take the piss out of each other at every possible occasion, calling each other yapping puppy dogs.

It seems Sharman's lust for blood is not quenched and he is now in a foul mood. He shouts, 'Right! I want you all to follow me over to the quad.' Sharman picks up a foot-long stick out of his desk drawer. It's in his hand; most are thinking, *Is that sodding stick for hitting us with?*

We all apprehensively follow him over the quadrangle build-ing, doing the usual messing about, pushing and kicking at each other's ankles, trying to trip one another up. We are led down the corridor, the familiar musty smell of geraniums sat upon the window ledges thick in the air. On we go, through the double doors, on to the square patch of grass that the chickens' coop is sat upon.

It soon becomes apparent that the stick is for a much grislier task than quick swipes at our arses. He opens the coop's wire fence door, then, quick as a ninja, grabs at one of the hens. Roughly, he grapples the flapping bird out of the confines of its pen. The poor thing! Only a few seconds ago, it was happily scratching at the bare soil for worms or any sort of grub in both senses of the word. I suppose the chicken was just doing the same thing Sharman is about to do to it. That's nature for you: the survival of the fittest and all that.

With a flurry of awkward wings and the soundtrack of distressing high-pitched clucks, quick as a flash Sharman pushes the bird's head to the floor and starts to squash the neck under the short stick he has deftly manoeuvred against the throat of the bird. The hen's beady eyes are fixed on all who are watching. The teacher then proceeds to step on each end of the stick with the chicken's neck trapped beneath his full weight. The petrified chicken is flapping and frantically squirming under the tubby Mr Sharman's girth. We all look on in horror as the chicken's breathing is choked and slowly the neck is crushed and then, with a distinct crack, snapped. He lifts the chicken – still flapping – and sets it on its feet. It starts to run about the quad, bashing into the wall and then the coop. This is the rather fun payoff, seeing the sad thing run about with its head loosely flapping around its breast.

After a couple of random laps of the quad, it keels over dead, and is now lying limp and still with its beady black eye on us all. This trick of the chicken's nervous system is the part Sharman gets the most joy out of. It seems to me that the poor creature was dispatched in an unnecessary vicious, convoluted and sadistic manner, designed to inflict as much distress, pain and horror as possible. In retrospect, it was more like a scene from a David Lynch movie than a gardening lesson.

Ah, the good old days.

Fortunately, no one fainted, so that was a plus; the bullying that would have followed a fainter would have been biblical. For example, I remember a girl in our class requested to go to the toilet. She had no chance. Asking in the middle of a lesson? Forget it. She was refused, then fainted and pissed herself on the floor. No sympathy was ever given to her. She was mercilessly picked on by all the lads, constantly told to 'Piss off' etc. I was lucky to not get bullied for my gardening fashion show earlier in the day. The gory events that followed must have made my glam-rock apparel pale into insignificance.

Not all the teachers were as nuts as Mr Cross and Mr Sharman. A couple of the younger ones seemed to still retain a little bit of enthusiasm for the profession. Mr Bell was one such teacher; his fragile spark had yet to be extinguished by the years of indifferent kids pissing about and staring out the window. Bell could be a bastard if he needed to be, but mostly he was a witty, lighthearted, portly, bearded bloke, dressed in psychedelic kipper ties, nylon suits, wide lapels and flared trousers. All of this sat atop a comfortable pair of beige suede Hush Puppy shoes.

I do give credit to this teacher; he was able to get my imagination ignited. The school owned several record players, items of equipment especially made for schools by the British company Garrard. They were very sturdy machines – only monophonic, but they sounded good. For many a year, I have kept my eye out at junk shops, antique fairs and car-boot sales – even searched on eBay – in the hope of obtaining one. I have never seen any since those secondary school days. Bell brought the record player into a lesson and played the Beatles 'She's Leaving Home' off the *Sgt Pepper* album. He went through the lyrics of the song and we analysed it as poetry. Which it is. A sensitive description of a teenager, an only child who sneaks off from the family home in the early morning to escape her stifled existence. It was not lost on me that it was exactly what my brother and sister had done, but without all the anguish and loss shown by the parents in the song.

This lesson went down well with the kids; it connected with us. Mr Bell was on a roll. The next lesson started with a tatty box of LP records under his arm as he burst through the classroom door. The records were a double album set of Dylan Thomas's 1954 production of *Under Milk Wood: A Play for Voices*, starring

Richard Burton, the great Welsh actor who breathed life into the words. The beautiful poetry told of the intertwined tales of the private lives of the occupants of a fictional Welsh fishing village Llareggub ('bugger all' spelled backwards), where both the living and the dead still existed side by side in different dimensions. We were particularly taken with the phrases, 'Nogood Boyo, up to no good in the wash-house' and 'Here's your arsenic, dear./And your weed killer biscuit.' We also liked great characters such as blind Captain Tom Cat, Organ Morgan and Gossamer Beynon. We would quietly read along with the records; it would mean something even if I never understood all of the words. I often bang on about this amazing BBC radio production to whoever will listen.

At this point in my life, I had only ever been to Wales for three days in 1965. Consequently, I was no expert on the Welsh and their mysterious ways. I had been forced on holiday to the Lyons Robin Hood caravan site in Rhyl. I hated it and always associated it with an unfortunate scarring event that occurred on that particular trip when my mum's mum had come with us. One soaking wet night while I was in one of the foldaway beds trying hard to get to sleep, my grandma had a shit behind a partition. There was no toilet in the caravan. The toilet block was a dark and rainy walk away. A galvanised bucket at the other end of the caravan was going to have to do. When you've got to go, you've got to go. I put my head under the pillow, desperately trying to block out the excruciating sounds of a slightly pissed eighty-year-old's plop, plop and splash. I still have nightmares about those little grey anaemic floaters squinting up at me in the morning, bobbing round in the shallows of the bucket. My dad had been not invited on the outing, but fortunately for me he did come to see if everything was OK on the following Wednesday, pulling up in his bright red Bedford minibus in which he ferried around the darts team from pub to pub. I pleaded with him to be sprung from this holiday from hell. I think my grandma wanted rid of me, too, so not much of a fight was needed.

The next time I would get to any other country, I would be twenty years old and on a Bunnymen mission to Belgium.

8.

Day Trips to the Spirit World

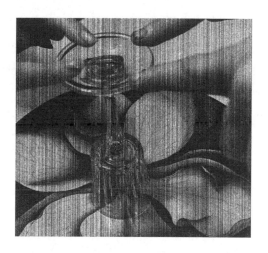

'Supper's Ready' – Genesis

As I got older, music was becoming more important, as it does with many teenagers. I was even getting my head around a few classical records. I had been hanging about with some lads that lived a street or two away from Station Road. Funny, in those days even a street away seemed like a big change in class. The houses were just normal semi–detached homes; but to me, they were very posh, all fitted carpets and open-plan living areas.

In those far off blue remembered days, most people knew or at least had heard of everyone in the village. If you were not a total bell-end (we had a few kicking around), it was pretty easy to make friends. Melling really was a small, friendly place. Around the corner from Davo's house, in a little road called Dunlop Drive, lived a kid about our age called Alan Roberts. Alan was unusual in Melling because he went to a school in Kirkby. This exposure to real hard-knock kids made him a little more worldly wise than us. He was a bit more resilient and faster witted, always quick with a comeback but funny with it. He and his brothers were all music fans. This was pretty cool as we all borrowed and lent records to each other, always returned after a few days, of course. Our knowledge of music increased. Between all of us, it was like a big music library that we were the exclusive members of. I can distinctly remember listening to a tape of the Who's album *Tommy* while we were sitting on Alan's front garden wall. I loved the bit that John Entwistle played on the French horn. It sounded like an elephant trumpeting.

Cassette-tape machines had just become popular – not the Sony Walkman-style ones that became all the rage in the eighties. These recorders were pretty clunky machines. I had one made by a Japanese company called Crown. It ate batteries and was the same weight as a small Rottweiler, but at least it was portable; we could take music with us.

A lot of wall sitting was done in those days, just hanging around on the streets. There was also the occasional youth club, where the girls would all dance in a line. We would just look on and dream, all of us too scared to approach them. All except Bill Bessant; he always was a suave ladies' man. I was as far away from a lady's man as could be possible and was in the Boy Scouts, which I enjoyed. I got to go on a couple of camping trips to Grasmere, a small village in the Lake District. The Lakes are a place that I still love and go whenever I can. I got kicked out of the Scouts for calling some posh woman who was visiting our Scout hut an old cow, after she started telling us off for the minor misdemeanour of chatting and having a laugh. But most of the entertainment was endless wall sitting, drinking tea or instant coffee, talking shit about girls that you fancied at school or in the village but you never stood a chance with. It was all fantasy.

My acne was really starting to become an issue for me mentally. At one point, I had a mini meltdown. I usually avoided mirrors as I was so self-conscious of it, but this time I looked. I saw the mounds of boils, red and sore. In between them were thousands of spots covering my face. I literally never had a patch of clear skin. I lost it and started to scratch at the spots, my long, dirty nails gouging and ripping, blood dripping, pimples left weeping. I let the blood dry and went to school like that: scratched to fuck and covered in dried blood. The frustration had got to me at a time when everyone seemed to be getting off with girls. I think this was the main driving force that later gave me the courage to start the band, to be noticed for something other than terrible acne. I know there are a lot of worse things for a kid to go through; but as it was part of the reason for start-ing the band, I must include it.

I'm sure a few of my friends' mums knew of the situation at 15 Station Road; village gossip takes no time to get about. There were plenty of curtain twitchers keeping round-the-clock surveillance on all in their view. I feel it would have been common knowledge about the situation between my mum and dad. All of my mates' mums and dads would show great kindness to me and sort of look after me. This was usually done by feed-ing me. I am only just realising this as I look back at this time with much older eyes. Billy Bessant's; mum Marie was a dab hand at egg and chips. This is still one of my all-time favourite meals. Funnily enough, Gordon Ramsay and the like have never featured this culinary delight on any shows I've seen. They would be shitting Michelin stars if they could get Mrs]Bessant's*pièce de résistance* on the menu. Dave Mazenko's mum Sylvia would make endless cups of coffee, and chocolate biscuits were always on offer. Even if Maz was out, she would let me sit with her and watch their colour telly, a refuge away from the hell house over the road. Davo's dad Harry was a baker and worked at a huge commercial bakery. His mum May was not bad at the art of baking either. She made really good fruit scones. Even though Davo never really liked them, she had made them just for me to scoff. Those fruity treats got offered along with morning coffee biscuits, perfect for dunking. Alan Roberts's mum Jean was also a really lovely lady, a real old-school mum – the sort you would see on gravy advertisements in the 1960s. The warm atmosphere in that house was a million miles away from ours. Her kitchen was always chocka with food on the go. If I went around there for a wall-based cassette-tape recorder playing session, she would find some spare grub and feed me up.

Up at the far end of Dunlop Drive was one of the kids who had been at Melling C. of E. He had passed the eleven-plus exam and now went to the grammar school. This was Richard Brunskill, the boy who had told us about getting paid to be in the church choir. He was mates with Alan Roberts from a few doors down, so we all hung around together. The Brunskill clan was defo posher than us. Richard's mum made me my first poached egg. 'What trickery is this? You can cook an egg in nothing but water?' I looked on in disbelief as the milky albumen started to solidify in the softly bubbling pan of water without an angry frying pan spitting molten lard anywhere in sight. 'Blimey.' The perfectly cooked egg was deftly plonked on real buttered toast. I can still remember this culinary revelation. To me, it was akin to discovering the secret of fire.

The Brunskills had a piano that we pissed about on. I couldn't play a thing, but Richard was learning bits and I was impressed with his mastery of 'Chopsticks'. His older brother Jeff was a lot better and could read music and play well. He would bash out the odd bit of pop music or happily play Bach or Mozart. They also had a large radiogram and a few records, one of which was the double EP released to coincide with the Beatles film *The Magical Mystery Tour* in 1967. This was more than likely my first brush with psychedelia. The tracks 'I Am the Walrus', 'Flying' and 'Blue Jay Way' stood out to me. These strange constructions were built with sounds that I'd never heard before and weird lyrics incorporating silly rhymes that we had recited as kids: 'Yellow belly custard' and 'Umpa, umpa, stick it up your jumper', etc.

The vocal sound on 'Blue Jay Way' is otherworldly and wobbly. This strange effect is created by sending the vocals through a Leslie cabinet. This is a large amplified speaker that usually comes paired with the mighty B3 Hammond organ. A switch on the organ's keyboard fires up this remarkable piece of equipment. When the switch is flicked, motors jolt into life and begin to rotate a metal drum contraption that sits above a bass speaker. The drum is whizzing around like a washing machine on spin cycle. This takes in the low end of the sound and jiggles it about. The whole thing then ejaculates the sound as it spins. Everything comes out washday clean with the sound of psychedelia. I would describe the effect as adding an underwater quality to the sound. I learn in future Bunnymen recording sessions that guitars can also be routed through the Leslie cab, and I employ this trick on occasion. This equipment transformed instruments into psychedelic staples of lots of sixties trip outs.

Meanwhile, in the dark and forgotten depths of the Brunskills' highly polished radiogram, there were designated areas for the storage of LP records. The obligatory Simon and Garfunkel albums were nestled along with a few pop singles: Petula Clark's 'Downtown', the Bonzo Dog Doo-Dah Band's 'I'm the Urban Spaceman'. I preferred the surreal imagery of the B-side 'Canyons of Your Mind'. They also had a couple of classical records (I told you they were posh): Tchaikovsky's *1812 Overture* – that's the one with cannons blasting off at strategic points in the piece – Ravel's *Bolero*, Holst's *The Planets*.

The Planets was my number one out of these LPs, though they all would have some influence on me. The bombastic nature of the planets orchestrations is brilliant, this classical work being the inspiration for countless movie soundtracks. The planets had titles such as 'Mars, the Bringer of War' or 'Saturn, the Bringer of Old Age'. Each track is inspired by seven of the then eight planets of the solar system. Holst never included Earth. The planet Pluto was only discovered in 1930, so that's not mentioned either; anyway, that tiny fella has since been relegated to the title of a dwarf planet, poor little blighter. Holst premiered the piece in 1918; surely this collection of tunes was one of the first progressive concept albums, decades before the concept of the concept album had ever been conceptualised. This could well have been my first brush with prog. Wow! Psychedelia and prog all in one beeswaxed and gleaming Pandora's box of sound.

Richard's dad was a great old seafaring fella. A few years earlier, when the craze for space hoppers was in full swing, he had found Richard a big orange rubber buoy that had been used in the River Mersey. It was about the size of a space hopper and that's exactly what we used it for, bouncing around the streets all day. It was better than a space hopper, built to resist the battering of boats and the tough conditions of the river, thus impossible to burst. It was a common sight back then to see the forlorn face of a freckled kid dragging the flabby corpse of a punctured hopper back home with a bright red mug wet with tears. Oh how we laughed. We shouted, 'Eat space-hopper dust, kid!,' as we bounded past them like a space-hopper-powered gang of Hells Angels. Such was the narcotic power of the uber hopper.

Richard's dad had been in the Royal Navy during the war. He was a bit of a wizard at making things. He worked at the BICC as an electrician and was a real electronics boffin. He had even built Richard a copy of a Fender Telecaster guitar from a kit advertised in the back of the monthly magazine *Popular Electronics*. In his laboratory (garden shed), he taught us how to use a soldering iron and wire up a few simple circuits. Here a fascination with electronics was born in me. This would come in handy later on in the early drum-machine days of the Bunnymen.

I had acquired a red plastic-coated Hofner Colorama electric guitar from some kid at the top of Station Road. It was fairly easy to find a guitar. It may have come from a swap for a bicycle. After the Beatles took over the world, everyone in Liverpool wanted to be in a band. Most failed, of course, hence there were stacks of disused guitars languishing under beds, forgotten, dusty and unwanted. However, I had no amplifier. By using my sister's record player, I could get the guitar to make sound. I don't know how I learned this; I would stick the wires of the guitar lead into the connections of the record player that would normally fit into the cartridge – this is the bit that the stylus sits in. It's a sort of microphone that works on the vibrations created when the diamond tip of the stylus is dragged along the groove of a record. I would nick my dad's electric razor and swing it across the line of the guitar pick up. I was fascinated by the rise and sweep that the hum emitted. It wasn't exactly playing the guitar, but it kept me amused for hours. I never learned a thing on this guitar – no chords, not even how to tune the thing. The whole idea of playing the guitar was a mystery to me. It all seemed so complicated. Eventually I got rid of it, sold it for £4. They now go for about three or four hundred online.

The Roberts boys had a few Stevie Wonder albums and one by John McLaughlin's Mahavishnu Orchestra, a very complex, guitar-based instrumental album with a jazz-rock feel. Not really my cup of tea, though; too many notes played too quickly. They also had the usual records we all had: Led Zeppelin, Jethro Tull, etc. I also remember being exposed to *Ralf und Florian*, a very early Kraftwerk record, at Alan's house. Alan has no recollection of this. I remember looking at the back-cover picture where Ralf and Florian are sitting facing each other in among many keyboards and items of equipment. This picture told me a band does not have to be three blokes with guitars and a guy at the back sitting at a drum kit. I would be fighting against this formulaic set up during the whole of my time in music. It's a mystery where this early Kraftwerk record came from; I think Alan's slightly older brother Richie may have borrowed it off one of his mates.

We played records – all the records – and would take turns messing about with the guitar, pretending to have a band that we called Poltergeist. A few of my mates had been getting a magazine called *Mystery and Imagination*, a monthly publication that dealt with all things occult, UFOs, Yeti, vampires, ghosts and all that. This strange German word *Poltergeist*, meaning noisy ghost or spirt, may have drifted into our orbit via this magazine's monthly arrival at Arthur Atkins's paper shop.

Richard, Alan, a couple of his mates that lived on Melling's main road, Waddicar Lane, and I foolishly began meddling with the dark side. We became fascinated with the Ouija board. We never had the real thing, of course; these 'toys' were pretty much banned in the UK. We improvised, using a coffee table lined with pieces of card on which we had written the letters of the alphabet. The cards were placed in order. At the top of the table and the bottom were numbers, zero to nine. At each side, we had the words 'yes' to the right and 'no' to the left. We used a glass as a pointer or planchette.

The first time, with the lights dimmed, we all lightly place our index fingers on the bottom of the upturned glass. Nervously we wait, all of us with fingertips resting lightly on the glass. One of us asks the spirits to join us for a chat, the usual invitation employed like the ones we have seen on the telly.

'Is there anybody there?'

Then again: 'Is there anybody there?'

Suddenly, the glass – with some force – drags our weedy little fingers to the right-hand side of the board. We are transfixed in fear. Is this happening?

The glass pulls up abruptly under the card with 'yes' written in bold black felt pen.

Fucking hell! That was very weird, I was not expecting this to work, I am chaotically thinking.

We are all looking at each other, hearts trying to beat their way out of our puny little ribcages. Accusations are hurled at each other: 'You are pushing!' 'No, I'm not!' 'It's you, then!' 'I'm not pushing; anyway, to go that way I would have had to be pulling not pushing, and the glass would have tipped over if you dragged it.' It's true: it would be hard to push or pull with fingers so lightly touching the glass.

The grimaces on our faces tell the story: we are too frozen with fear to laugh. We have embarked on this frivolous adventure. Not knowing how to chicken out of the proceedings, our stupid teenage bravado keeps all fingers on the glass.

Trembling, I mumble, 'Who are you?'

The glass sets off again, darting from letter to letter: first C, then quickly on to A, and onwards. It turns out we had contacted an old sea captain who was lost at sea. But who knows? If the dead are liars, just like the living are, he may have been just bigging himself up and that. He could have been anyone: a bin man from Croydon or a fishmonger from Fleetwood or a sausage maker from Hull. The ghoul could have been a wind-up merchant. 'Well, today I'm a sea captain. Yes, that sounds more impressive to a gang of spotty kids still wet behind the ears.'

We ask a few inane, adolescent questions: 'Where are you from?' 'How old are you?' 'How did you die?' – all pretty bog-standard communicating-with-the-dead kind of stuff. The glass circumnavigates the coffee table with some urgency and, letter by letter, spells out the answers. He's from Greenwich; he passed over at sixty-one years of age; the sailing vessel sank near an area of water where a line of vicious jagged rocks breaks the surface of the English Channel – known as the Needles because they protrude from the water vertical and very sharp.

I know you will find this hard to believe and I understand. I too find it hard to believe and I was there, crapping myself with the rest of them. I do not believe to this day any one of us was pushing the planchette, at least not willingly. Minds might have been controlled by some unseen force but that in itself is fairly creepy. I clearly remember the glass pulling my finger along with an internal energy. Sometimes it was hard to keep up with the instant direction changes. At one point, one of our gang thought it would be funny to ask if the Bible was true. The glass flew over the little ridge of the table's edge and smashed against the wall. If that was pushed, it was some party trick. Harry Potter would have had trouble pulling that one off. Plus, to have the nerve to smash a glass, and in someone else's house? I certainly wouldn't have had the balls, bravado or bad manners to do a stunt like that. I don't think the others would either.

The lights went back on and that was the end of that night's communing with the spirit world. We cleaned up the shards of glass up from the shagpile carpet. But the fear subsided and curiosity took over. It wasn't long until we returned to our paranormal activities. A strange thing was happening to our little gang. We were intoxicated. It was almost becoming an addiction. We were starting to have no choice in the matter. When the chance arose, we would meet up and have a not-so-pleasant evening dabbling with the forces of evil we were too feeble minded to understand. We alternated whose house we would use next to conduct this tabletop communication with the other side. We carried on for weeks, having about ten sessions in all.

This went on until a large standard lamp fell over of its own volition during a rather animated séance involving a thief that had been hanged in the nineteenth century. This disgruntled deceased fella with a terrible stiff neck had decided to get all poltergeist on our asses. The atmosphere was a bit odd from the start. Most entities we got in touch with were kind of glad to have a chat with the living. This fella, however, was a little confrontational from the start. (It was always male spirits we contacted. It seems we were not attractive enough to interest even dead females.)

After that, we all decided to pack it in. If any of our little gang was messing around and trying to push the planchette, they never owned up to it. By the end, we were all scared shitless. I think if it had been a prank by one of the members of our secret teenage coven, they would have been keen to carry on the fun. I know I never cheated; it would have been easy to spot me if I was doing it. My spelling was atrocious, it was worse than Slade's.

At the end of the final session, we were so scared stiff we had this notion that we should ritually smash the replacement glass we had been using, just in case the vessel still held fragments of ectoplasmic energy from some entity on the other end of the line. It was a bit like in the TV show *Breaking Bad*, where the characters are always smashing the burners (mobile phones) after they do their dodgy business, to prevent being tracked by the Feds. It would have been most distressing if you were drinking a glass of water and an paranormal entity slipped down your throat as you glugged.

I'm not sure if we contacted the dead or there was a crossed line from the astral plane. We might have been subconsciously controlling the glass's movements. We contacted something weird and we were lucky to be able to break free of the addictive grip of the spirits. Whenever I have told this story to people, some have said, 'Come on, let's have a go at it now.' The fear that it still puts in me means I have never been tempted to try it since. No chance. I shudder thinking about the stupid things you do as kids. Take my advice: don't be tempted to chat with dead people.

As the 1970s progressed, music progressed too, taking influences from the classical world. Bands had become more virtuoso. Just a few chords and a simple tune were no longer enough. The LP format demanded something more than just a catchy single. Bands had begun to stretch out their songs, which were developing into epics, sometimes skipping from one time signature to another, just for the hell of it. They had broken free of the two-minute pop song. No longer was music just designed for dancing to, unless you were the strange village hippie girl swirling around in a flowery dress with half a florist's shop strapped to your head; every village had one back then.

The lads — and it was mainly lads — would sit down and thoughtfully listen to the records. Each time, you would find something new in the melange of sounds. I don't think people listen to music the same way now. There was none of this listening for a few seconds of the song then skipping to the next track malarkey. If you wanted to change the track, you would have to get up off your arse and turn the LP over or lift the stylus over to the next tune. So we just played the albums in their entireties. If there were one or two tracks you didn't like, you would have to hate them a lot to be bothered to skip them. Instead you would just sit through them. Tracks that you maybe didn't like as much on the first listen would eventually become growers; after a short time, your mind gets used to them and you end up liking them as much as the rest of the tracks. That worked with me, anyway.

Layer upon layer of sound becomes unpeeled the more you listen. Emerson, Lake and Palmer, Yes, Genesis . . . all these bands manned by well-educated, far-out toffs. Most were from private schools, music schools or universities. This lot had been taught music properly. It seems someone forgot to tell Keith Emerson that sticking daggers in your organ (painful), crawling underneath the thing, tipping it up and making it squeal like the proverbial pig wasn't the correct way to tickle the ivories. Plus there is a good chance you might get your sequinned cape ripped or dusty. Such were the antics of Mr Emerson when I saw him and his muso chums at the Empire. I loved all this progressive rock. I could lose myself in the deviant and often sci-fi worlds the bands would conjure up.

I had managed to get myself a reasonable hi-fi from the Freemans catalogue, along with a set of headphones. To save money, I even made my own speakers, my soldering iron skills coming in useful. I could buy all the components in kit form, greatly cutting the cost. They sounded pretty good, too. All of this was bought with payments from my weekly paper-round cash. I would go to sleep every night with the headphones on. The electronic sequences of *Phaedra* by Tangerine Dream was a favourite at the time. I have listened to it lately; it's still a great record, but I wouldn't let it lullaby me to sleep now. There are lots of dark, creepy areas of that album which I would now deem as nightmare fuel.

When Roxy Music emerged in the seventies climate, they fitted right in with the more experimental of the bunch – although now you would never think of them as progressive music. I had seen them at the Empire and was spellbound by this gang of human peacocks. The alien presence of Brian Eno in particular took my attention. Rumours were going about that he was from outer space. His alien forehead convinced us it might be true. His name, we decided, had to be shortened to Eno because humans were unable to pronounce his full name.

At the Empire, he struts about, twisting dials and injecting leads into sockets like a film noir telephone operator. The synthesiser he pilots with a joystick, deftly teasing out the burbling noises like thick aural jelly. Eno never seems to be playing anything in a normal way. His input is the creation of smooth then suddenly angular gloopy bubbles along with white noise and clattering swoops of sound. He has to be from another planet! (Maybe the poor little lonely planetoid Pluto. Now that it has been demoted and shunned by the astronomers, it would make the perfect place for him to be able to conduct his experiments, tucked out of the way in a less desirable area of the solar system.) At his back is an expensive and much converted, Swiss-made, precision Revox reel-to-reel tape machine. I have seen similar cheaper Japanese machines in the Freemans catalogue. I put that on my list of things I want if I ever manage to get a job.

The crowd heave and churn as singer Bryan Ferry belts out, 'There's a new sensation/A fabulous creation', the opening lines of 'Do the Strand', a track off their new LP entitled *For Your Pleasure*. Later, as the beginning of 'Ladytron' from their first album creeps upon us in a sea of white-noise reverb, sax player Andy Mackay's electric oboe sweeps across the cavernous Empire's plush seats. Suddenly a chant starts up: 'Eno, Eno, Eno!' I'm quick to join in: 'Eno! Eno! Eno!' It is greeted by a curt glance across the stage from Ferry in Eno's direction. This tells me he's getting a bit sick of this Eno hero worship. His ego is bruised, Ferry's got a cob on, but it's mainly the lads who are calling for Eno: 'Don't worry, Bryan, all the girls are still yours; they still love you.'

I think the lads got into the mechanics of it all, a hero that could not play much but knew his way around a soldering iron and a VCS 3 synthesiser or something like that. I can't imagine Bryan Ferry fucking around at the back end of a faulty amplifier, with a cigarette holder in one hand and a crosshead screwdriver in the other, no chance. Eno, on the other hand, would be right in among the hot valves, diodes and capacitors, wires and parts flying all over the place. At least that is how it was in our imaginations and that is all it took; imagination is way better than facts any day of the week.

Soon after, at a gig in York the same scenario unfolded, the crowd shouting for Eno. This soured the atmosphere and Eno decided to leave the band, being quickly replaced by Eddie Jobson from Curved Air. We had helped kill the thing we loved. I'm sure there were other factors involved, but that's how it looked to me. Roxy went on to make a few more decent albums. The squares would say better albums, but think again. It may have been Ferry's band, but Eno was the force that stopped it becoming just another rock 'n' roll outfit. For me, the magical element was gone. Eno went off and created many great albums and a whole new format: ambient music. He produced vast amounts of records, and has worked with every man and his dog, so it all turned out OK in the end. I love Eno for what he has done to open minds up and am still buying his records to this day.

9.

Venus in Flares

***Andy Warhol's Velvet Underground featuring
Nico* – The Velvet Underground**

It's now coming to the end of 1973. The IRA are bombing the shit out of towns and cities the length and breadth of England. In a matter of months, disgraced President Nixon will resign in a cloud of shame, the Vietnam War drags on and I have reached the final days of my fifteenth year.

During this time, I would go with my eternally cantankerous old man to Walton Vale on his search for meaty products. These trips were exclusively on a Saturday morning, after he had consumed a skinful on the night before in the Horse and Jockey, our local pub. Thus he was more than likely hungover. This would inject superpower into his black moods, spurred on by high octane fuel from the grumpy pump. 'Oi, Will, if it was that bad, why bother going?' I hear you ask. I was prepared to suffer these trips because, a) I never went anywhere and, b) there was a small branch of NEMS record shop in the Vale. While my dad went off in search of chops, I was left to head straight to the record shop.

I'm looking through the neatly alphabetically ordered racks of the records. David Bowie, *Ziggy Stardust* – got that one. Alice Cooper, *Killer*– no, already got that one, too. Jethro Tull, *Aqualung* – just got that classic off Maz in a swap for the lime-green Ben Sherman shirt with the massive penny-round collars, so nope, don't need that. *Meddle* by Pink Floyd? Yep, got that one also. Hmm, I think I'll play that when I get home. What a great album; probably my favourite post-Syd Barrett Floyd album.

On I go past the Rolling Stones, T. Rex and the *Who's Next* LP with the cover shot of the band after just having a piss on some weird concrete obelisk down on the beach . . . classic. I flip the albums forward; they make that satisfying frrluurup! sound as they fall into line behind the front record. I've skipped the Vs, so I go back, quickly skirting through Van Morrison and then Van der Graaf Generator. No, I don't think so; they're even too weird for me. (I've since been training my brain to deal with Van der Graaf; it's coming on slowly.) Suddenly a double album with an amazing graphic cover draws my gaze. It's a rip off of the block colour screenprint style of Andy Warhol. The image is on a simple white background, the nine square frames of a sensual, luscious girl's mouth opening to receive a protruding straw out of a coke bottle, the mouth then closing around the straw and beginning to suck the delicious brown nectar. It is phallic symbolism at its saucy best.

Across the front in a handwritten style: *Andy Warhol's Velvet Underground featuring Nico*. I have heard of Andy Warhol. After all, he had designed the cover art for one of my all-time beloved albums, the Rolling Stones' *Sticky Fingers*. The record featured the innovative close up of a pair of well-packed (with a banana more than likely; we all know of Warhol's love for the symbolism of that particular fruit) Levi's jeans, complete with working zipper. *Sticky Fingers* is one of the albums that from week to week either belonged to me or to Dave Mazenko, depending on what was being bartered: a pair of jeans, a corduroy Wrangler jacket, a shirt or simply another album. (I still have this album; it's a little battered and the zipper has been up and down a few times, but it is getting on for fifty years old. I haven't got any pairs of [not so well-packed] Levi's jeans that have lasted that long, so it's not doing too badly.)

I love the artwork of the Velvets album so much. It is such a fresh idea, even though sort of stolen. I'm sure Mr Warhol was OK with it. He stole all his work anyway. Andy Warhol was the one who said, 'Art is what you can get away with.' I buy the record, having not heard of the Velvet Underground. When we get back to my house, I rush to the little parlour where my record player now lives. Floyd's *Meddle* is put on hold; I'll play that one later. I'm dying to hear what's on this record. I put it on. 'I'm Waiting for the Man' is the first track. I'm hooked. It has got a rawness that the progressive music I have been listening to doesn't have. The production is weird. It sounds like it has been recorded too loudly and unprofessionally. The sound is hard, cheap and rhythmic. There are grating feedback squeals, all are kept in the mix. The drums are simple and pounding, like a steam-powered piledriver. On it goes without let up. Track after track, they are amazing; why the hell have I never heard of this mob before? The lyrics are dark but tuneful and memorable. The album goes on through 'Candy Says', a slightly distorted recording with a little glockenspiel sound as the introductory hook. So many great tunes. Fuck me, this is ace. A new obsession of mine is being born.

I subsequently learn that a lot of my favourite bands are into this – at that point – mostly unknown New York combo. Bowie, Roxy Music, Mott the Hoople all have recorded tracks by the Velvets. It seems I have been sleepwalking right past what is now deemed by many to be one of the most influential groups of all time. Bands left, right and centre would be formed under the direct influence of the Velvets once word had got around.

We are now in the last year of school. The extra year is known as RSLA: raising of the school leaving age. A new block has been thrown up over the summer holidays, and is christened the RSLA Block, built on Mr Sharman's vegetable plot. There will be no more tribal hunting adventures for him. He will have to make do with his other bloodthirsty pastimes. I fear the quad-rangle will soon be running low on chickens.

The class has moved to a new form room. We are now in 5C4. This is the new way of categorising our thickness: 5 as we are in the fifth year of school; C because this was the stream in alpha-betical order (A being the best) and 4 the level of our stupidity in a slow-flowing C stream. There is also 5C5, and then the old favourite for dumping the numpties, R. Our new form room

– the place where you have your desk – is high up on the second floor. That's three, not two storeys up, as the name would suggest. We always call the ground floor 'ground' in this country; must be because it is on the fucking ground.

The aforementioned Pupil X makes use of this elevated height of the classroom. He is hanging the smallest kid in the class out of the window. He is known as Smelly Melly because his surname is Melvin. As far as I am aware, he gave off no great aroma other than that of a mildly grubby schoolboy, which more or less we all did. If anyone should have been given the title smelly, it should have been me. I was still a scumbag with no one at home to make sure I washed. I'm sure I must have given off a pungent whiff to rival a musk ox. Seems I still am standing upwind of my chums and getting away scot-free on the bullying front.

Having said that, in those halcyon days, nobody got too close to get a sniff. There wasn't all this hugging crap that goes on now with the youth. These unnecessary close-contact greetings favoured by the continentals need to be stamped out. In those days, no one touched anybody unless you included getting the boot in. The closest to a high five or fist bump would have been a dead arm or leg, Chinese burn, shin scrape or ankle tap – the latter being most effective with the sharp sole edge of the locally favoured Como. Also popular at that time was the stealthily artistic act of silently spitting on the back of a classmate's blazer or, for the very bold and reckless headcases, a teacher's unsuspecting suede elbow-patched jacket. Kids with gaps in their front teeth were the undisputed masters at this favoured form of disrespect. Unfortunately, I had pretty much worn my teeth flat by anxious night-time grinding while sleeping, hence this covert operation was not a viable option for me.

119

Here's the scene as I enter the classroom late: the class is gathered at the far side of the room by the large windows. Getting a good fill of fresh air is poor Smelly Melly. Pupil X is hanging him by his wrists out of the window, and the victim is wriggling like a worm on a hook. Inside there is an uproar, slamming desks, shouting, laughing and general mayhem. Some (girls mainly) are saying, 'Get him back in, get him back,' but most are baying for Pupil X to let go of the poor little bastard. I can't remember what I was shouting, so it could have gone either way: peace negotiator or executioner. After a few minutes of terror, Smelly Melly is dragged back inside to peals of uproarious laughter. Smelly himself is smiling too, not sure if it's relief or some sort of thrill-seeking symbiotic deal he has with Pupil X. Impossibly, nobody on the outside of the building has a clue what has been going on fifty or sixty feet above the ground. All the teachers must have been busy in the staff room dunking chocolate biccies and topping up their coffee with a little brandy or Valium, getting ready to face the day.

This is not the first time Pupil X has nearly done for Melvin. A year earlier, when we were in the fourth year, our form room doubled as a physics lab. For that reason, it happened to have long and heavy floor-to-ceiling curtains for experiments that required the classroom to be blacked out. Melvin had been almost hung with the draw ropes that worked the pulley device responsible for opening and closing these drapes. With the heavy cord coiled around his neck, he was hoisted a few feet above the floor, his little legs dangling. The really weird thing was that, after X's regular attacks throughout the school day, as soon as the 4 p.m. bells sounded – the welcome signal for freedom – all these heinous crimes were forgotten. They must have lived in the same part of Maghull as they walked home together, Smelly with his little neat brown leather satchel on his back and X with his sinister black briefcase: the sort a hitman would use to carry a broken-down sniper rifle. Off they trotted like Winnie-the-Pooh and Christopher Robin as if they were best mates and it was just another day in the Hundred Acre Wood.

The year creeps up to 1974. I am in an English lesson situated on the first floor of the old building. The teacher is a Mr Corcoran; he's OK as teachers go, I suppose. He suddenly throws a board duster at Davo. He more than likely deserved it, knowing Davo. The thing whizzes past me and, quick as a flash with cobra-like reactions, Davo flips his desk lid up, deflecting the duster completely. Davo has been paying great attention to the techniques employed by the character Kwai Chang Caine in *Kung Fu* when deflecting nasty-looking wooden spears during the opening titles. As Master Po from this show would say, 'You have learned well, Grasshopper.' The heavy wooden and felt projectile ricochets off and smashes through the window, creating a large plume of white chalk dust on its exit like it's some sort of intentional pyrotechnic display. The duster clatters through the glass towards the car park and shards rain down on the cars below. The duster sails on, narrowly missing the car of our music teacher, Mr Lee. It's a Moskvitch A34, a strange little Soviet van.

No, I'd never heard of them either; but there it was, sitting next to the colourful cars of the day. The thin steel bodywork is forlornly dressed in a rather depressing coat of proletariat grey paint, no doubt left over from Battleship *Potemkin*. Proudly she is sitting on the imperialist tarmac, with the optional extra of, erm, agricultural corrugated pig-iron side panels, like something the French would make a Citroën out of and call it style. To cheer the dowdy motor up, Mr Lee has deployed the old trick of red vinyl stick-on bits to give it that *Starsky and Hutch* makeover feel, with go-faster stripes that every Ford Capri up and down the land was now sporting. I'm kidding, of course. Mr Lee *has* customised this lethargic, battleship-grey lump in his own special way. In large, red plastic stick-on letters placed on the panels, he created a warning: 'DON'T BUY MOSKVITCH MY GUARANTEE NOT HONOURED.' This appears on both sides of the van. When I first saw this sign, it took a while to sink in that Moskvitch was the make of the vehicle.

It all just seemed so odd, but Mr Lee was a rather odd chap. He had a large frizz of grey, out of control hair, his corduroy-clad shoulders dusted liberally with dandruff, the obligatory seventies colourful kipper tie tightly noosed around his neck. Mr Lee's music lessons were a disorderly free for all. As with anybody with the name Lee, it is the tradition to add the prefix 'Leapy'. I think this came from a singer called Leapy Lee who had a hit with the

song 'Little Arrows', but I digress. Leapy Lee had no control what-
soever over the class, and we knew it; it was mayhem. Things not
nailed down got thrown about. Fights and messing around were a
constant carry on; it was absolute chaos. The classroom was a clut-
tered mess of cased instruments, music stands, piles of books,
tambourines and percussion bits and bobs, general music-related
crap everywhere. We had no orderly seats or desks; we were sat on
wooden stage plinths that were stored in the room. I don't think
this free-range approach helped with the control of kids' behaviour – not with class 5C4, anyway. Zero interest was ever shown
in music lessons. No one was given any instruction on how to
play an instrument. It was obvious to Mr Lee that this lot wouldn't
know one end of a violin from the other, so why waste his time?

The lessons generally consisted of Leapy playing the piano
and us pretending to sing along to these shitty old songs, rather
strangely about donkey riding, mainly. As they say in the States,
go figure. He did at one point try and interest us in the notes of
the scale as written on a stave.

He is completely shocked by the answer when he asks the
class, 'Does anyone know what the letters representing notes
are?' Leapy has drawn the five horizontal lines with a treble clef
to the left on the blackboard. I pipe up and say, 'F. A. C. E., sir'. I
then continue, 'E. G. B. D. F.' This is easy to remember as it
stands for 'every good boy deserves favour'.

Leapy stares on, his mouth open; a smile starts to form. The
class quiets down and they look at me; all are in shock.

Sarky Phil sneers and questions, 'How the hell do you know
that, Beethoven?'

The class chuckles, but I ignore Phil. Richard Brunskill had
shown me this when we were messing about on the Brunskills'

upright piano, and I had remembered. Leapy is so shocked, he reaches in his pocket and throws me a copper tuppence piece. It's a prophetic gesture.

Leapy says, 'Well done, Sergeant. Maybe you will earn some more money by music one day.'

To celebrate this minor triumph, Leapy Lee picks up his violin and starts to play the theme tune to *The Beverly Hillbillies*. He often employs this trick to try and gain some control over the class, when things are getting too crazy. It's very much like in the Frankenstein movies when the monster is distracted from throttling an old blindman that he has stumbled across, the imminent throttling avoided by the poor sod luckily picking up his violin and playing. (It also reminds me of a later time when I was driving through our local safari park at Knowsley. We threw out some food from a small crack in the car window in an attempt to coax a gaggle of wanking monkeys off the car's bonnet when the horrible hairy primates were trying to eat my windscreen wipers.)

This diversionary violin-playing tactic also works for Mr Lee. Suddenly the mayhem stops and it becomes a more acceptable kind of uproar. We stamp our feet and clap our hands like some happy-clappy, God-bothering congregation. We are almost in time to the music, all bellowing out the words:

Come and listen to a story 'bout a man named Jed
Poor mountaineer barely kept his family fed

I learned a valuable lesson that day, and I have remembered his words ever since: I have never bought a Moskvitch A34.

★   ★   ★

Back in Mr Corcoran's English class, the chalk dust settles. The red-faced teacher goes to the car park to check for damage, and we all strain to look down to see Corcoran reach under the Moskvitch's rusty chassis and collect the duster. On his return, we are quietened down by him and the class continues. 'Right, you will be going for job interviews soon. You will need to gain confidence in speaking. The best way for you to do this is to stand up at the front of the class and tell everyone about an interest or hobby you may have: collecting stamps, perhaps stealing birds' eggs, training kestrels, getting ferrets to jump through hoops . . . whatever floats your boat.'

The only thing floating my boat that week was the Velvet Underground.

I shout out, 'What about snogging girls, sir?'

We all laugh and Corcoran replies, 'As if you have ever snogged a girl, Sergeant. Shut up! You idiot!'

As expected, Sarky Phil chimes up and sneers from the back of the class. I'm grinning so much after the window-smashing incident that his sarcastic grunt is water off a duck's back. My witty interjection has pleased me. I liked being the centre of attention even if it was slightly ridiculing.

I go back to dreaming of the image of the girl's lips on my new Velvets LP cover.

I am at home when I realise that the sleeve notes on the back of the VU album are perfect for the upcoming front-of-the-class talk. All I have to do is copy it down. Easy! The next day I bring the album with me to school.

The teacher has provided one of the school's much coveted (by me) Garrard record players. A few other students have brought albums in to talk about and play, mainly Motown. One lad has brought a butcher's outfit, complete with knives, hat and apron. He has a Saturday job in the town square. Another kid talks about fishing. A girl is droning on about the Bay City Rollers. Soon, it is my turn.

I nervously play the record at the front of the class. 'Waiting for the Man' is first up. It gets no real reaction. I move the record on to track 2, 'Sunday Morning'. This goes down a little better; but to my mind, it is just pearls before swine: they won't get it, anyway. I slip on 'Venus in Furs' with the intention of freaking the class out; it works. This is enough to get a strong reaction. I am pelted with rolled up bits of paper and jeers. I turn to my handwritten notes cribbed from the back of the album. Corcoran asks if he can see the cover. I hand it over thinking, *Shit, he's going to spot that I just copied all this stuff*. My nerves are increased tenfold as I try and keep it together and continue my speech.

Then he says, 'Sergeant, you have just copied that from the back of this record cover, haven't you?'

'Yes, sir. Is that a problem, sir?'

Corcoran blurts, 'Sit down! I thought it sounded much too eloquent for you. See me later.'

I sit down but am relieved that I don't have to finish the speech.

Corcoran points at Marc White. White is a new recruit to our little gang in the corner. He has been held back a year and he fits in well with us. He is a good laugh, always up to pranks and messing about.

Corcoran instructs him: 'Get up here.'

White is keen and can't wait to tell us all about the piglet he is rearing at a pig farm he works at on the weekends. After this talk, we have a new nickname for Mark: 'Swamp Pig'.

White is a comedian and not as thick as he looks. Once, in an environmental studies lesson conducted by our new form master, Mr Ellis, he made a bet with most of the class that he would do a jig on the desk in front of the teacher, right in the middle of the lesson.

We all line up with sweets, pens, erasers, penknives, cigarettes, chewing gum, cash and collectable football cards. When all the promised booty has been laid out, we eagerly wait for White to get on the desk and jig as promised. There is a shiver of nervous excitement going round the class. We are giggling with the anticipation of him clambering on the table and the teacher going ballistic.

But White has figured it all out. He simply raises his hand. 'Sir?'

Mr Ellis looks up from his notes on the desk and grunts, 'What is it, White?'

'Sir, would it be OK if I did a jig on the desk?'

Ellis looks bemused, but we can see he is intrigued. We are all stifling laughter; we can't believe what we are hearing.

White repeats, 'Sir, would that be all right if I did a little jig on the desk?'

Ellis looks at White's big, pleading eyes as they peer from behind the thick lenses of his aviator-style glasses.

Then Mr Ellis surprises us all. 'Yes, go on, White, you jump up there if you must – and it better be good!'

By this time, the class is in hysterics. All eyes are on White as he clambers on to the desk. He's a big lad; the desk squeaks with the weight of this trainee pig breeder. (If this had happened today, it would have been an internet viral sensation, like some sad fucker's pet cat moonwalking or something.) The music starts and the lumbering dance begins. This consists of White lurching from one foot to the other in a slow hop that would undoubtedly constitute the description of a little jig if it were ever to become a legal issue.

He continues his jig and the class is incandescent with joy. One lad starts to choke, his breath stolen by laughter. He gets bashed on the back and ends up in a red-faced coughing fit. The girls try to clap along with White's arrhythmic slog. Mr Ellis looks on in disbelief, but he is grinning from ear to ear. The teacher from the technical drawing class next door knocks on Ellis's classroom door, drawn to see what all the commotion is about. He is ready to give the class a good bollocking. He pops his head in and sees that his colleague is grinning; his attention is now drawn to young White, who is still on the desk. He can't help but smile at the surreal sight of a boy hopping about on a desk.

He chuckles, 'Hello, Mr Ellis. I see you have everything under control here,' and goes back to his class with a snorting chuckle.

Ellis says, 'OK, White, that'll do. And White . . .'

'Yes, sir?'

'If you feel the need for more jigs, you will have to do them in your own time and out of school hours.'

We all cheer and clap as White climbs down and gets back in his seat, directly behind me and Davo as we turn around and congratulate him on his daring. The booty is delivered to White's desk. He slumps back in his seat, beaming and happy as a piglet in shit.

10.

Zookeeper and Supernatural Elsie

Taking Tiger Mountain (By Strategy) – **Brian Eno**

It's 1974. President Nixon finally bites the bullet and quits, before
he gets booted out. Muhammad Ali goes looking for trouble in
Zaire, in the fight that's christened 'The Rumble in the Jungle'.
Ali's opponent is heavyweight champion George Foreman. By
round eight, Foreman lies spread-eagled on the canvas with little
birds flying around his head. It seems he gets some sense knocked
into him, as the hot Zairean air gives him no relief: 'Fuck this for
a lark, I'm going to go into the production of grills.' Millions get
sold but their destiny is to lie cold, unused and hidden in kitchen

cupboards all over the world. They rest alongside the Breville sandwich maker and the Ronco Chop-O-Matic®.

It's April and I have just turned sixteen years old. My time at Deyes Lane Secondary Modern is coming to an end. The class have taken all the final exams, CSEs, Certificates of Secondary Education. It's a forgotten qualification now; CSE exams were bargain basement, a little bit shit. They pretty much acknowledged that you bothered to turn up to school. O levels were the prize for the smarter kids, but these too have passed their sell-by date. They have been renamed GCSEs.

When the results are in, it's no great shakes; I do OK. At least I haven't failed any; there are some close shaves, but I get a pass on all I take. My grades are in the middle scores, grade 3 or 4. I must have done better than Pupil X. He refused to participate and just sat in the examination room, never looking at the exam paper. My best grade is in woodwork: grade 2. It must have been my artistic mastery of form and function that manifested itself in the cerebral beauty of my varnished pine pipe rack. A tour de force! Such dowel work has never been seen since Tilman Riemenschneider was a lad.

In the coming days, we are sent to see a careers officer. This interrogation will be in the sixth-form common room, a place I have never even been inside. Rumours have been going around the school all year of the crazy stuff the sixth formers have stashed in this room, from a stack of jazz mags to hot chocolate machines to beds, even a telly. This room is a total no-go zone for fifth-form divs like me. To be found trespassing in there would surely have meant death or a good kicking at the very least.

We are sent over from our form room to the mysterious common room. Some kids are on chairs waiting in a corridor.

Soon my turn comes and I enter the room. Sitting there with notes on the desk and a briefcase at his side is a grey-haired chap. He is sporting a checked nylon suit and the seventies staple of a kipper tie. He is smoking a fag. He tells me to sit down.

This careers bloke is going to try and steer me in the right direction based on a few questions and the aptitude I have shown while in the school system. The only aptitude I have actually shown is the ability to be able to grow a daily crop of boils, spots and pimples, with a liberal scattering of blackheads and yellow-heads along with an increasingly bad attitude. Unfortunately, this is not going to get me anywhere in the real world.

'OK, lad, what do you want to be after school?' he asks me.

I come up with the most obscure job I can think of at the time.

'Zookeeper, sir,' I reply. I was being stupid, of course, and trying to be funny.

The careers officer isn't laughing.

He looks at me, then quips, 'What about the army? Do you fancy that? I know the Liverpool regiments are recruiting at the moment.' He thinks I would make a good target for the IRA.

I'm thinking, *And I know why they are recruiting too.*

So, I reply, 'No thank you, sir. I don't like the footwear, sir.'

He glances down at my fake patent leather, wedged, purple and black Marc Bolan-esque shoes, complete with neatly bowed candy-striped laces threaded through oversized shiny silver lace holes. These shoes peer out from under Birmingham bags trousers. 'Burmos', as they have been christened, are all the current rage. Wider than flares, the vast acreage of loose-fitting polyester and cotton mix sits in folds about my legs, all kept in place with a high three-inch waistband. This new trouser style has danced its way into the shops via the northern soul scene. They have been adopted by many of the youth cultures regardless of their ability to do acrobatic backdrops, spins, high kicks, flips or even the basic northern soul dance, the shuffle, all of which are the staple moves to be witnessed every weekend on the well-sprung dancefloor down at the Wigan Casino all-nighters. The look is finished off with large patch pockets stitched on the thigh, presumably somewhere to keep a stash of the favoured soul-boy drug of choice, amphetamines. Black Bombers, Purple Hearts, the energiser to power the dancing until dawn's early light kisses the cobbled streets of Wigan.

The careers officer is becoming impatient with this spotty smart arse's attitude. I don't blame him; I would be too. For some reason, you think this sort of thing is hilarious when you are full of testosterone and hormones are surging up through your loins. I am grinning like a moron, which is exactly what I am. All lads at this age are morons.

'OK.' He looks at his notes. 'Sergeant, I'm sending you for a test at the Liverpool Royal Institution on Colquitt Street. This will ascertain if a welding course would suit you.'

'What about the zookeeping, sir?'

He looks at me with the resigned scowl of someone that has had enough of his job. He grunts, hands me some bits of paper with the information about the welding course and says, 'Send in the next boy.'

The sixth-form common room has been a disappointment. Far from being the promised land of all kinds of goodies, it's a pretty bland room with a few soft-cushioned chairs, a couple of tables. On the wall, pictures of Liverpool football stars and some pop posters plus a crappy transistor radio – the only item that

might suggest this was a groovy hangout for the sixth formers
– sits atop a cupboard. I'm thinking, *This is the place everyone was
talking about?*

As I leave, I notice that pinned on the wall behind me is a
large poster for Lou Reed's album *Transformer*. I come back on
the last day of school and steal it. I still feel bad about doing this.
I ease my conscience by convincing myself the kid who it
belonged to had probably left years ago.

The weekend shopping trips with my dad have stopped abruptly.
This is because I have managed to get a Saturday job. I am now
a catering assistant in the kitchens at a rather swanky department
store. Henderson's is in the centre of Liverpool and owned by
the same people that own the poshest of posh shops in London,
Harrods. Maz has been working there since he left school at
fifteen. I have landed the position thanks to him putting in a
good word for me with the head chef, Mr Holt.

It is my first day in the kitchens. It's all new to me: so daunt-
ing, so confusing and so bloody hot. The head chef tells Maz to
show me what to do. I am given 'whites': this is what the jackets,
aprons and lightweight, pale blue and white gingham-checked
trousers – the uniform of a chef – are collectively called. They
might have started out white in the morning but by the end of
the day they are filthy. We also wear the large traditional chef
hats, pleated and stiffly starched, standing tall on our heads. As
we are a pair of long-haired troglodytes, Maz and I wear hairnets
under the chef's hats. The laundry man is a little chubby chap in
charge of dishing out the uniforms. We called him Mr Magoo as
he is a doppelgänger for the short-sighted, bumbling bloke off
the cartoons voiced distinctively by Jim Backus. Unlike the

cartoon version, who never seemed to let his temper get frayed, our Mr Magoo is a grumpy old git.

Henderson's was a Liverpool landmark, occupying a prime spot right in the middle of prestigious Church Street. The store was one of the few buildings still standing after the excessively ambitious Herr Hitler had thoughtfully bombed most of Henderson's rivals out of business. The Victorian stone-carved facade looked down on the competitors' piles of rubble. The store still retained the snobby air of superiority post-war. That is until 1960, when an electrical fault caused a fire that gutted the place. Eleven people died in the blaze, even though the fire brigade was there in two minutes. By the next day, the building's shell was all that was left. It was fully demolished and rebuilt in a modern style. Today, they would have had trouble getting the plans past the planning officer.

Back in the sixties, it seemed like heritage meant nothing. After all, the council had pulled down the Beatles' second home, the Cavern Club. The former Fab Four haunt was left a scabby, gravel wasteland for years; there seemed to be no point in its destruction. Shoppers would park their cars on top of the birthplace of the Beatles, the mystical, magical sweaty cellar entombed just a few feet below. Weirdly, it was directly opposite the club Eric's, which would eventually be the nursery of my band the Bunnymen. All of this sat on a little cobbled lane called Mathew Street. Later, in the 1980s, realising what they had done, the city tried to reconstruct the Cavern and threw up a small shopping centre, calling it Cavern Walks. Someone must have woken up and realised the potential of making a few quid out of this legendary beat combo's iconic status.

The Cavern and Eric's came from the same energy surge, a flowing ley line of supernatural power. The leys straddle the country between sites such as stone circles. Our future manager Bill Drummond insists one such surge of energy shoots up Mathew Street. It is very possible he's not talking shite. This little cobbled lane spawned so many successful bands that there must have been higher powers at work. Bands such as Frankie Goes to Hollywood, the Teardrop Explodes, Orchestral Manoeuvres in the Dark, Dead or Alive, all desperate to shake off the shadow of the Beatles that pervades every aspect of Liverpudlian life. I think something may have happened to the ley line. The flow must have shifted, been diverted. The street only spawns stag and hen parties now and the only things created are back-alley knee tremblers and oceans of vomit washing the granite cobbles.

When I worked at Henderson's, the tragic fire was still fresh in the minds of a few of the long-standing employees. It would be mentioned from time to time in conversations between the waitresses.

'Do you remember the fire, Elsie?' asked Rita.

'No, sorry that was well before my time; I'm not old enough.' She was lying; she had been there since the year dot, as my mum used to say.

Elsie was the unofficial head of all the waitresses. A slender lady in her sixties, I would say; but when you are only sixteen, anybody that looked over thirty looked ancient, so it is difficult to say. She was certainly getting on a bit. A very warm-hearted character, always rushing about, always there to say, 'All right love, don't worry, I'll do it,' before darting off to do whatever needed to be done. She never stopped; her energy was incredible. She was like the mum of the waitresses and, on occasion, kitchen staff. If any of them had a problem of some difficulty, she was there to help. The regular customers loved Elsie. She had many that she had been delivering tea and food to for decades. Her supernatural superpower was reading tea leaves, which she would do for her favoured regulars. In turn, they would cross her palm with silver in the form of a few shillings' tip.

After leaving school, my Saturday job just sort of morphs into a full-time job. I am now given the title trainee chef – or, if you want to get all French about it, commis chef. I work a five-day week. I have Thursdays off. It is never possible to have a Saturday off. This is by far the busiest shopping day. All shops are closed on a Sunday so Saturday is *the* day!

The kitchen is situated on the fourth floor of the building. There are several areas, each with a designated purpose: butchery, prep, roast, pastry, etc. There is a pan wash area with massive sinks manned by the very Irish Danny, with an accent so thick it's hard to understand him half the time. A couple of massive walk-in fridges and freezers, a storeroom, plus a huge dishwasher the size of a Moskvitch A34. At the far end of the kitchen complex is the stillroom. This is where tea and coffee are made. A small area for wine and spirits is kept locked and only accessible by the wine waitress who holds the key. After all the preparation is completed, the action moves to the area called the service. This where all the meals are put together as the orders come in. The food is kept warm in bain-maries and hot cupboards all built out of shining, stainless steel. At breakfast and lunch, this is the hub where everything is put together.

As time goes on, I get used to the kitchen pressure-cooker atmosphere. The heat is a killer, but after a few weeks, you learn to cope with it. It's a scary environment; but Maz has been working here full time for a year or two; he knows the ropes. This job will eventually change my life beyond all measure. I will now have a few quid in my pocket; that means clothes and records. I give my dad some money, as is normal practice, for my 'keep'. But I still have a few quid left.

I am just a small part of a team that knows what needs doing without being told. The routine becomes the norm. We get all the ingredients ready for service and this is called *mise en place*, in French, which means simply everything in place, or as you or I might say, getting your shit together. We prep salad in the morning then put together the old seventies favourite, prawn cocktails, and cook off trays of bacon and pork sausages. Tomatoes by the truckload are sliced and grilled. Eggs by the trayful are cracked one handed and two at a time into a steel bowl, done with the manual dexterity gained by repetition. The eggs are then quickly whisked and stored in the fridge, along with the preparation of grated cheese, mixed vegetables, mushrooms and ham – all ingredients needed for the various omelettes ordered in the breakfast rush. I make trays of poached eggs, thirty at a time. Once they are just cooked, the eggs are plunged into ice-cold water; this immediately stops the cooking process. They are added to the top of toast or plonked on a freshly toasted Welsh rarebit, a sort of mustard- and Guinness-enhanced cheese on toast. With the addition of a poached egg this dish is transformed into a buck rarebit. This is still one of my favourite breakfasts. The eggs get a quick flash under the powerful grill broiler called a salamander and they are served up piping hot and still with soft yolks. All pretty basic stuff, but the quantity dictates speed and efficiency.

The fast pace and rough nature of a working kitchen is quite a shock. Barking orders and getting sworn at are normal (just like home). Think Gordon Ramsay without the kind, gentle attitude he sometimes portrays, and that's pretty much what it was like. The service area has a wide, stainless-steel shelf: the pass. Chef Holt or, more often, one of the second chefs, Billy or Frank, mans the pass. This is where the waitresses give the written orders to the chef and then they are shouted at us, and we put it all together.

One of the waitresses brings back a salad and hands it to the head chef. He passes the plate to me and says, 'Put chips on that.' I have never heard of anyone putting chips on a salad before and I look a little bemused. I'm thinking this must be some kind of wind up that they play on the new bloke in places like this. I hesitate. The chef looks at me, leans in and slowly and deliberately says in a low, menacing voice, 'Put some fucking chips on that salad or go and collect your fucking cards now!' To spare being sacked, I scoop up a portion of chips and put them on the salad and realise the head chef is not one for a joke.

One day, I am sharing the preparation area known as the roast with the second chef named Frank. He's Scottish and calls all the women 'hen': 'Are you all right, hen?'

Billy, the other second chef, is kind of in charge of the pastry department. He's a bit square and slightly condescending, but a nice-enough guy. He's a neatly turned out chap. His whites are always very clean; I am not sure how he manages this. I am usually very messy after an hour or two. If I try and get a set of clean whites out of Mr Magoo, it's like asking if I can have a go on Mrs Magoo. Mr Magoo keeps a tight grip on the bloody things. You would think he's doing the washing of them himself. The whites are well stashed and locked behind a seven-foot high wall. Maz often climbs over the wall and passes out the jackets when Magoo isn't about.

Frank is making a large steak and kidney pie in a shallow steel tray that fits in a bain-marie. He is busy with a huge frying pan, sealing the steak chunks. He tells me to fry off the kidneys he has prepared. I get myself another giant cast iron frying pan off Danny the pan man. Above the industrial, enamelled cooker, there is an old tin full of what looks like vegetable oil, sitting on the cooker's shelf. I add a small amount of cooking oil and throw in most of the kidneys to cook off a little before adding to Frank's mix. He is making a rich gravy. The kidneys are not reacting to the oils as I would have expected; small bubbles are forming.

'Hey, Frank, this look right to you?' I ask. I can now smell a strange aroma emanating from the pan. Lemon?

Frank reacts quickly. 'What the fuck have you done? Where did you get the oil from?'

'Just up there in that old tin.' I'm pointing to the tin and I'm starting to panic.

'You fucking dickhead. That's liquid soap for floors,' he squeals. 'Quick, get rid of that and get a clean pan back over here fast!'

He doesn't have to ask me twice. If Chef Holt sees this mess, he will go berserk. I will more than likely be sacked on the spot. Holt, as has already become clear, is not one to suffer fools and sacks people at the drop of a hat.

The gritty-looking kidneys are now swimming in the soapy mess that is bubbling up and creating a frothy pink spume over-flowing the hot pan. I do as I'm told. I quickly dump the pan in one of the large bins we have dotted about the kitchen. Frank covers it with some vegetable peelings and adds what's left of the kidneys to a now properly oiled pan. He cooks them off for a short time just to get a bit of colour on them, then mixes the kidneys, gravy and steak chunks in the bain-marie tray that the pie will be baked in. Billy from pastry rolls out the crust and seals the mix before anyone can see that the kidney content of this pie is a little light. For the next few weeks, my nickname is Soapy Sergeant, but I don't mind. The relief of them getting me out of the shit is worth a little friendly name-calling.

Frank is always up to some stunt or other, usually designed to freak out the older waitresses. On one occasion, when we have large spirals of Cumberland sausage on the menu, he takes a generous length of the porky treat and calls me over. I am unwittingly to be the straight man is this choreographed prank. Everyone else in the prep area is primed and ready. They know what Frank is up to. Frank always wears his apron short. He folds it in half, then half again, then ties the strings around his waist. He is the Mary Quant of the kitchen staff with his micro mini apron resting high on his thighs.

He instructs me to, 'Go tell Rita I want her for a minute,' while he sets the trap.

I do as I am told and trundle out of the kitchen to the area of the breakfast bars near the pass. I find Rita tidying her station and replenishing the glass Cona coffee maker. The shop is quiet; it has not quite opened up yet. She is getting ready for the influx of hungry shoppers.

'Hi, Rita,' I say. 'Frank was looking for you.'

Rita turns to go into the kitchen and sees Frank, who is crouching down on one knee, like he is looking for something on a shelf under one of the large stainless-steel preparation tables.

He has positioned the sausage out of the fly hole of his chef's checked trousers. As he crouches lower, the short apron rides up and reveals the huge Cumberland dangling between his legs.

Rita's eyes zoom in on the mighty, flaccid sausage swinging around, screams and runs out of the kitchen. Frank is pissing himself laughing and the whole kitchen is in an uproar. The sausage is added back to the rest and cooked up for an unsuspecting recipient of bangers and mash on the lunch menu. I'm sure stuff like this goes on in kitchens to this day. You never know who's had your sausage down their keks.

The kitchen was in a constant battle against rats, flies and weird little cockroaches that lived behind all the close-fitting units. The kitchens at Henderson's are the only place in England that I have ever seen a cockroach. Any small space was home to them. They were everywhere: behind the fridge, under the sink, all over the place. Every few weeks, they were sprayed with some sort of DDT pesticide, but it was an uphill struggle. They can rather disgustingly jettison egg sacks all over the place that could stand a nuclear bomb. DDT . . . no problem! Often, we would spot dying rats that had scoffed an overdose of poison, a gift from the ratman. The toxic bait was left under tables and hidden corners. The rodents would drunkenly wander out from various secret hiding places, staggering about, more out of it than the Pink Fairies were at their last gig at Liverpool Stadium. They would deliriously pop their little whiskered noses out only to be quickly dispatched with a floor-sweeping brush to the head or drowned in one of the huge steamers.

Early one morning, before opening time, Frank put a small dead rat on a plate and covered it with one of the metal cloches that were used to keep the food warm. He gave it to a waitress called Sheila. When she lifted off the cloche to see the dead creature, everything went up in the air and another screaming fit followed. He was a mad bastard. I think Holt never sacked him because he was as hard as nails and Scottish. He would probably have stuck one on Chef Holt.

Maz wasn't so fortunate. After a few months of me working at Henderson's, my mate Dave Mazenko got the sack for not turning up on a Saturday, although he had squared it in advance with Chef Holt a few months earlier. It was very busy, and the kitchen was left in the shit or, as we used to say back then, up the wall. Orders were getting on top and people were waiting on food. There were not enough pairs of hands behind the pass in the service area so Holt had to jump in and help. He was not too happy about this. Normally he would be in his office all day, sorting out the menus for the upcoming week, ordering stock and drinking coffee. He had forgotten that he had given the day off to Maz. When Maz turned up on the Monday morning, his protests of, 'You said it was fine!' were ignored. He was given his cards and left the kitchen.

'Where ya going, Maz?' I called to him as I saw him walk into the restaurant. All the customers were looking at this long-haired chef with a dirty apron. He shouted back, 'Holt's given me the sack. Will see ya later.'

As time went on, I learned lots of culinary skills and even went to night school on the same street that I had attended to take the test for the welding course that the nylon-suited careers officer had sent me to. As you can probably guess, I never passed the test to become a welder. My life would have been so different if I had.

11.

Battling the Grim Sweeper

'Riders on the Storm' – The Doors

It's 1975 and Maggie Thatcher becomes the leader of the Conservative Party. The Sex Pistols perform their first ever gig at St Martin's College. Both events will change the land forever. One good, one bad: I'll let you decide which is witch. I myself am unaware of the Pistols at this time; not many are. I am still in the progressive rock world. The big news in my orbit is that Dave Maz and I are going to see Pink Floyd at Knebworth Park in Hertfordshire, though we miss most of the set as we are in a massive queue for chips when the Floyd go on and have been waiting far too long (three hours) to abandon the line and the hope of something hot to eat.

I had been into motorbikes for a while. Now that I was working, I had the funds to buy one. It was possible to ride a bike up to the engine size of 125 cc on a provisional driving licence, without passing a test. I got myself a trail bike, a Suzuki TS 100 cc. This small bike was a sort of semi off-road ride with high suspension, knobbly tyres and wide handlebars. The bus got the boot and now this became my way of getting to work, for a while at least. After a few months, the bike was stolen from a car park in Liverpool. Unusually, the cops recovered the bike and I got it back after a week or so. I was back on the road and this time even faster; I'm not sure what the thieves did to the little bike, but it was a good deal quicker. As with all motorbikes, there was a danger element, mainly from other road users; but there are some pricks who ride bikes too and, at that young age, I was one such prick. I had a few close calls.

I am on my way to work, riding along Melling Road as it weaves its way through the home of the Grand National racecourse at Aintree. I'm thundering along round a bend when I see a road-sweeping truck and a car stopped on either side of the road. I'm doing about sixty, more or less flat out, and the little two-stroke motor is screaming a painful, high-pitched squeal. I slam on my brakes and the back wheel locks and goes into a skid, the burning rubber of the chunky off-road tyres leaving a plume of blueish smoke in my wake. I'm too close, I'm too fast and I'm not in control. Instinctively, I release the brakes. I will have to try to squeeze through the small gap between the car and the sweeper truck. Oh shit! No turning back now. I hit the gap at some speed and clatter through the tight space. I grimace as I feel the end of the handlebars scrape down the side of the bright yellow sweeper lorry. As I come out of the other end, I smash off the car's wing mirror. Jesus Christ! I've managed to get through; I don't know how I made it. I should be dead. I pull up and look behind at the scene. The car and the truck are still in the same spot. The driver of the car is wondering what the hell was that. I decide to go, and I twist the throttle and disappear.

I also did all kinds of stupid stunts including trying to catch up other small bikes in some sort of macho race mentality. I came off around a corner too fast and lost it on a build up of gravel, most of which became embedded in my palms as I scooted along on my gloveless hands. I ended up in an area of stinging nettles with a fractured arm and red raw palms. I was left with dangling flaps of skin that I had to cut off with a pair of scissors.

Davo and my mates in the Deyes Lane gang were all into bikes as well. Bikes gave us the freedom to explore. We would use them as our transport to get from Melling to Southport for the rock night at a club called Dixieland. There, I heard rock records played so loud my body shook from within. I can remember the DJ playing Led Zeppelin's 'Whole Lotta Love' at a ridiculous volume. I was standing dead centre in front of the speakers. Greasers were jumping about and the odd leather-clad girl would be swirling around as I stood still, getting washed with rock, the speaker stacks pumping out a sheer wall of power. I drifted into a sublime, trance-like state, my whole body shuddering, but that could have been something to do with Newcastle Brown Ale we were guzzling down. After several more Newkie Browns and lot more rock, we were sufficiently lubed up to set off home. Pissed-up seventeen-year-olds on bikes; how we had survived those nights of stupidity, I do not know.

It was life-changing to hear my heroes Led Zeppelin at a ridiculous volume. Led Zeppelin was a very important band in my youth. The Mazenko boys had all the Led Zep albums from the get-go, and they had even seen them at Liverpool Stadium when they were on the way up. I was exposed to the LPs from the beginning, and they had soon become my favourite band. The other big band back then was Deep Purple, but I was never that convinced by that mob; you were either into Zeppelin or Purple. The organ put me off. I wanted loud guitars, that organic crunch that has a physicality other instruments can't provide. Also, Zeppelin's mysterious vibe, with the overtones of witch-craft, was fascinating. There is an enigma behind them that appealed to me. I carefully embroidered the Zoso symbol off the fourth album's inner sleeve on to my denim jacket. I read *The Lord of the Rings* because of the references to Mordor, Sauron and Gollum in their songs. I liked the fact that, from the outside at least, they had no interest in chasing transient chart positions; they never released singles, it was all about the album to them. They managed to keep themselves separate from the pack; they were, in my opinion, well above the rest. This attitude was some-thing that coloured my concept of the early Bunnymen. I wanted us to be separate from the pack.

I get to see Led Zeppelin in 1975 at Earl's Court in London. I have arranged for my brother, who was living in London, to meet me off the Liverpool train at Euston station. He then helps me navigate the Underground and get to Earl's Court Exhibition Centre where Led Zep will, in a few hours, blow the roof off. Brother Steven is going to hang around the local hostelries of Earl's Court until the gig is over. We have arranged a spot to meet afterwards.

I enter the throng of hairy Zeppelin fans and eventually get up the steps and into the hall. It is massive, the biggest indoor gig I have ever been to up until then. I climb up to my cheap-option seat, high up and on the right-hand side of the stage. I see my row and my seat number.

There is a gang of bikers on that row, one of whom is sat in my seat.

Oh, crap, what am I going to do now?

I'm too frightened to claim my spot. Even if they would have given up my seat, I don't fancy being in the middle of that lot doing the wanking dog (rocker's dance) all over the place. No, I don't think so. I decide to sit on the stairs.

The lights dim and the spotlight hits DJ Alan 'Fluff' Freeman, who is the BBC's Mr Rock Radio and spouter of the slightly tongue-in-cheek catchphrase, 'Not 'arf, pop pickers!' He gets the crowd clapping. The feeling of anticipation is welling up in me, the butterflies in my stomach are desperately trying to escape my skin; the build-up is immense. The crowd are doing exactly what they are told by Fluff and are obediently clapping, stomping, screaming and shouting. Then the moment comes: Fluff announces, 'Music lovers, here is Led Zeppelin!'

John Bonham has a quick thump around the drums, then comes the familiar snare/hi-hat intro. The poor drums are getting the total shit pummelled out of their trembling skins. Zeppelin are out of the traps and the whole of Earl's Court are out of their seats. The sonic attack of rock 'n' roll from the *Led Zeppelin IV* LP with the four mystical symbols is thundering out of the giant PA stacks, the Golden Gibson Les Paul then the ancient Danelectro guitar tuned for the slide on the go until the mighty Gibson EDS 12 double-neck guitars all make an appearance. John Paul Jones abandons the bass and beautifully transitions to the ethereal string-section tones of the mellotron. The song remains the same, but I'm not sure if I will.

Zeppelin has a big screen projecting all the action and I have a pretty good spot, a side view, and I'm on Jimmy Page's side of the stage. I can see his massive, sequinned flares sporting glittering Chinese dragons on the yards of velvet. The familiar dark red Gibson EDS 12 double-neck guitar is in his hands and 'Stairway to Heaven' begins. The common misconception and why some idiots dismiss Led Zeppelin – the thing that most people don't get – is they think they are heavy metal. But they are so much more; they dip and twist from crashing thunder to the ephemeral flap of a moth's wings as it bounces off a lightbulb. All this is deftly demonstrated by the latest epic track, 'Kashmir'. They are pushing vibrations through the air to my lonely spot sat high on the steps of Earl's Court. This is seeping into me. I don't know it, but this will colour my songwriting in the future. It's all about the dynamics of the sound, the surge and sweep, the cliffs on to the slow drift of a warm breeze.

It was one of my most memorable concerts. I floated out of the hall and met up with brother Steve who had been killing time and pints at a pub over the road. It was brilliant.

12.

Beanbags and Dead Goats

Tubular Bells – **Mike Oldfield**

I have my lunch break at 2 p.m. The restaurant has usually quietened down by then. I spend most lunch hours wandering around Liverpool. The fact the city is built on the banks of a wide river means you can't easily get lost. If you are going uphill, you are going away from the river, and downhill towards the river. There are two massive cathedrals at the highest points, roughly to the north and south, linked by Hope Street. You can usually see one or both of them bobbing up through the streets. These buildings are guiding you to where you need to go. With a definite central shopping area concentrated down at the lower areas of the city, Liverpool is very small and easy to get around. I get to know the streets. A good few of the backstreets are still cobbled, flanked by a bad compilation of sixties and seventies shop buildings; boring blocks. Some of the old Victorian ones are still standing: Adolf's boys managed to miss a few. All the old structures wear a century-old overcoat of soot. Down by the river, the Royal Liver Building and her neighbours the Cunard Building and the Customs House are black with grime. I roam away from Henderson's, upwards as far as the hour of my lunchtime freedom allows me. It's the record shops and clothing stores I am seeking out. I carry on up Church Street and on to Bold Street. A narrow bohemian lane creeps uphill towards St Luke's Church, still roofless and bald after the Blitz.

As I walk, I see familiar faces that I have passed on my lunch-time perambulations. The old fella with his sandwich boards proclaiming, 'Repent ye your sins' and 'Jesus is Lord'. He is busy Bible bashing in his regular spot, rather aptly on Church Street. Across the street is a bottle-scarred wino turned rock 'n' roll busker. He's wearing a black leather rocker jacket, thrashing at an acoustic guitar and bebopping his way through Chuck Berry songs. He gyrates in the old Elvis jerk. On top of his battered face, his heavily greased, dyed jet-black quiff is dancing to a different tune. After a while, I become very comfortable in the city atmosphere. I start to love the place.

Liverpool is an easy place to fall in love with. Its grubby face and tough image conceal a heart of gold. The people are friendly. Everyone refers to Liverpool as 'town'. 'Are you going into town?' And 'Does this bus go to town?' 'Single to town, please.' Town becomes very familiar and all fear of the unknown is vanquished. At the bottom of Bold Street, there is a post office and former gentlemen's club called the Lyceum. At the latter, Victorian gents would sit around sipping Benedictine and reading *The Times* newspaper while sucking on stoked pipes of tobacco. It was not the gentlemen's club of today – that's a different kettle of fish entirely, as are the gentlemen that frequent such establishments. By the time my teenage self walks these streets the Lyceum has become a café and has a famous florist stall in front of its ornate facade. An old flower lady and her assistant sell blooms to lovestruck office clerks who wait in doorways for wedge-heeled and maxi-skirted shop girls to take their lunch.

I am heading in this direction for one reason only: Richard Branson has recently opened his third branch of Virgin Records at number 90 Bold Street. Virgin Records is being built on the runaway success of Mike Oldfield's *Tubular Bells*, the label's first album. (That album, released in 1973, sold millions and was in the charts for about a billion years. Mention it now and most won't know what you are on about.) I often make this trek up to Virgin on my lunch break. The small shop entrance belies the amount of vinyl inside. Two floors are brim-full of racks of LP records. There is an area upstairs for listening with headphones and comfy beanbags to crash on. Many Liverpudlian hippies are taking advantage of this luxury and are crashing on them in a mess of tangled hair and curly wires that are attached to the bin-sized headphones. Bearded and beaded freaks are sprawled about the colourful cushions, languishing in a stoned blissful stupor, reminiscent of an opium den Sherlock Holmes might have frequented. All are listening to underground sounds such as the Edgar Broughton Band or even *Tubular Bells*. Like all hairy hangouts, it is obligatory to cloud the air in a thick plume of the distinctive scent of Nag Champa incense. The pop music you generally find in square record shops is banished; Virgin only stock the out-there sounds of the underground, the records you would usually have to send off for by mail order.

I am a frequent visitor to Virgin. A few weeks earlier, I found the double album *Images* by David Bowie, on Deram Records. I am already a Bowie fan and have been collecting his records for some time. After the breakthrough album of *Ziggy Stardust*, all his previous releases become readily available and quite easy to track down. At one point, Bowie had about five albums in the UK chart all at the same time.

Images 1966–1967 is a compilation of all his early songs. It seems to me Bowie was still trying to find his way when he recorded these tunes – more the cockney cheeky-chappy style of Anthony Newley's musical theatre. It is a mix of amusing ditties with characters such as Uncle Arthur, Silly Boy Blue and Laughing Gnomes. Bowie's old works make up an interesting collection of songs. Even through the silliness, it is clear Bowie is the greatest of songwriters. These tracks are all part of his journey and I love it. There is a dark edge appearing in the form of 'London Boys'. It tells of a young runaway mod trying to fit into the scene and reminds me of a song by a young Al Stewart, way before his hit 'Year of the Cat'. The track is called 'Pretty Golden Hair' and is about a young lad that ends up used and abused as a sixties London rent boy. Pretty out-there subject considering Floyd's song 'Arnold Layne' was banned by the BBC just for a reference to Arnold's strange hobby of nicking women's clothes off washing lines and possibly cross dressing.

I also bought *The Faust Tapes* by Faust; this is on Branson's Virgin label. It has a brilliant op-art painting called *Crest* on the cover (I do like a good cover) by the fantastic artist Bridget Riley. It's the sort of thing that makes your eyes go a bit weird and disorients your mind (easily done in my case). Not bad and that's just the cover! What's the music going to be like? It is only forty-nine pence, worth the punt. Turns out to be pretty unlistenable but as time goes on and I mature in my tastes, I have begun to understand it. Part sound art, part music, it incorporates found sound, sound effects and I realise it's a work of assemblage. It becomes an influence on my future recordings. It sold about 60,000 copies, so the 49 pence price tag worked.

As I leave the shop, I see a tall lad in a belted cardigan as favoured by Starsky from the smash-hit TV cop show *Starsky and Hutch*. It's Paul Simpson. He was a pupil at my school Deyes Lane and a friend of Les Pattinson, the Bunnymen's future bass player. He was a cool kid, always with the latest trends in clothes. At school, he dressed in a soul-boy style that was popular at the time: neat and slightly flamboyant with button–down collars and much coveted cuffed two-tone trousers.

Now Paul is looking a lot more hippie or, as they were known locally, trog. The two-tone trousers are now replaced with wide flared jeans. He resides in a sweet-smelling haze of patchouli oil and the rattle of many bracelets. All this is topped off with a supercool haircut known as a feather cut. I suppose Rod Stewart was the most famous for this style. It has been creeping around the long-haired scene for a while. I even had a go at one point, but our village barber was not quite up to the job and it looked more like a hairy Viking helmet than something Rod the Mod might sport.

Paul has just bought Ian Hunter's solo album. Hunter is the singer from Mott the Hoople. Their biggest hit had been 'All the Young Dudes', written by David Bowie. Bowie's brilliant guitarist Mick Ronson is heavily involved in Hunter's solo effort and Paul, just like me, is a huge Bowie fan, therefore a Mick Ronson fan too. I am there to buy another solo LP. My choice is from Steve Hillage, the guitarist of psychedelic Anglo-French hippie tripsters Gong. This is his first solo record after bailing out without a parachute of Gong's Flying Teapot. It's called *Fish Rising*: lots of guitar effects and layering. This dates this encounter to 1975. We chat for a short time about school days and remove our latest purchases from the groovy Virgin Records plastic bags and show off the contents to each other. I never knew all through school that Paul was into similar music to me. Besides a mutual love of Roxy Music, I had him down as one of the soul boys in our school. I won't see him again until the first time I go to Eric's in a couple of years. Weird to think that we will be instrumental in the formation of two iconic

Liverpool bands, the Bunnymen and Teardrop Explodes; but on this day, we are just building up our knowledge of 'other' music and finding our way in a post-school world.

Another favourite haunt of mine on my lunchtime meanderings was a boutique that was just around the corner from Henderson's. It was an interesting hippie clothes shop called Cape. They had that seventies bubble writing favoured by graffiti artists at the time for a logo, hand-painted in bright yellow on a blue background. Cape sold tie-dye grandad shirts along with colourful flower-power shirts with huge collars and, the big trend back then, the penny-round collar. Some of the shirts are made from semi-see-through cheesecloth. Cape had an area for outlandish shoes, showcasing platform boots in the various shades with gold and silver stars. Clogs were in at the time, and Cape had taken this idea to the ultimate point of ankle-twisting fun, creating platform clogs. Huge wooden soles and the cobbled streets of Liverpool are not a good combination. They sold all the hippie regalia too: beads, bracelets, hippie hats, patches and badges, not forgetting the massively wide-bottomed split-knee loon pants. The split knee gave the chance to be twice as psychedelic, two shades of purple being the 'norm'. The shop was awash with the familiar, sickly scent of patchouli oil. Wispy lines of smoke drifted upwards from joss sticks, settling in a musky cloud that hung above our heads.

This must have been to quell the rancid hum of scores of ornately embroidered Afghan coats that had become a hippie staple item of outerwear. A few dozen were hanging around the store in racks like some sort of groovy abattoir. Maz had bought one of these stinking Afghan coats at Cape and I had acquired it in some deal that, as usual, more than likely involved bartering with records. Afghan coats are made from a mountain goat skin turned inside out so the fur is on the inside of the coat. Add a bit of embroidery around the cuffs and at the front opening, and there you are: instant hippie. They were very warm in the winter but stank badly when it rained, giving off a pungent hum of rotten meat and matted goat fur. Come to think of it, they stank even when it hadn't been raining. What did they smell like? You guessed it: a dead goat. This had only one advantage: you were always guaranteed to have a seat to yourself on the bus.

13.

Motorbike Goes for a Swim

Me and Davo out and about on our motorbikes.

Meddle – Pink Floyd

My job at Henderson's is bringing in regular cash and I have managed to buy myself a slightly bigger motorbike, a lovely bright red Yamaha Dt 250. It's another trail bike, but this time I buy it brand new and on a payment scheme. My mate Billy Bessant has got a job at Mike Weston's motorcycles over the other side of the River Mersey. He helps with the deal and even gets me a little discount.

I love this bike. Unless you have ridden a motorbike, you will not know the joy it brings. There is a time of the evening, the twilight time; these are the hours I love to tootle about. I don't know why the need grabs me and makes me want to ride. I have to feel the wind on my face. I ride into the west along the coast road towards the setting sun. The sun will be on its final descent to the horizon, around 7 or 8 p.m., even later at the height of summer when it can still be bright at 10.30 p.m. in the north-west. The sun's fading light embroiders the sky in impossibly red, pink, golden and purple hues. The workday rush has subsided, and the fresh cold air will kiss my face and freeze my hands.

The smells of the night are blasted up my nostrils. I'm riding high in the saddle. I can see over the hedges and grassy banks. The bike swoops low into the bends as I accelerate through the corners. The engine's revs and speed are increased, causing the gyroscopic forces to glue the tyres to the tarmac. I'm eating up miles of Lancashire's country lanes. As the light fades, the head-lights are turned on and moths are attracted to the beam, a divine wind of fluttering suicide pilots.

I love to ride on my day off from work. One such Thursday, I've got my off-road biker kit on: waxed waterproof Belstaff jacket, knee-high motocross boots, fleece-lined gloves, open face helmet with a large peak attached by three heavy-duty popper fasteners. I just point the bike in a direction and twist the throttle and off I go, escape for a while. I'm in search of all the muddy tracks and waste grounds in the area. Eventually, I'll go slightly further afield and head to the beach. (To ride on the beach was permitted back then; now you have to pay to get on the sand and that is purely for parking. Motorbikes are no longer allowed to blast up and down, like a demented Evel Knievel.)

As I ride, slowly everything is changing: the scent of fresh cornfields, rich soil and cut grass are being crossfaded to the salty ozone bite of the Irish Sea. I'm like a dog with his head out of the car window; the olfactory information of the area is forced up into my head. In no time, I am riding along the beach with the wide sky above. I can hear the crash of waves and call of seabirds. I'm standing up and out of the saddle, bouncing on the pegs, my knees acting as shock absorbers. The wading seabirds by the waves take to the air in close formation squadrons, changing direction in an instant, a moving cloud of glitter flashing in the distant sunlight. I rattle across the ripple patterns left in the sand by the tide. The beach is exactly how I like it, bright and deserted. The shoreline is bordered and protected by large sandhills, home to the rare natterjack toad.

I stick to the incredibly wide area of the shore beyond the sandhills. It is a massive expanse of sand. The tide goes out for miles here but can come in quickly due to the flat nature of the shore. I'm hurtling up and down, spraying wet sand off the back tyre. I hit a narrow stream of brown, sloppy, rather shitty-looking silt. The momentum of the motorbike carries me through this hazard with no problems, other than some splashes of mud upon my freshly polished Czechoslovakian bike boots. I'm about to learn that these soft areas where little streams finish their journey and trickle into the sea are extremely dangerous, no matter how knobbly your tyres are. If you pick the wrong point to cross, you are doomed. This will be my hard-learned lesson for today.

The tide is out, and I ride a little further up the empty beach before turning around and gunning the two-stroke engine. I am following my tracks left in the sand. I hit the shitty stream at a slightly wider point at quite a lick. The bike nosedives and grinds to an abrupt halt, nearly ejecting me over the bars. The soft, muddy silt has me in its grip. My heavy black leather motorcycle boots have half-a-dozen straps up the sides of the leg; I am in the mud to the top buckle and slowly sinking. I'm stuck; my bike is stuck. Then I notice the tide is coming in. With some effort, I extricate my legs from the gloop and get off the bike. Bad idea. I try and drag the bike out, but it's no use: the bike is getting embedded more and more. The bike is still running so I click it into gear, twist the throttle and the rear wheel turns. It has no grip and spins furiously, flaying sticky shit everywhere. This only makes things worse and digs the bike further in the mud. The more I struggle, the worse it gets. The reality of the situation is starting to sink in. I have to get myself out now; the tidal flow is hitting a sandbar a few hundred feet away.

The tide comes in notoriously fast around here. A little further up the coast, the tide can outrun a horse. I decide to use the bike to help drag myself out. By holding the bike, I get a leg free and manage to climb on a foot peg poking above the sloppy mud. Now using the bike for leverage, I can get the other leg out of the mud. I scramble on to the seat and decide I have to jump. Standing on the seat, I launch myself as far as I can. I hit the ground with a splash and sink in a little, but not much. I am free now and on the reasonably hard sand of the edge of the stream. The bike is standing bolt upright, the wheels, and now the bottom of the engine, have sunk into the silt. I look around; I am starting to panic. I can see the water fast approaching; the unstoppable swirl of foaming eddies of Irish Sea are creeping up. If I don't move soon, it'll be King Canute all over again. The crafty sea will sneak behind me and cut off any escape route I may still have.

I have to abandon the bike and go for help. I can see, just above the tip of a dune a little distance away, a building, the coastguard station in the sandhills, Her Majesty's ensign rattling in the stiff breeze. I get my breath and start to try and run towards the building, the bike gear, helmet and boots making extra heavy work of it. I'm continuing to run up the soft sandhills. I look round at the bike, wheezing and exhausted. I can see the red bike in the brown swampy rivulets, the sea not far behind it now. I'm hot, sweaty and scared. I have only had the bike for about six weeks, and I will be paying off the payments for years to come. I am clambering up the dunes, my heart bursting from my chest. I get to the coastguard lookout post. I bang on the door; a chap in a double-breasted navy peacoat with shiny brass buttons answers and lets me enter.

I manage to splutter the words, 'My bike! My bike! It's stuck in the sand!'

His mate is looking through some fancy binoculars that are fixed to the ceiling with a long, swivelling bracket. Still viewing the scene through the binoculars, he says, 'Too late, lad. The sea has covered it completely.' He then adds, 'Oh, hold on, no, no my mistake. I can still see the headlight.'

I can't help thinking that he finds pleasure in informing me of this terrible situation, as he delivers the news with some glee.

Coastguard number two turns and gestures for me to have a look.

I take the binoculars and scan the cold, grey sea and catch the tip of the bike's chrome headlight bezel glinting just above the tide, reflecting the wide, sunny sky. A second or two later, and it's gone. Below the surface, small crabs with eyes on stalks are no doubt eyeing up my exhaust pipe as a possible new home.

I have to walk, wet and cold, for a couple of miles to the nearest phone box and call home. My dad – after calling me all the fucking idiots under the sun, somewhat deservedly – drafts in my uncle David. David is just about the only brother, or relative for that matter, that my dad still speaks to. David is a lover of all things mechanical and is keen to help. It is agreed to leave it for now and come back the next day at low tide.

We pick up Uncle David and head back to the beach with a ladder and some rope, driving down the beach as far as possible. The bike is around a headland, and it's too wet to drive a car that far. I lead the way. The tide has retreated and left the bike keeled over and almost swallowed up by the ebb and flow of the water; a few more tides and it would have been gone for good.

Using the ladder as a walkway, we get the rope on the bike. With all the strength of three men, we pull. The bike is on its side, the handlebars digging into the silt like anchors. The bike fights and grips the muddy sludge; it doesn't want to leave what will be in a short time a burial at sea, becoming a sodden, salty crouton half-submerged in a briny soup. Slowly we heave-ho like pirates hoisting a mainsail, the freezing bite of the coarse and soaking-wet rope blistering our palms. With a mighty effort on the count of three, the sodden lump squirms.

Uncle Dave calls out, 'It's moving, pull, pull!'

As one, we put our backs into it. The lumpen mass starts to slide through the muddy quagmire. A few more heave-hoes and we have it in the harder sand and out of the inlet, the bike dripping and waterlogged. There is no trace of the red livery that Yamaha had dressed it in. Now it is clothed in a thick skin of stinking mud with kelp seaweed wrapped around the bars like a soggy scarf. We have recovered the bike from Davy Jones's locker. The gulls hover above our heads and call, expecting these strange fishermen to discard the odd mollusc or crustacean; but all they have to feed on today is two-stroke petrol and gearbox oil that have leaked from the tank and sump and are now beginning to create swirling rainbow patterns in the sandy pools left by the tide, shining, glistening in the fading light.

I wheel the bike off the beach and up to near the train station. I knock on a random door. The door is opened by an old woman. I tell her my sorry tale and ask if I can leave the bike there until I can organise a van to come and pick it up. She kindly lets me stash the bike in her garden. I wheel it into the backyard, prop it up against the wall and head for the train.

On the following Sunday, I call on my mate from over the road –Bill Bessantt – who has use of a van from Mike Weston's. Without hesitation, he offers up the van and himself.

'Yes, OK, I'll come. I'll get some straps to tie the bike up in the back.'

Off we go to Ainsdale and retrieve the bike. We take it directly to Mike Weston's motorbike shop on the Wirral, where the mechanics can't stop pissing themselves laughing at the story of this prick who nearly drowned with mud encrusted all over his jacket and boots. After a few weeks, they eventually begin the job, flushing the slush of corrosive seawater, crabs, razor clams, limpets, cockles and mussels out of my engine. They get the bike going again, but it's never quite the same; the electrical components have suffered the worst. I still use the bike for about another year until Davo's brother Mark offers me a few hundred quid for it and I sell. It's the end of an era and I abandon the bike world for a while. Come the next Monday, I'm back on the bus and on my way to work again.

14.

The Birth and Death of Punk

'Anarchy in the UK' – Sex Pistols

The year is 1976. Harold Wilson resigns as the British prime minister. He's had enough and is now sixty years old. Jim Callaghan steps in to run the Labour government. The summer has seen a serious drought and hosepipe bans are in force across the country. One of the hottest summers on record is announced with the now-classic headline, 'Phew, what a scorcher!'

On the telly and radio, it was pretty much wall-to-wall disco music. Soon *Saturday Night Fever* would be in full swing. All the nightclubs played was disco music. On the radio, you couldn't listen for half an hour without hearing Abba's horrendous europop; I wasn't a fan then and I am not now. It was late 1976 and punk was lurking in the shadows, yet to creep into the population's consciousness. Even the music press at the time pretty much ignored it, or more than likely were unaware of it. I was a regular reader of the music papers *NME* and *Sounds*, even *Melody Maker* would be floating about. But I can't remember seeing much in 1976 about punk. I was still into Dr Feelgood, Bowie and the Sensational Alex Harvey Band. There was no 'punk' movement as far as I knew. Maz had bought the first Ramones album but they appeared to be just another gang of scruffy, long-haired kids – just like us. The Ramones' music was stripped-back rock, no big, drawn-out solos. They seemed to be adopting Status Quo's approach: they had the long hair, they had the faded jeans, although Joey and the boys had ditched the flares that Quo were still sporting and in their place wore battered Levi's 501s. Like Quo, the band's sound was built around a few chords. They rocked like hell and were as tight as fuck. Somehow, even though a lot of the ingredients were the same, the taste was so different. Status Quo were becoming uncool and the Ramones were very cool; how does that work? It can only be down to the attitude, the blatantly moronic lyrics contained in such songs as 'Beat on the Brat' and 'Now I Wanna Sniff Some Glue'. They sounded like a twisted Beach Boys if Charlie Manson had been welcomed into the fold as a chief nihilistic lyricist.

I had heard the Sex Pistols 'Anarchy in the UK' at a Dr Feelgood gig. The sound engineer played it over the PA system, and it stood out among all the usual pre-gig rock tunes from 10cc, Supertramp, Led Zeppelin, Queen and the like. I'm sure they played 'Anarchy' a few times that night. It made me feel weird: my heart was racing, I had a strange feeling in my stomach. How can music make you feel this good, create this amount of emotional joy? After all, it's only sound, the ephemeral touch of vibrations in the air. This effect has always fascinated me. From the days of Melling Youth Club and the grimy, fuzzy, cracked riff of Norman Greenbaum's 'Spirit in the Sky' or Bolan's mystical string orchestration and Gibson growl on 'Hot Love', it can all make my body tingle and guts bubble with excitement.

I could feel a change in the wind, and that's not because my guts were bubbling. The Pistols were as yet an unknown band but 'Anarchy' had wormed its way into my memory and taken up residence in the area of my brain known as the amygdala. It had become something impossible to forget. When I heard it later, more than likely on BBC Radio 1's John Peel show, I remembered: 'Ah, so that was that fucking (sorry, said a rude word) amazing track they had played at the Feelgood gig.' This is the sheer power of music that touches you deeply. There must have been a buzz in the Feelgood's camp, a thirst for this stripped-down sound. Now it all makes sense. Dr Feelgood are on a similar quest; after all, their first album was released in mono and so stripped back it was almost naked. Unfortunately, Feelgood's records could never match up the visceral energy of the live gigs.

So the seed had been planted, but I didn't know what it was. 'Punk' was yet to reach me and my sleepy village of Melling. This all changed in December 1976 when the Pistols famously said some rude words (fuck, shit, fucker, bastard, you dirty rotter, etc.), all broadcast at teatime in an interview with TV news stalwart Bill Grundy. Johnny Rotten looked a bit like a naughty schoolboy and was pretty quiet but Steve Jones the guitarist was the fearless one that day. The whole movement under the moniker of punk didn't really become a thing in the news until the Pistols had been on that *Today* show. The next day, the Pistols were front-page news, the *Daily Mirror* printing one of the greatest headlines of all time: 'The Filth and the Fury'. Everyone was talking about Rotten and his merry chums. The more they outraged the establishment, the more they were loved by the youth, including me. You have to remember that these were the days when pop musicians were hardly ever in the newspapers. Newspapers back then had news in them, not speculations or what bands were up to.

★   ★   ★

The best youth cults are the ones that are created by the youth. They grow naturally, without a manifesto or plan. They do not seek the approval of adults, the press or anyone else: 'It's our thing and we ain't giving it to you; if you don't like it or don't get it, good. Now fuck off, it's ours.'

Things had been slowly brewing just out of sight of the mainstream, rising like sourdough bread, quietly growing until it all came together . . . and wham! We were unstoppable. The progressive rock acts were getting more and more up their own arses, residing in mansions in the home counties, sitting around surrounded by elfin beauties swathed in flowers and colourful chiffon. At least that's what you would think looking at the photographs on the inside covers of some of the records. They inhabited another realm, a strange dimension of the freaked-out superrich hippie fringe. Meanwhile, they were planning elaborate stage shows with ten-ton revolving drum kits, flying inflatable pigs and twenty-minute drum solos. Come on now. Something had to give.

Punk was a true zeitgeist moment. Up and down the land, bands were falling into this coverall of punk rock. Playing ability was no longer an attribute necessary to be in a group.

There were a few transition bands that broke free of the progressive rock format, including, as mentioned, Dr Feelgood, along with the Heavy Metal Kids, the Sensational Alex Harvey Band, Doctors of Madness and Bebop Deluxe. They were soon left behind; with one foot still in the past, they could not be accepted by the new regime. Over in the USA, although progressive rock was chiefly a British or European movement, AOR or adult originated rock was on every FM radio station. The colonial cousins over in the States countered this bland assault with bands such as Suicide, the Modern Lovers, Television and Talking Heads. These bands were following on from a more garage-band ethic pioneered by MC5, Iggy Pop and the New York Dolls. Although all these groups were very different and not punk in the UK sense of the word, I suspect they never wanted to be tagged AOR.

In 1973, the New York Dolls performed on the BBC's late-night music show, *The Old Grey Whistle Test*, hosted by beardy Bob Harris. Bob, with a wry smile, thought he'd seen through the glam shine sparkling off singer David Johansen's polka-dot blouse. Bob christened them 'mock rock'.

I thought, *What's he on about? They were great!* as did a lot of kids at just fifteen years old. We were already well-versed in the crossdressing style of Bolan, Bowie and Eno, so what was so mock rock about it?

The songs were a garage band trash-thrash with a large portion of Jagger's swagger thrown in. Bob's whispered, snide, 'mock rock' put down suggested it was some sort of joke. In my book, if it upset the squares, even the bearded ones dressed in neat BBC wardrobe department regulation 'freaky' clobber, it was good. The Dolls had stood out, as had Bowie and Alex Harvey's sensational gang of futuristic vandals. These bands shone brightly among all the others that were appearing on the *Whistle Test*. I religiously watched the programme and also the earlier music shows such as the now pretty much forgotten *Colour Me Pop*, an offshoot of the BBC arts show *Late Night Line Up*.

The progressive scene was fast becoming tired. I think Peter Gabriel of Genesis had seen the end back in 1974. It was time for a change from the hairy-fairy songs about giant hogweeds. Gabriel had created a much more urban hero, Rael, the chief protagonist from the concept album *The Lamb Lies Down on Broadway*. Dressed as a leather-jacketed punk kid with jeans and sneakers, he could have easily been one of the Ramones. Don't get me wrong, I do not hate progressive rock at all; I still love it for all its pomposity and ridiculousness. Unlike some, I do not deny my past obsessions. I went to see the *Lamb Lies Down* show at the Empire and Genesis were fantastic. I also saw Emerson, Lake and Palmer, Pink Floyd and Yes. Prog fired my imagination when my imagination needed to be fired . . . I had nothing else at the time. It was an escape in my life when all I had was my imagination.

I sometimes ruminate that in the unlikely event that I was ever to be asked to appear on the BBC Radio 4's extremely long-running show *Desert Island Discs*, what would I choose? You can choose just eight records to accompany you on the imaginary, lonely island. How the hell do you choose eight songs that mean something to you?

I ask myself, *Would I take two-minute throwaway pop tunes or punk-rock songs?* I think not. I am a practical fellow, so I would be trawling through my progressive rock albums for epics of at least twenty minutes or more, something to get my teeth into and wrap my ears around. There is only so much complete silence I can tolerate. Revisiting the progressive rock music of my youth, I listen now on a different level. I have even ventured beyond my collection and am now buying records I never had as a kid. This exploration is interesting to me; I'm a split personality. I can appreciate the raw power of Raw Power, the trippiness of Pink Floyd, the electronic evocations of Tangerine Dream, Kraftwerk, rhythm and blues, soul, folk and modern jazz as well as the mystical stories that Peter Gabriel, Yes and Emerson,

Lake and Palmer can conjure up. The combinations of instruments often augmented by a mellotron; ah, the mellotron, a kind of early sampling keyboard used on numerous records. Think Moody Blues' 'Nights in White Satin' or the flute intro to the Beatles' 'Strawberry Fields'. The organic and ethereal nature of the mellotron sound became an entity in its own right and a great addition to many sixties and now lo-fi and post-rock records.

Along with the mellotron, super-phat Moog synthesiser sounds floated my boat. Emerson, Lake and Palmer were particularly good at making great-sounding records. Considering they were only a three-piece, they could push out quite a racket. I'm not too fussed on the weird western saloon bar plinky-plonky piano stuff that Keith Emerson was so very fond of. This aversion is possibly a throwback to the torture of the art lessons with the migraine-inducing background of ragtime piano dripping in my mind like a leaky tap, doing my nut in. Oh God, change the subject. Quick.

The punk movement was important to vast amounts of the youth trying to breathe their own air. It was like when you grow up and find that things you were terrified of as a kid are not in the slightest scary now. The establishment's mask slipped. We had seen that they were shitting themselves. Rock 'n' roll has always been threatening to the squares; this time it was different – there was no real drug threat. Now I think of it, what the hell were they scared of? Punk was no threat to anybody. The art of punk is harking back to Dada styling, when rough cutups and collage formed a lot of the artwork. No matter what you think about Malcolm McLaren along with Sex Pistols, cover art genius Jamie Reid and Vivienne Westwood, they were inspired by the work of the Dadaists and they all dowsed punk rock with a soaking of this strong artistic aesthetic.

Dada was an art movement from the early twentieth century and had a lot more to do with punk than any other movement. Dadaists, like punks, understand self-destructive and self-loathing processes; part of the manifesto states that 'Dada Means Nothing'. They were referring to the word and the movement; they had freed themselves to be Dada. Dada saw the stupidity of the First World War and reacted to it. It was never meant to last; it was a spat swearword that would fade, but it has left many clues behind, like DNA at a crime scene. It contaminated future forms of art with ripples that are felt without most people even realising. Punk took this Dada ethic and, as Dada reached into the future, so did punk. The effects are still resonating today. Now kids have a vague idea of what it was. But they will never really know what punk was about. The kids wear a Ramones T-shirt that they just bought in ASDA. It reminds me of the scene at the end of the great film *Withnail and I*, when the freakish drug dealer Danny says wistfully, 'They're selling hippie wigs in Woolworths, man.'

Likewise, when thousands of high-street shops are selling tartan punk pants and kids with Mohawks are posing for photos with tourists on the King's Road in London, it's all over. Punk became too mainstream, the end of a dream. After punk, we all woke up better for it, refreshed and aware of where we were going or at least where we were not going. The so-called punk bands that came after were all fake in my eyes; most were dreadful. The punk scene I was a part of only lasted about a year. There is no point in trying to be punk; it was dead by late 1977. The Pistols' album, released in October 1977, took so long to materialise that the momentum had already gone. I never even bought it.

Talking Heads, Pere Ubu, Television, even Devo are not really what people should describe as punk, but they were all in the same camp; they wanted a change. Pere Ubu were experimental rock verging on progressive music or even Krautrock. Now they are included in the punk gang, too, which has retrospectively been made much bigger than it ever really was at the time. It's a very odd, thin line. Pere Ubu were not hippies or denim-clad rockers. All freaks, yes; but not punks. More akin to a weird street gang from a David Lynch film.

Punk was so short-lived it was over in the blink of an eye. I think it was meant to be a brief kick up the backside; how could it drone on like the music it was trying to replace? This extremely powerful movement was designed to purge the old and sweep the decks ready for what was to come next. Punk did at least shake things up a bit. Fortunately for me, I was to be in the right time and right place.

15.

Discovering Eric's

Eric's

Mathew Street, LIVERPOOL 2
Tel: 051 236 8301

MEMBERSHIP CARD

Name *William Sergeant*

Address *15 Station Rd.*

Melling

Signature *W. Sergeant*   Signed for Eric's *J. R.*

MEMBERS MAY SIGN IN TWO GUESTS
Valid until DECEMBER 31st 1979

Marquee Moon – **Television**

Early summer, 1977. I am on my lunch hour wandering about the streets. I generally head uphill, but this time I have decided to walk in the opposite direction . . . no reason other than just for a change. I head out of the annexed block that houses the locker rooms. First stop: I look in at a hi-fi shop. Beaver Radio is very close to the side entrance of Henderson's, with its large window-front facing on to Whitechapel Street. I browse about, looking with envy at all the latest expensive hi-fi equipment. I slip out of the shop and make my way through the throngs of shoppers, mainly older women dragging loaded tartan shopping trollies, wearing too thick coats for summer and those funny little sheepskin-lined suede booties with a zip up the front – all very popular with all the old dears. Some of the posher shoppers are heading to Liverpool landmark café the Kardomah for a well-earned brew and an egg and cress butty.

On I go across Whitechapel towards Button Street and into Probe Records. Probe have not been at this location for long; they migrated downhill into town from up on Clarence Street, not far from the Catholic Cathedral. They were situated in a small shop; it could almost be called a kiosk. I had bought Gong's album *Flying Teapot: Radio Gnome Invisible, Part 1* from there. Probe has now set itself up in a grand building in a much more central position. It is a time when many of Liverpool's grand buildings stand empty and are fairly cheap to rent. A few steps up to the door and I'm inside, flicking through the records for a short time, then off I go; I'm only browsing today. I move on past the radical bookshop October Books. Liverpool has two such bookshops. We called them the communist bookshops, so that kind of tells you what the political scene in the city is like right now. I walk on past the open area that was once the Cavern, still a gravel car park.

Then I notice a poster pasted on the wall on the other side of the street. Eric's Club: XTC. Friday, 10 June. I think to myself, *That's tonight.*

I have heard of XTC but I'm not sure what they are all about. At the bottom of the poster, it reads, 'Tickets available from Probe Records'. I am intrigued and decide to go. I nip back into Probe to buy a ticket. This is a strange thing to do; I am still very shy, mainly because of the state of my acne-ravaged face. For me to go to an unknown club or anywhere on my own for a night out is very unusual; it is just not like me. Something has made me do it. This chance lunchtime deviation would prove to be the real beginning of my adult life.

When Friday's working day comes to an end at 5.30 p.m., I take my time getting over to the locker room and getting dressed. I have a few hours to kill before the club opens. I get my bike from the car park and ride about aimlessly, and then get chips from a chippy. I ride down to the pier head and watch the New Brighton ferry arrive. The passengers stream up and down, going home after work. I'm wearing the uniform of the average biker: jeans, biker boots, black leather jacket with a studded collar and a few enamel badges pinned through the tough hide. I have made a stencil by tracing Lou Reed's face from the *Transformer* poster that I purloined from the sixth-form block. Using some old house paint, I daubed the back of the biker jacket. Lou's lips are picked out in red with some nail varnish my mum had left behind when she fled. I used a small paintbrush to carefully write 'Velvets', mimicking the font style used on the Velvet Underground album I had bought a few years earlier. This is my outfit for Eric's. Not exactly punk but scruffy enough to sort of fit in. Not that I even think of such things; my main concern is where the hell am I going to stash my helmet? I am pretty unkempt, and my greasy hair still smells of the deep fat fryers from Henderson's kitchens.

Eventually, I head back towards Mathew Street and I park my bike on the gravel car park opposite the club. Twenty-odd years earlier, just a few feet below the surface, the Beatles would have been taking to the stage in their leather jackets and quiffs. My destination is on the other side of the little backstreet. A pair of thick metal doors are at the entrance; at some point, this place must have been part of a warehouse or workshop. Above the doors sits the large black sign proclaiming Eric's Liverpool. A few punks are milling about outside, trying to get in for free.

Eric's is such an odd name for a club. I have heard tell that the club was named as a reaction to all the other clubs with names such as Tiffany's, Amanda's, Samantha's. These were glamorous names that would conjure up some sort of jet-setting wonder-land populated by the beautiful people, who somehow would be drawn to a dive club down a stinking, piss-soaked back alley in a forgotten part of Liverpool. Roger Eagle and Pete Fulwell, along with Ken Testi – the partners in starting the club – thought such names were ridiculous. They were being playful and wanted to stand out; their club would be juxtaposed to all that nonsense. A much more down-to-earth name, a little in-joke between themselves. So Eric's it is.

I hand my ticket to a vaguely familiar blonde woman and walk down the stairs to the dim, sweaty club. There is a cloak-room and I hand over my gloves and helmet, so at least that problem has been dealt with. It's getting full and the heat's intensity is building, though I keep my leather jacket on. As I venture deeper into the darkness, I'm greeted with a whiff of something not that pleasant. This place has its own smell, a combination of stale beer and bad plumbing; my hair being flat-tened by my helmet and stinking of a day in the kitchens is no longer a problem. There is a carpet by the bar area that my boots are sticking to. Even in our shitty house back in Melling – as bad as it is – you never stick to the carpet. The place is a bit of a dump – not that I have much to compare it to. I'm no John

Travolta, disco dancing my way around the city's nightspots. Apart from gigs, the BICC social club and rock nights at the Dixieland show-bar in Southport are about as far as it goes with me and nightlife up to this point. The club scene is not something I was familiar with.

The gents toilets are an inch deep in water – possibly piss. The walls of the club are painted black with odd bits of red furniture dotted around. There are some stools and a raised area of seats by the bar. The place is not really for people that want to sit and talk. The DJ is blasting out what I soon learn is 'Roadrunner' by the Modern Lovers, 'New Rose' by the Damned, Talking Heads, 'Love Goes to Building on Fire', Television, 'Marquee Moon', the Ramones, 'Blitzkrieg Bop' and, of course, the Sex Pistols, 'Anarchy in the UK'. All classics now. The DJ is behind a pair of ancient disco decks. His head bobs up and down as he crouches to fish for the next forty-five to play. He wears little round glasses. I recognise him from working behind the counter at Probe. His name is Norman Killon; it's an unusual mix for a nightclub at the arse end of the 1970s when disco ruled the world. He plays the punk records with the occasional Jamaican dub and the odd Velvet Underground or Stooges track mixed in. There is a low stage and at the far end a little seated area for eating what is passed off as food: chips and wafer-thin burgers of dubious origin.

I go to the bar and get a beer; they only seem to have one type, Pils lager and just about everyone is holding a bottle in their hand. It's not cheap and I'm not rich, so I don't go nuts; I make it last. I am leaning on the wall, waiting for something to appear on the stage, when a friendly face appears: it's Paul Simpson, from my schooldays. I hadn't seen him since bumping into him outside Virgin Records on Bold Street in 1975.

'All right, Will, what are you doing here?'

I reply, 'Dunno. I saw a poster; thought I'd come and have a look.'

I'm still being surprised that Paul is here when Les Pattinson from my class at school also appears from out of the darkness.

Les is looking very cool. He is wearing beige sixties Sta Prest slacks and a vibrant green crew-neck jumper (his mum's) but most striking of all is his pure blond, almost white hair, cropped short and with the punky spiked flat top. It looks brilliant; he's like the singer from Generation X, Billy Idol. The last time I saw Les, he had light-brown hair styled into a feather cut. He was sporting a Ben Sherman button-down collared shirt with his Deyes Lane school tie fashioned into a ridiculously large knot. To be fair, at the time we were all trying to master the art of the Windsor knot, whereby the length of the tie is wrapped and folded round itself a few times, then pulled into the neck to create a knot the size of a house brick. This was an attempt to match the style of the much more opulent kipper ties that were à la mode at the time, worn the length and breadth of merry old England – mainly by student teachers, BBC weathermen and hippies that had gone straight. The only problem was that school ties were short anyway – not much cloth to play with. The little dangling bit was only a few inches in length. This stubby tongue needed to be tucked into the V-neck of a school jumper. Tucked in equals cool; dangling out and flapping like a fishtail, not so cool.

Les has changed quite a lot; I sense his Windsor knot days are well behind him now. Les and Paul are both transformed from the 1970s soul boys I had them down as back in the old school-days. I hardly recognise them; they are very comfortable and looking quite at home with the other punks wandering around. They wear no obvious punk stylings like bondage pants, Vivienne Westwood T-shirts or thousands of safety pins all over the place. The northern punk aesthetic is very different. It's all homemade, as was the idea of punk from the start. Les looks like some sort of sixties hipster or villain from *The Avengers* (not the crappy comic book films that are all over the cinema now – more like a slightly suave, psychedelic henchman who is about to feed John Steed or Emma Peel into a vat of acid).

Les says, 'You'll have to get your hair cut if you want to knock about with us.'

'I don't suit short hair,' I say, not sure if he's being serious.

'Well, you are not kicking around with us then,' continues Les.

Paul pipes up. 'Ha-ha, don't worry, Will. Everyone suits short hair.'

I'm not convinced, although Paul seems to be pulling it off with no problem. He also has very short spiky hair, coloured and standing up like hedgehog spikes. His clothes are an interesting mix. It seems like he has taken a blowtorch to his white cotton shirt collar and cuffs. They are singed and blackened, with several holes in the cotton. He looks like he's just walked away from the burning wreckage of a plane. The ensemble is completed with what must be an old suit, pilfered from the darkest reaches of his dad's wardrobe, all wide lapels and baggy trousers. A small zip-lock bag with various items of detritus – cigarette butts, an old apple core and a rusty razorblade – is safety pinned to the pocket like the campaign medals of disillusioned youth. As I talk to them through the gloomy lighting, more flamboyant and crea-tively dressed inhabitants of this underground world materialise. They all seem to know Les and Paul. I am sort of nodded at as a greeting, though they seem unsure if they want a long-haired biker in their clique.

Paul is a little more friendly and shows me about the place. We chat and have a lot of common ground. He's asking me if I have heard this band or that band. Most I haven't. The club opened in October 1976; the first band to play was the Stranglers. Paul tells me he has been going to Eric's since November. Eric's did not start life as Eric's. The club was originally called the Revolution Club and it was in a completely different part of the building. It was rebranded as Eric's as 1977 got underway. Things started to build up to a regular weekend of gigs as more and more bands began to form. The music press started to take notice of punk and the swell of new bands was incredible. It felt anything was becoming possible.

The first bands to play at the venue after the Stranglers were the Runaways and Sex Pistols, all before I began to go. Paul's first gig was the Manchester band Slaughter and the Dogs; they are riding in on the first wave of punk groups. I go to Eric's as much as possible and I see them a few times as they are regulars at the club. The singer's gimmick is that he covers his hair in talcum powder. Every energetic jerk or fast movement results in a cloud of talc billowing out in a choking, dense fog. He bathes the place in the heady scent of a granny's parlour. After the gig, hairy-arsed punks from the mosh pit are trotting off home, dusty and smelling of lavender. For the price of some cheap talc, Slaughter and the Dogs manage to fill the stage up better than any smoke machine. This has the added advantage of masking the club's rancid sewer stench.

Over the coming weeks, I start to instinctively know what bands I will like just by the look of them, which ones I deem to be uncool and what I see as very cool. Top of the cool list has got to be Television. This New York combo have virtuoso skills that are never overblown and always fall into the area of good taste. No extraneous wankfest here; just raw-edged guitar inter-play. They stand out to me among the punk shots of one- or two-minute angry thrashes. Television's melodic content shines high above all the dross. On paper, if you said a punk song was ten minutes and forty seconds long with several guitar solos, you would be forgiven for thinking that's more akin to prog rock than punk rock. Television has two great guitarists, Tom Verlaine and Richard Lloyd. They instantly embed themselves in my mind. These New York City neon boys weave a meandering journey similar to Ravel's *Bolero* rather than any punk combo. They fight a deadly duel to a climactic crescendo. Couple this with a chorus containing no vocal hook – just guitar licks that slither up and down the scale like you are riding a cheesed off Sasquatch in an out of control elevator, next stop the thirteenth floor. Television's *Marquee Moon* contains a lot of the elements that put the final nail in the coffin of progressive rock. It can never in a million years be called prog. How did they pull this off? Television is my new favourite band and will remain a major influence on me for the rest of my life.

Eventually, on my first night at Eric's, XTC amble on to the stage and kick off with their jerky angular take on pop music along with a slight hint of jazz-rock. It's all a bit too wilfully quirky and clever for me, and I'm not that into them, to be honest. I quickly learn that the band performing on any particu-lar night is almost secondary. It's the club you come for; it gets into your veins like the heroin that is starting to flood Liverpool's streets. There is supernatural power in the bricks and mortar of the place. It seeps into you and can keep drawing you back like a salmon fighting its way upstream. You have no choice; it is like a survival instinct. The combination of youth, music, belonging and this movement called punk has become entwined as one force.

There are some nights when the band is so good, so powerful, it leaves the regulars reeling. The Clash had played about a month before my first visit and the place was still buzzing with talk of this event. Paul and Les tell me about how great it was. Les is a keen photographer and had taken some pictures of the Clash that night; I have seen one or two of them. He still has quite a few he hasn't even printed.

There is nothing I can do to free myself from the club's grip. It only takes the one night of being there and I'm now addicted. The appeal of being an insider in this outsider scene has me by the bollocks.

16.

Punk Royalty

THE LATEST
NEW WAVE GEAR

FAST DELIVERY.
PVC STRAIGHTS. In the following colours: Black, pink, lemon, snakeskin or orange. State alternative colour if possible. Sizes — Men 26W to 38W; girls size 8 to size 18.
£6.90 + 60p P&P
The same style **STRAIGHTS** also available in **COTTON DRILL.** Colours black, grey, khaki, navy, maroon or green. State alternative colour if possible. Mens 26W to 38W; girls size 8 to size 18.
£5.90 + 60p P&P
PEGS. Cheapest in Britain? Colours black, maroon or navy. Sizes — Mens 26 to 38 waist; girls size 8 to size 18.............£5.90 + 60p P&P
PVC MOTORBIKE (PUNK) JACKET. In black, pink, snakeskin, lemon or orange. State alternative colour. Sizes 30 to 44 chest.
£9.90 + 60p P&P

Money-back guarantee if goods are returned unworn within 7 days. Send cheques, Postal Order or cash to

MAINLINE (N), 51 TWO MILE HILL ROAD, KINGSWOOD, BRISTOL BS15 1BS.
Callers welcome Friday & Saturday only

'Damaged Goods' – Gang of Four

Over the coming weeks, I become a familiar fixture at the club. I'm now a member and a regular. The unfriendly faces from my first few visits are starting to be a little more friendly. Punk fashions are embraced and embellished. Most outfits are homemade or adapted from charity-shop buys. Some have the odd item from Vivienne Westwood but with not much money around in Liverpool, a trip to London and the King's Road is out of the question. It seems to be an unwritten law that to be seen twice with the same look would be an outrage. The clothes become ever more inventive. One of the most creative is Paul Rutherford – punk name Maggot. He is the singer of the Spitfire Boys, the local heroes of the punk scene, and later will be a massive part of Frankie Goes to Hollywood. He is the club's deadliest dancer and dub is his weapon of choice. Norman and the other DJs at the club spin cuts off African dub albums that have been pressed in a shack in Jamaica and imported by Probe Records. Paul's looks stood out. One such was an army fatigue jacket with one of the sleeves removed. It was either a radical look of non-conformity or it had been pulled off in a street fight that often took place between Eric's regulars and the tracksuited scallies (short for scallywags) wandering the streets. These times are the punk rock wars. There is an element of running the gauntlet walking from the station to the cobbled backstreet that Eric's lived on. Once safely inside, not much violence is witnessed at the club. Some skinheads kicked off when the Specials were on but that's about it.

There is a hierarchy of coolness in place at the club. At the top are the King and Queen: Holly Johnson and Jayne Casey from Liverpool's art-punk band Big in Japan. They always look the coolest. They have a small gaggle of friends, courtiers that are always with them. These are the more inventive members of the club. Holly and Jayne change their image daily. One night, Jayne and Holly are sporting cropped white hair, their National Insurance numbers inked into the remaining fuzz. They brilliantly sum up the mood of the youth, reducing themselves to a commodity. It's pretty much how everyone feels. Jayne Casey is one of the most inventive and creative dressers in the club. I first noticed her at a Deaf School (Legendary Liverpool art-school band) gig at the Philharmonic Hall. She was down the front with a throng of creative types. You couldn't miss them all wearing extravagant clothes and embellished with Roxy Music chic.

The Larty sisters Lori and Sue, both regulars at Eric's, look like sixties space-age dolls in colourful mini-skirts; both are incredibly beautiful. An arty girl called Hillary who helps in the kitchen of the club always has a camera. I'm never a subject; she wouldn't want to crack her camera lens. All the regulars that come to the club are trying to stand out, to be someone, but not in the naff way that Z-list celebrities want fame and fortune at any cost. This is more of a creative way of saying *Look at me! I am important.*

Another of the denizens floating in the higher echelons of the club is the formidable Pete Burns, later to be leader of the number-one selling artists Dead or Alive. If Holly and Jayne are King and Queen, Pete is their Witchfinder General. He and his girlfriend Lynne both rock the gothic look years before it is invented. They all seem to have an art-school vibe, though none of them went to Liverpool Art School. I think their style is under the influence of Bowie, Roxy Music and Liverpool glamour boys and girls Deaf School. It is all part of the formation and development of the punk-rock ethic.

Pete stalks the city and is draped in a long black robe reminiscent of the cassock I wore in Melling church choir. He pairs this with strange black canvas Ninja Tabi boots that have a split at the toe, giving the foot a cloven-hoof quality. With full-eye contact lenses as black as death, he looks like a crimp-haired Nosferatu or a demon that's got on the wrong bus and just popped into town for a few bits. In reality, he emanates not from hell but the Wirral. He wilfully cuts a scary persona and is not by any means friendly. If anyone of the general populace look at him for a little too long, he shouts them down with an acerbic wit that it is difficult to recover from. He exudes menace, I think as a defence mechanism. He must have had to put up with lots of shit from the scallies in Liverpool on a daily basis. I admire him for that; he is a tough kid. He works behind the counter at Probe. When he is on duty, most of the regular customers kill time and wait for someone else to serve them. I myself have seen some sorry soul come up to the counter clutching a 10cc album.

Pete spat out, 'What do you want that shit for?' then threw it at the poor kid, who scurried off out of the shop in fear of his life.

After that, I'm not taking any chances. I choose to wait, clutching the Damned's first album. I am skulking in the dusty and neglected jazz section of the shop, nonchalantly leafing through the Miles Davis LPs until Pete goes to the back room for a brew. There is a rush to the till as he vanishes. I'm not sure if the Dammed are acceptable to Pete, but it's not worth the risk. Relief comes as Norman – the Eric's DJ – takes over the counter and serves me without so much as a frown.

'Duck Stab' by The Residents.

As 1977 moves into 1978, the club is my second home; in fact, it is more like my first home. I'm sure I spend more time in its grubby cellar than at my grubby house.

Les Pattinson and Paul Simpson are friends with a bleached-blond posh kid called Julian Cope.

Paul introduces me. 'Come and meet Julian, he's brilliant. He likes all that weird shit we like.'

He means the Residents. I have recently become obsessed with this obscure art ensemble. BBC DJ, the late great John Peel, played an extract from the first record, *Meet the Residents*, on his show. I had my cassette recorder set to record, as I did most nights he was on. I was fascinated; the oddly discordant renditions of classic songs distorted and regurgitated into a melange of sound almost unrecognisable from the original version. Uneasy listening? But for me it strikes as beautiful discord.

Cope – or Copey, as he is known – is an enthusiastic lover of all things out there and we get along pretty well. He is incredibly passionate about music, more than anyone I know. He is very animated. When he speaks, he's jumping about and being over the top but it's an infectious exuberance. He just about manages to transcend being really annoying . . . just.

It's another night at Liverpool's premier punk hotspot. I hear a shout as I enter the club. The distinctive and slightly posh accent cuts through the sonic assault of the Venus and the Razorblades song Punk-a-Rama that is playing in the main room.

'Will! Will! Have you heard the new Residents record?'

I turn to see Julian galloping towards me, his blond mophead hairdo flopping about.

He has my attention now.

It's an EP called *Duck Stab*. We waste no time and rush over to the DJ booth and ask Norman to put it on. It's unthinkable now that such a record could be played at a nightclub and even more weird that Norman had the record to play. Norman does indeed play a song off the EP. The track is called 'Constantinople'.

We are grinning as the Residents chant in a weird redneck swamp-dweller hybrid accent 'Here I come Constantinople' in a repetitive chant, while an oddly angular backing track stutters along like a three-legged dog.

The Residents' concept is to remain anonymous. The main fact about the Residents is that they do not show their faces. An art ensemble living in San Francisco, they are not doing this for personal attention. They are doing it for attention to the work. No one knows their names or their faces. They perform most famously with giant eyeball masks covering their heads or swathed in costumes that hide the identity of the wearer. The music is not palatable to everyone but if you stick at it and let the weirdness evaporate, it will become sweet as sugar. This seemed to happen almost instantaneously with me. I am completely into the Residents' world. They take the normal stuff of life and death, give it a little squeeze and everything is changed and otherworldly. The mysterious nature of the band is a fascinating aspect and they have a cottage-industry ethos. They make and sell their own products via a catalogue called Buy Or Die. They are always coming out with new concepts, imagery and records. I'm straight down to Probe the next day to buy the record (and I still have it).

It's an X-Ray Spex gig and I am wearing my motorbike boots with lots of buckles up the side and black shiny plastic jeans tucked into the boots with my Velvets leather jacket on. I am wandering around the club waiting for Poly Styrene, Lora Logic and the rest of the band to kick off. A couple of the other members have arrived and are also milling about in the club. Suddenly, the bass player is speaking to me. 'Where did you get your boots, mate?'

I tell him, 'An advert out of the back of *Motorcycle News*. They're Czechoslovakian motocross boots.'

'Nice,' he says.

This sort of thing is a normal occurrence – not that someone likes my boots but that a member of the band is seen to wander around and is just like us. We are all punks and in it together. No one bothers them or demands anything from them. To us, they are famous people but punk is a leveller that has done away with all that 'I am a star' crap.

Paul and Julian are always hanging about in town. You can generally find a few Eric's regulars in a tearoom called the Armadillo. Paul works there on and off. Groups of post-punks hang out with a pot of tea, generally spouting shite about the next band they are starting. It seems that's the new thing: inspired by the punk revolution, everyone is starting bands. Most of it's just talk; the next week it will be another name, another concept and another line up.

Paul gets wind of me wanting to try something musical and says, 'Hey, Will, are you after a guitar? I have one. I'll swap it for those black plastic pants you were wearing at the X-Ray Spex gig.'

'Yes, OK. You're on,' I say.

The guitar is a Kay and has a sunburst finish. I have nothing to compare it to, so I don't know they are pretty crappy; but it's

a start. I order a combo amplifier from Mrs Mazenko's catalogue. It's a called a FAL Merlin. The FAL bit stands for
Futuristic Aids Limited. The Merlin bit stands for Merlin as in
the . . . er, wizard or maybe the type of hawk. I'm now in business and buy a book with all the chord shapes dotted on the
relevant strings and frets. The fingers are given numbers to help
identify which to use on which string. I practise moving from
chord to chord and painstakingly convince my uncooperative
fingers to creak into position. Tuning is a big issue and I have a
small silver pipe thing that has the notes of the guitar strings E,
A, D, G, B, E. You blow into the designated pipe and out
comes the note . . . more like a duck than anything useful. It's
a nightmare. The slightest knock on the guitar and it's out of
tune again. I uncharacteristically persevere. The fingers are sore
– the tips especially – the skin is too soft and the muscles in my
hands are aching. I seem to get the strumming part of the guitar
down pretty quickly. I start simply by moving from one chord
shape to the next. After a few weeks of making an awful racket,
the fingertips become a little harder and the movement from
one position to the next becomes easier. This is how I learn to
play.

All this time, I am recording bits on my tape recorder and
working out how music all fits together. I'm still learning about
the construction of songs. I can come up with a cool riff and
thrash away at it for hours.

It becomes apparent that I need a better instrument. I decide to
buy a 'proper' guitar. Something in the back of my mind is telling
me to start a band. Can it be that hard if some of the divs that
frequent Eric's can get one together? My guitar of choice is a
Fender Telecaster. I choose this because that is what Wilco Johnson

from Dr Feelgood uses and also the Clash are fond of the Telecaster. I wander into Rushworths musical instrument shop, right next to Henderson's. They have a black Telecaster hanging on the wall. It's brand new and £160, and it's about to be mine.

Under the counter in the glass case, nestled among the various effect pedals, strings and guitar-related ephemera, sits a little wooden box with several silver push buttons in a line and an on-and-off volume knob.

'What's that thing?' I ask.

The guy behind the desk says, 'That? That is a Mini Pops Junior. It's a drum machine. It plays drumbeats and you can play along with it.'

I have heard of drum machines. I have heard them used on various Eno albums, most notably on *Another Green World*. The punk band Métal Urbain, from Paris, uses one, and one of my favourite bands from the New York punk scene – Suicide – also has a drum machine, but they are pretty unusual. I stored the info in the back of my mind. As soon as I have saved another £35, I buy the Mini Pops Junior drum machine.

It's 1978. Paul sometimes borrows his mum's car and comes over to visit me in Melling, bringing his latest records plus his guitar. We would inevitably try and record things. After a couple of these rough sessions, on 8 February Paul comes up with the name Industrial/Domestic. He's got the name from the back of a BBC sound effects album that he found in the Oxfam shop in Ormskirk that he regularly haunts. It fits in with the love of the strange, proletarian music coming out of Sheffield: the Human League and Cabaret Voltaire; and from the industrial wastelands of Ohio's rubber town of Akron (Devo) and Cleveland (Pere Ubu). It all seems to fit with the industrial grimy world we all are living in.

It is all talk, of course, and we never actually get around to recording anything properly. We have a song – I use the term loosely – called 'Timothy' about a creepy kid. Everything as usual is sent through the FAL amp to give it an otherworldly effect. I fancy a girl called Julie Marsh, who is a regular at the club, and her name inspires another 'lost gem'. It seems that the songs mainly consist of names mournfully shouted though the amp's cavernous reverb sound. The other alternative is making noises on the guitar and having the drum machine ticking away in the background. It is just a kind of messy jam. (I hate that word 'jam'; it's contaminated with the soft rock and blues-based wankfests that punk set out to get rid of. Unfortunately, it's the only word to use on this occasion, so I'll wash my hands after typing it.)

Sometimes Les would also come over and we would listen to records. Now and then, I would ride my motorbike the three or four miles to Aughton, to Les's house, where we would, guess what, listen to records. I often took my Doors records, but he wasn't that keen. I would play tapes of the John Peel show; these went down a lot better. Les would tell us about the bands he was going to form. They all sounded great to me and Paul. One such was the now legendary and very psychedelic Love Pastels consisting of an all-girl backing group and Les would be the singer. He seemed to have an endless supply of groups residing in his imagination, including the Jeffs. Everyone in the band had to be called Jeff, and Les's name would be Jeff Lovestone. He even went so far as to make up amazing song titles that made our 'Timothy' and 'Julie' seem rather boring. For example, 'Apples from France' or 'Mr Cambridge Wells' or the sci-fi futurist 'Outer Time Outer Space' or, my favourite, the mysterious and ambiguous 'The Balloon Man Will Know'. If only he had seen it through, I'm sure they would be classics now.

We would drink gallons of tea and scoff down his mum's amazing apple pie, then head over to the local quarry. Les would ride his Spanish Montesa trials bike over impossible obstacles and skirt along high rock outcrops and ledges that would put the fear in me. Les had been competing in trials riding for years. The aim was not speed but about manoeuvring the bike across ridiculously difficult terrain without having to steady the bike by putting a foot on the floor. Points were added for these 'dabs', as they were called. The rider with the least points won. Les was good at it and won many competitions high up on the moors of Lancashire, Cheshire and Yorkshire in disused quarries and waste grounds, fearlessly gunning his bike up almost vertical hilltop tracks. It was a cold and muddy carry on; I went to a couple of events to watch his skills.

The musical explorations, or more accurately sound experiments, come to an abrupt end when Paul gets a flat in town (Liverpool) at 14 Rodney Street. He had also joined forces with Julian Cope to create a band called A Shallow Madness. This time it might even be a real band.

Rodney Street is conveniently nestled on the edge of Liverpool's city centre. The opulent and attractive Georgian facade belies the freezing damp bedsit within. Directly opposite number 14 is an imposing but unused and pretty wrecked Scottish Presbyterian church, not surprisingly called St Andrew's. In the grounds sits a pyramid where legend has it a man named William Mackenzie rots inside. A gambler, supposed to have lost his soul to the Devil in a game of cards (Happy Families?), he sits with the winning hand in his brittle, skeletal grip. It all sounds unlikely as the monument was erected about ten years after he died. It's a good story and adds to the groovy location of Paul's flat, which soon becomes one of the hangouts for our growing gang of punk chums. Many records are listened to and many cups of tea are consumed here. It's only a five-minute walk to the city-centre shopping areas. Unfortunately for Paul, it's also first stop for someone looking for a couch to kip on after a night in Eric's and their last few quid spent on lager. On many nights, his sleep is broken by muffled cries of 'Paul, Paul!' I am as guilty as the rest. The sash window would open, and he would throw down the key.

Julian and I are hanging out at Paul's flat. We arrange an expedition a mile or so out of town. The destination: Great Homer Street. The city-centre shops have little to offer; we are after more exotic booty. Just a short bus ride away is a clothes market called Greatie Market by the locals aka Paddy's or St Martin's Market. Housed in a large, corrugated iron building, the market is only open a few days of the week. Luckily one such day is Thursday, my day off work.

The plan is set. Our mission: to check out the piles of dead men's suits, jumpers, shoes, shirts and trousers. All are sold by older women who are permanently in rollers pinned and permed into neatly curled hairdos, all kept in check by tightly tied headscarves. These women would sell clothes for pennies, or at the most maybe a quid or two for a good condition Merseybeat suit.

The musty air is thick with the smell of smoke, ancient dusty wardrobes and mothballs, and that undefinable pong of history. Dozens of trestle tables are piled up with mountains of old clothes. A really nice sixties vintage suit or tweed jacket could be picked up for a bargain price, if you didn't mind that it might be coated in the previous owner's dandruff and stink of sweat and roll ups.

There is no pussyfooting around in the market. Nothing is neatly piled or sorted into sizes or even items. You just have to dive in and see what you can fi nd. I have spotted a pair of trousers in a striking green colour; a little more digging and I have a matching jacket. Bingo! A suit and it's from John Collier, a fashionable tailor. The TV ad has the tag line: 'John Collier, John Collier the window to watch.' The suit is dark green flecked with black threads.

I will pretty much live in that suit for the next year or two. When most young kids are only seen in jeans and T-shirt, with a bomber or denim jacket, someone wearing a dead man's suit cleared out of a dusty wardrobe would tend to turn the heads of the tracksuit-wearing hordes of Liverpool scallies. You may even get a, 'What the fuck are you wearing, you knobhead?' from them. This would of course be the compliment we were aiming for, as we were so cool. Braces, walking boots, brogues and thick woolly socks were also the height of sartorial elegance.

This Scott of the Antarctic style with a bit of old colonial refinement is all Paul Simpson's creation. He has the uncanny ability to enter a charity shop that seems like a barren wasteland of shitty polyester and rayon, then miraculously proceed to pull gold dust out of nowhere: the best jacket or pants you've ever seen.

Items could be found in all the charity shops, but it took a lot of searching. I never managed to get the bloodhound skills of Paul. The juxtaposition of these post-punk youths dressing in old clothes was a ground-breaking artistic statement that would be completely lost on the passers-by as they fl ocked into Marks and Spencer's. Now, at my age, if I wore an old man's suit, I would just look like an old man, possibly on his way to the chiropodist or off to Boots to get a prescription for the piles.

On other clothing expeditions away from the familiar hub of the town centre, the thirst for fashion would lead us to London

Road. This is still classed as the centre of town but not the epicentre. Every so often we would wander en masse and embark on the trek up through uncharted areas, past Lime Street Station towards the Odeon Cinema, turn right and on up London Road. It was a slightly rundown area of Liverpool. Most of Liverpool was rundown in those days, but London Road was even more neglected, populated by winos, smackheads and dodgy-looking blokes in leather jackets heading for the bookies or off licence, roll ups permanently stuck to lower lips.

The reason we would venture to the dark side of Liverpool was the lure of a very special shop, run by one John Edels, and known only in the parlance of the time as the 'Jew's Shop'. Yes, you can stick your Vivienne Westwood – we had something better. It was a dingy, old-fashioned throwback to a time from Liverpool's glorious past. It had the feel of an episode of the magical shopkeeper cartoon *Mr Benn* about it. Through the once stylish now grubby window could be seen all manner of wondrous things, still brimming with stock from the Merseybeat period and earlier. The great thing about the Jew's Shop was you never knew what you would find. It seemed like Mr Edels and his missus had an endless supply of goodies in the back, that every now and then they would bring out and have on show. Victorian shirts with detachable collars, braces (the type that you needed buttons on your pants to attach to), strange thin ties with geometric designs . . . gold dust! And the ultimate dream of the post-punk hero: impossibly pointed winklepicker shoes still in stock from the rock 'n' roll glory of the fifties and sixties. Haggling was the name of the game at this emporium of the past. I say haggling, but it was not that involved. The brown winklepickers I had my eye on were for sale at six quid – still pretty cheap even then for Italian-made shoes.

'How much are the shoes please, mate?'

'Six pounds,' the tired old shopkeeper replies.

I feign disappointment and stare at the floor.

Edels sighs. He knows the routine well and asks, 'How much have you got then, lad?'

'I only have two quid.'

Now this was the thing that was the most amazing thing of all: 'OK, you can have them for two quid.'

This was what we all knew would happen. Tell them you only have a few quid and suddenly the price would come down.

'Brilliant,' I chirped. 'Thanks, mate,' and off I would go to squeeze my now size nine feet into a size-eight winklepicker.

It was apparent the owners had endured enough of the rag trade and just wanted to get rid of as much as they could to these strange young blokes that bought all this out-of-date shite.

Now, in the twenty-first century, London Road has had a major makeover and gone upmarket. It even has its very own Cash Converters.

17.

Frozen Chips and Pasty Nightmare

Low – David Bowie

Back at work, things are changing. Henderson's has been sold off and now becomes Binns. It's a shit name for a shop and it fits the new regime: trash. It is a much more downmarket affair. The kitchens are reduced in size and are getting refurbished. I am allocated to the staff canteen – a definite demotion. It's all Kraft cheese slice sandwiches, frozen chips, sausage roll and pasty nightmare. When I eventually get back to the kitchen on the fourth floor, all is different; any pretence of culinary creativity is quashed. We now serve up cheap and mostly bought-in food; it's more a case of just heating this crap up. There are only a few of us left; all the real chefs have moved on to new places. We have no head chef; a supervisor is now in charge. A few of the waitresses are still here, but they now serve from behind a counter as you might see at a service station on the motorway. The food is of very low quality, basically shit.

Now and then we have a chap come down from head office, somewhere in the north-east of England. Mr Farr is his name. He's a bit of a cunt and looks like a rat. Everyone is on edge when he shows up. Farr instructs us to put any food left at the end of the day through the mincer: dried-up meat from the middle of sausage rolls, mummified sausages and the innards of meat pies that have been kept warm all day in the hot cupboard and are now hard and crispy. You wouldn't give it to a dog. Any sort of meat we can salvage, we add to a dried packet of some sort of low-grade mixed minced meat. This second-hand sludge is topped with a bit of instant mash to create a masterpiece of food pretending to be cottage pie. It's a disgusting practice, but we have to do it when Mr Farr is on patrol. What a penny-pinching shower Binns are. My flagging interest in cooking is now at an all-time low. To be fair, it was never on a high; but there were things to learn, at least at the beginning.

The gloomy existence in the late 1970s consisted of no interest in me from any girls, hardly any cash and my face looking like the surface of the moon. I have always been a moody sod so I could easily have plunged into a deep depression. The nights at Eric's were just about the only thing to keep me from going into that hell.

★   ★   ★

It's early 1978 and punk has pretty much moved on. The bands that were happy with belting out a few chords and a bit of angry screaming are tiring of the format. Wire, the Fall, Subway Sect and Gang of Four are some of the front runners that are now cementing their own true identities and have become so much more than punk. I wear scruffy jumpers and old trousers, topped off with a battered leather suit-style jacket from Oxfam. I have made a leather tie with the thin black leather I bought for patching up jeans. I glued it together and am pleased with the result, but it's a bit too much on the New Wave side of the street. 'New Wave' is a phrase I hate. I dress with no concessions to fashion for the ailing punk scene that is dying all around us. Trends in clothes are ignored and that in itself becomes a trend. This bland conformity seems odd on a young lad like me. While most scallies are head-to-toe in Adidas sportswear, I earn the nickname 'Manchester' due to my drab dress sense and the fact that I seem to be following the Manchester bands a lot more. The Buzzcocks and the Fall are among my favourites.

Around this time, there is a kid on the periphery of Paul Simpson and Julian Cope's little gang of mates. I am aware somehow that he is a Fall fan and his name is Ian McCulloch – or Macul, as we refer to him. Some say he likes to be called 'Duke' after Bowie's persona, the Thin White Duke. Macul knocks about with a lad called Dave Pickett. Dave is a little shorter than Macul. He wears an old tweed jacket and has a pockmarked face not too dissimilar to mine, poor sod. I hear that Macul, Dave, Paul and Julian are all in a band now, but not much notice is taken. Is this the Shallow Madness thing Paul has mentioned? It's probably just all talk.

Macul is thin and tall, has shaggy hair and is wearing aviator glasses. On his feet are plastic transparent sandals that are known as jellies. He has stretched elastic bands around the bottom of his navy-blue corduroy flares. This is done to bring the uncontrollable swinging material into some sort of controlled, tight-fitting jean and in line with the punk-rock aesthetic. I expect, just like everyone else with very little money, he was inventively adapting the clothes that he had. If punks are dotted with safety pins, I don't see anything wrong with using rubber bands, so I'm not judging here. I actually think it's the very essence of punk in a way.

At this point in time I had never spoken to Macul, though he is always hanging about the club, and was one of the few to see the Pistols and he was also there at the opening night. Like lots of the kids that are regulars he's just another face and not really in my orbit. It is known that he is friends with Mark E. Smith from the Fall and would hitch over to Manchester with Paul Simpson to stay with them. He does look cool in a Bowie-ish way; the clothes are more thrift store than Kabuki theatre, though.

Early summer 1978. I have still been hacking away at the guitar. The help of the Mini Pops Junior drum machine's steady tick of the beatbox helps me play along, keeping time as I'm repeatedly changing from chord to chord. I am getting fairly competent rhythmically. On one occasion, Paul Simpson and Julian Cope, from the freshly formed A Shallow Madness, make the trek to my dad's house in Melling to have a fuck about with some musical ideas, play some records, and talk shite.

Julian says, 'Let's do "Satisfaction".'

' "Satisfaction"? Oh God.' Paul is not that into the idea. 'It's a bit normal, isn't it?' he says.

I'm not that into the idea either. I have never been into learning the guitar by playing other people's songs. I have no interest in it. I always think why bother? It seems a waste of time that could be used to make up your own tunes. I am not as confident as I should be and go along with Julian's suggestion.

Julian starts the riff on the bass. I have no clue how to play the song. I start a riff I think is the rough approximation of what I have heard the Stones chugging out. I have a terrible ear for tuning; nevertheless, we are having a rather random attempt at 'Satisfaction'. Both Devo and the Residents had covered this, so we feel it is sort of an OK choice from the old world we were confident punk had seen off. Julian is the most musical among us and is pumping the riff. Paul is on percussion, backing vocals and melodica. A melodica is pretty much a staple of the post-punk scene. It's a sort of large harmonica crossed with a keyboard that you blow into in order to make the sound. Dub-crazed punks had nicked it from the dub reggae records of Augustus Pablo.

It turns out I'm not in the same key; my guitar is out of tune and it is all wrong, but I don't let this stop me. I keep going to the point that the others think I'm doing it on purpose in an attempt to be avant-garde; maybe if I'd known what that word meant, I may well have been. The real reason is that my already twisted sense of melody has been altered by hours of listening to the Residents, who can formulate an even more twisted take on melody. It actually sounds fine to me. We record the tune using a cardboard box as a drum; an old guitar pickup Sellotaped to the box acts as a microphone. Everything is sent through my new mail-order amplifier, the FAL Merlin. With the reverb setting on maximum, it is way beyond lo-fi – more like no-fi. With the arrogance of youth, we are pleased with our day's work. Cassette tapes are copied, and everyone goes home thinking we had created something important. Indeed, we have: the spark of collaboration is ignited in my mind without even realising it. I have set off on a trip that will take me hurtling to this very moment that I am writing it all down, which is a bit surreal.

Birth of the bowl-cut.

Devo had played Eric's Club on 9 March 1978. The day after the gig, I meet up with Paul on my lunch break. We are hanging about in Liverpool, just mooching. We end up in the Army and Navy surplus store opposite the entrance to Lewis's department store. Always on the lookout for outlandish outfits that could be adapted to the punk format, we head for the first floor where the military kit is kept. Here we spot Devo singer Mark Mothersbaugh. We are skulking behind the navy peacoats and peeping around, trying not to look like we know who the Devo kid is. The floor is patrolled by a miserable old bloke. He's on the lookout for kids on the rob. The misery approaches the Devo singer. Mark is holding up a massive pair of black rubber, sewage-worker trousers with huge wellington boots fused to the legs as an integral element to this very Devo-ish apparel. He is studying them with great care through his bottle-end glasses.

'All right, lad,' the misery guts says.

Mark does not flinch and continues to examine the latex for gig-ready durability.

'Eh, lad, the jeans are downstairs,' chimes the assistant grumpily.

It seems he is keen for his floor to be empty of customers as soon as possible so he can spark up a fag or get a cup of tea.

Mothersbaugh turns towards Grumps and strains his myopic gaze in his direction. He says in that polite way of speaking Americans have when addressing their elders and betters:

'It's OK, sir. I'm not looking for jeans today.'

Behind the clothes rack we are thinking, *As if this four-eyed sci-fi spud would ever wear jeans.*

The cheesed off assistant snaps back, 'Well anyway, they're no good for you, lad. Too big, mate.'

Mark, still in awe of the massive garment, retorts, 'I like them big.'

At this, Mr Grumpy gives up, shoots him a very baffled look, scoffs and wanders off towards the sailor boy bell bottoms.

Meanwhile, Paul and I are stifling our giggles behind the coat rack. After a short while, we approach Mr Devo and tell him we saw the gig at Eric's and thought it was great (it was).

The overriding image still in my mind is of Mothersbaugh astride a western saddle mounted on a wooden A-frame structure. He is centre stage, waving a kiddie's cowboy hat in an exaggerated rodeo jerk, as the rest of the band are belting out the twang fest that is 'Come Back Jonee'. After the show the humpers (roadies) are loading out the equipment. It's late and the club is about to close. The main room is scattered with bottles, plastic cups and other detritus, the aftermath of another sweaty night. Suddenly, in a flash of skin, a kid goes shooting past me. Shirt off, the kid is running about like a dog on the beach. Norman the DJ is playing the song 'Petrol' by the Vibrators. In a flailing erratic dance, the kid hops over and picks up a stool from the edge of the club. A few regulars gather to watch this crazy spectacle. He places the stool in the centre of the floor and loops around it. He then takes a running jump and clears it easily, crashing to the bottle-strewn floor. Instead of writhing around covered in blood like Iggy Pop's party piece, he curls up immediately and rolls forward, and in a flash is up and off again.

On his next circuit, he scoops up another stool, heads towards stool number one – still dancing to the Vibrators punky speed-freak tone – and proceeds to stack this next stool upon the top of first one. He then continues to frantically circle the larger structure. Off he goes, leaping over the two stools and lands among all the spilt beers and general shite left on the floor. He morphs it into a forward roll that Olga Korbut would have given her favourite leotard to pull off. The crowd is growing and he's loving it. He grabs a third stool and adds it to the other two. Now the thing is about five-foot-high; the kid is only about five-foot-four, so this next leap is going be interesting. He belts around the target and takes a few laps of the room. The crowd are now anxious with excitement: is he going to make it? He takes his final leap headfirst and smashes into the top stool. It all comes tumbling down around him. He skids across the floor. Stool legs have caught him awkwardly and painfully. As if it were nothing, he's up again and incredibly is still going. It seems the crash is all just a part of the spectacle. He has the 'don't give a shit' attitude that punk nurtures. At last the song finishes, and before the little whirlwind can do himself any more damage, Norman knows what to do and drops the needle on 'Croaking Lizard', a much more sedate Jamaican dub record from the Upsetters and Prince Jazzbo. The frantic leapfrog show is over. The kid is called Ian (not that one) and he does this attention-seeking act on numerous occasions. He never seems to do himself much damage. It seems he is happy with his bruises.

I return to the front bar area and hear some news hot off Eric's grapevine. All the talk of Paul and Julian forming A Shallow Madness, with Macul on vocals and his mate Dave Pickett on drums, seems to be true. Also joining on guitar is Mick Finkler. Mick is one of the unsung heroes of the scene. He is the best and most imaginative guitarist around. It's a loose and fragile situation. They have had a few rehearsals in a flat on Belmont Road that Macul shares with some kid called Paul Ellerbeck, also known as Smelly Ellie. I never got close enough to this lad to confirm or deny if he stinks or not.

A few weeks pass and it doesn't take long until all is not well in the A Shallow Madness Camp. Macul is soon booted out for not turning up to rehearsals, even though the rehearsals are in the same flat that he is kipping in. The lazy sod can't be arsed to get out of bed and join in the fun. You have to admit that such dedication to idleness on this level would make a sloth seem hyperactive. It would never have worked: Macul and Julian in the same band? No chance; Julian diving about like a kid on too many E numbers and Macul on beauty-sleep duties. Dave Pickett goes too. He is replaced by a drummer called Gary Dwyer. Gary is a romantic in love with all things from the golden age of Hollywood: Humphrey Bogart, Lauren Bacall, the clothes and all the film noir classics. He is into Roxy Music and Deaf School. He even draws a mascara line above his top lip to mimic the thin moustache that Deaf School singer, the gloriously flamboyantly named Enrico Cadilac Jnr (real name Steve) has fashioned. These personnel changes are no big deal. Nobody thinks it's going to be anything anyway. Even the name is replaced by the much better-sounding the Teardrop Explodes. This comes from a panel in a *Daredevil* comic that Paul Simpson has found in the disused basement of his flat at 14 Rodney Street. It's a great name and reflects the psychedelic records that we are all starting to discover.

I feel it's important that the sixties are mentioned here. We are looking backwards now, beyond progressive rock when things were a lot simpler. The garage-band music of that time is the perfect companion to the burgeoning post-punk scene. Bands such as Love, the Seeds, the Chocolate Watchband. Question Mark and the Mysterians, Mouse and the Traps, the Third Bardo and a lot of one-hit-wonder bands are all starting to be tracked down by our little gang of punks via Probe's record rack of psychedelic reissues.

We get to delve deeper into this wealth of great records via the double LP compilation *Nuggets* put together by Lenny Kaye. (Kaye will be the future guitarist with Patti Smith's group.) *Nuggets* was originally put out on Elektra Records in 1972. It was re-released in 1976 on Seymour Stein's Sire record label. Lenny Kaye points out on the liner notes of *Nuggets* that the bands on the album were called punk rock back in the day. This is possibly the first written use of the phrase. The ripples of this record are still being felt today in Liverpool.

One of Eric's favourite punk bands was the Electric Chairs. Fronted by Wayne County (soon to be Jayne County) they always started with the Strangeloves track 'Night Time'; the lolloping chug of the bass riff would announce the set, building the atmosphere in the time-honoured tradition of rock. This could go on for quite some time, whipping the crowd into a frenzy until at last the rest of the band kicked in. Norman had been dropping the odd garage-band classic into his DJ sets for a while. The Standells 'Dirty Water', the Chocolate Watchband's 'Let Talk About Girls', the Count Five 'Psychotic Reaction', along with the usual suspects: the Velvet Underground, 'I'm Waiting for the Man' and the Stooges, 'No Fun'. We knew the sixties wasn't just Merseybeat and Lulu. I was becoming aware and intrigued by this then forgotten underground music. I was already a fan of the early Pink Floyd records and the psychedelic side of the Beatles, such as 'Tomorrow Never Knows', and the Doors album *Strange Days*, in my view their most trippy effort.

Julian was pretty knowledgeable about psychedelic music and we would endlessly talk about such things, trying to outdo each other with tracks and albums we knew or had.

'Have you heard the Fugs?' he would say.

I would counter his Fugs with, 'What about the Strawberry Alarm Clock, Tintern Abbey or H. P. Lovecraft?' It was a sort of childish Psychedelic Knowledge Top Trumps, but it kept us entertained.

The MVCU in its heyday.

Paul, Gary, Mick, Julian and I are in another of our haunts, the Open Eye Gallery Café. It's a sort of art and photography workshop run by artists and various Liverpool heads. It's part of a collective called the Merseyside Visual Communications Unit or, to save about ten minutes saying that, just the MVCU. There is a small four-track studio here, housed in an old dilapidated pub once called the Grapes. They also run the hippie café we are now sitting in.

Over cups of tea, there is talk of a midweek birthday party for a girl called Penny, which is to be held in an upstairs room of Kirkland's wine bar on Hardman Street. Kirkland's is one of the bars that we go to now and then. It's a bit more of a funk-soul scene; people are usually dressed smartly in there. The party is an open invitation to any one of the regulars from Eric's. I don't know Penny, though I have seen her around. I think she works as a contributing journalist for *Sounds* music paper. She is the girlfriend of DJ Norman. As I don't know her, I am in two minds whether to go or not. The others are going, so after a bit of deliberation in my mind, I decide to go too.

On the night of the party, Kirkland's is busy as usual. It's a place where Liverpool hardcases go, looking to cop off. Hordes of them are several feet deep at the bar. Neat, open-necked shirts revealing bad taste gold chains can be seen paired with the fashion disaster of the rolled-up suit jacket sleeve or, even worse, a pastel jumper over the shoulders. These tough nuts have been on holiday to Spain and the tan is getting full exposure. All are scrambling for bottles of the current trendy bevvy, Jamaican Red Stripe lager. I am avoiding all that and slip straight past the crowds gathered around the pool table. I head for the door that leads to the steep stairway up to the party. I never even knew this part of the bar existed until now. I reach the top and it opens up to a room with a small dancefloor. It's very dark, save for a few disco lights. Norman is on the decks playing familiar tunes. 'One two three four five six': the Modern Lovers take us on a road trip through the suburbs of Boston. I get a beer to keep me company as it looks like I am the only one of our little circle of friends to have turned up yet.

With a beer in hand, I turn around as a disco light catches the glasses of someone sitting in the gloom. It's a familiar face: Macul. He's alone at a table in the shadows. He's nursing a beer and looks pretty bored. Like me, he's early. This is probably the only time he's ever been early in his life, so it is rare good timing. With no one else there that I know to talk to, I approach him and say, 'All right, Macul, who you waiting for?'

He replies quick as a flash as though he had been rehearsing the line all night: 'I'm waiting for the gift of vision.'

I know he has pretty bad eyesight. His glasses are extremely thick and are testament to that anyway, but this clever retort also refers to a record by David Bowie, *Sound and Vision*. Bowie sings, 'I'm waiting for the gift of sound and vision.'

The track is off my current favourite Bowie record, *Low*. My two biggest heroes – Bowie and Eno – had teamed up in Berlin to create this masterpiece. I'm impressed by Macul quoting this; it is a sign we have a mutual bond in the love of Bowie.

As we chat about stuff (more than likely Bowie), it comes to me he is a singer that has recently been kicked out of a band. He claims he left because they were crap. I'm not going to get into that; either way, he's no longer a member of A Shallow Madness, now re-christened in its Macul-free state as the Teardrop Explodes.

I'm thinking, *I wonder if he would be interested in coming around to my house to mess about with guitars. If I'm to get this music thing off the ground, I will probably need a singer.*

I ask him, 'Hey Macul. I'm off work on Thursday – do ya want to come over to mine in Melling and mess about with guitars, see what happens?'

He perks up a little. More than likely, his feelings are still smarting from being kicked out of the band by Julian.

He says shyly, in his soft scouse accent, 'All right, yes, sounds good. I'll bring me guitar.'

My phone number and address are offered. A few of our mates are now filtering into the party and I head over to talk to them. I think nothing much of it after that, not really expecting him to show up.

18.

Nutjobs

Bill Drummond's 'Filofax'.

'Repetition' – The Fall

After the party at Kirkland's, the weekend comes and goes. Back at work and the days are dragging by now. There are only three of us commis chefs working in the kitchen. The more professional pass has been replaced by a serving hatch. Working behind a wall with only a small opening to see the café feels detached, lonely and dull. I like to see the customers chatting and hear the banter with the waitresses.

At the weekend gigs at Eric's, I don't think it's even mentioned that Macul is coming over to my house on the next Thursday. It seems no big deal. It is just an attempt to quell the boredom of life in the late seventies. I have no master plan to take on the music business, to gain fame and fortune – these concepts never enter my head. Really, it's all just done to be a part of something interesting, something creative, on my part at least.

I am awake early for my day off. I usually just lie in bed until mid-morning, but today I'm up and dressed by 8.30 a.m. I hear the door slam as my dad is off down the road to the woodyard. Time to set about tidying up the house. Along with the general dust and grime, there are stacks of old newspapers all over the place. Leafing through, I see that my dad has been at them with his marker pen again.

Better hide them away, I think to myself, *I don't want Macul to think we are all nutjobs.*

Let me explain. Anyone my dad did not like – usually some person in the public eye (when I say, 'some person', I mean just about everyone) – would get a scribble over their faces with a marker pen before he would read the paper.

He would say out loud, 'And you can fuck off, and you, ya bastard,' as he scribbled the faces in with the pen. I'm still not sure why he did this. Any image of famous faces seemed to set him off, a build-up of anger in him boiling over. The only way to get back at these people he had never met or had any dealings with was to reach for the felt-tipped marker pen.

'That'll teach 'em, the fucking yard-dogs!'

Prime Minister Ted Heath, religious leaders, Cilla Black, comedians Mike and Bernie Winters (I must say, I'm with him on that one: they were shite), actors, TV weathermen, chat-show hosts . . . all got the inky-face treatment. Any rivals of Liverpool

Football Club; Everton and Manchester United got particular attention. Managers, players, coaches and supporters. Nottingham Forest's mouthy manager Brian Clough – don't even go there. I would say the only people he had any time for was anyone involved in Liverpool FC. Manager Bill Shankly was the godhead and his players were revered as saints, unless they left to join another club, of course; then they would be excommunicated instantly and would be getting the marker-pen treatment with the rest. But by far the people he hated more than anyone else was the royal family: Princess Anne, Charles, Andrew, the Queen, the Queen Mother, Prince Philip and all the others – what they call now minor royals, the maggots that are hanging on in the wings. He would often say if he were in charge, they would be first against the wall for the firing squad. All of which was extremely odd as he was a very patriotic man. He supported England above all others and hated all other peoples of the world. He had volunteered to fight for king and country at the outbreak of war. He was a very complicated chap, I must say.

Either way, the defaced papers are quickly hidden out of sight and stuffed under the seat cushions. The kitchen floor is mopped, the dishes washed and stacked. We only had about three pre-war chipped plates, a few mugs and two sets of knives and forks, the odd spoon, and that was about it, so that's not hard; all are very quickly washed. The asthmatic vacuum cleaner is dragged around like a uncooperative sausage dog. Its wheezing electronic lung sucks up the accumulated dust as best it can. This major clean up, however, didn't go as far as buying a toilet roll. Scraps of neatly torn pages of the *Liverpool Echo* are still in place on the toilet window ledge. Our shithole of a house is a mess, but I manage to get it reasonable and it's more tired than dirty now.

All is ready and the clock is ticking towards noon. Another cup of tea, a few more records and it is now 12.25 p.m. Still no sign of Macul. The clock's approaching 1 p.m. now – no sign. I have commandeered the little back room my mum always called, in a rather Victorian way, the parlour. That makes it sound a lot nicer than it is. My hi-fi is set up in there with just me and my dad in the house now. This little back room is my domain and I have furnished it and painted over the hideous textured anaglypta wallpaper with an equally hideous dark-blue, silky sheen paint. It is now my music room. It looks pretty good in a gloomy sort of way. Albums are housed in a flatpack cheapo wardrobe my sister had left behind. I have turned it on its side and adapted it with the inclusion of a few pieces of plywood to partition the vinyl. My album collection has grown now and is stored in alphabetical order. I love getting my records tidy.

I pull back the tatty curtains and see the mass grave of dead flies on the windowsill. The windows are all welded shut, so there is no escape. Once in, they can never get out. My dad is always packing the Vapona fly killer; they don't last long. He hates flies almost as much as the royals. With wings burning from the acid vapour, they head for the light and crash into the window glass, croaking in buzzing agony on the windowsill. The featherlight, dried-out insect corpses are no problem to the prehistoric Electrolux vacuum; all are soon gobbled up.

A couple more cups of tea and some toast later, 2 p.m. arrives and passes and I'm giving up on Macul now.

I think to myself, *Oh well, probably would have been weird and shit anyway.*

I go over to my neatly ordered albums and pull out *Transformer* by Lou Reed. Time is flying and dragging at the same time, the way it does when waiting for someone. The record player's diamond needle soon makes its spiral journey to the centre and crackles into the runout groove. Time to turn the record over and side two begins with the track 'Make Up'. Lou and the gang are accompanied by Herbie Flowers's tuba.

I'm trying to sift through my mind to find another record that features a tuba – it is not an instrument you often hear on a rock album, that's for sure. It adds a comedic element and images of funny, lumbering, blobby aliens are brought to mind. I'm up again and the kettle's back on the stove for the umpteenth time. Next on is *Another Green World* from Brian Eno. I slump back in my chair to let Eno soothe my mind; I am enjoying the ship-shape order of the room, getting sleepy when my doze is suddenly interrupted. I jump up to the rat-tat-tat of the knocker on our front door.

I answer . . . and there he is, only three hours late. He is sort of shy and I show him into the back room. He has an acoustic guitar in a bin bag with him. He removes the plastic and sets the acoustic down on one of the little corduroy-covered seats I have in the room. It is all a little awkward and we are both nervous. Up until today, we had never really spoken. All I know is that he is mates with Julian Cope and Paul Simpson, and I've heard he was allegedly singing with Julian and Paul – but that's it.

'I had to get about ten bleeding buses to get here,' he says.

'Ha-ha, yes, us woollies like to keep out of the way,' I reply nervously.

He only lives a few miles away as the crow flies, on the other side of the rather fantastically named Fazakerley in Norris Green. It's not on a direct bus route, so it's possible he might have had to get on two buses, maybe three. (I never thought about it at the time; but knowing him now, it must have been something he really wanted to do, to make that trek.) We seem to have a lot in common: a couple of intense and insecure kids with a council estate background, a love of the Fall, Bowie, Velvet Underground, Iggy and the Stooges and the New York Dolls. It's all good. He is quick as a whip and sharp as a razor. He's funny too – we are getting on well. We are slagging off all the bands from Liverpool we hate. Anyone who he thinks is embarrassing – which is just about everyone – is in his words, 'cherry on'.

On the deck goes the Fall's new single. I choose the B-side, 'Repetition'. We marvel at the rough edges of the Fall's sound, the simple and strange guitar of Martin Bramah, Mark E. Smith's poetic and sometimes incoherent ranting words, each sentence ending with a working men's club-singer lilt, 'Repetition-nyaa!'

The kitchen at 15 Station Road.

After a few more records and chat, out come the guitars. We proceed to my least favourite part of playing the guitar: getting the bloody thing in tune. After a long and difficult tuning up, we reach an approximation of what we think is in tune. Macul is as crap as me at tuning. I get the drum box ticking away, sending the signal though my hi-fi amplifier. We simply just start to chug away, mainly at the E and A chords. We don't really discuss this, it just happens. Off we go; the chords get a good hammering for what's left of the afternoon. We follow Mark E. Smith's advice and repetition is the order of the day. We are going in the same direction but taking different avenues of the rhythm, and it works in a Velvet Underground way. In fact, all I hear is the Velvets being channelled through me and Macul's choppy guitar patterns. He is direct and serious when he plays. The staccato nature of his style bites deep into the strings.

After a while of this chugging, I abandon the chords but keep it simple and start a one-string, sub-Fall riff that goes 'da dada-dada da dadadadada'. The FAL amplifier reverb on maximum helps to give my naive noodling a mystery that hides the simplic- ity of it. I get great joy from that. It is nice to play along with someone and it seems that Macul is enjoying himself too. This E to A chug-athon keeps us entertained for a couple of hours. My dad gets back from the works and that is the end of that. We call it a day; it has been a good one.

We arrange to make the Thursday session a regular thing. With his acoustic – or as he calls it, his 'acky' – back in the bin bag, off Macul goes, back to the bus stop.

19.

Welcome David

'She's Lost Control' – Joy Division

The summer of 1978 is crawling past and it is still only June. Macul has been coming over to my house on a pretty regular basis. He is always late; I'm getting used to it now. We are getting a little more confident, as you would expect. We have been experimenting with a choppier style; guitar strings deadened with our palms, the rhythms we are making are percussive. It could almost be called funky. In fact, we have christened one of these scratchy and very loose songs. 'Funky Whelps'; God knows why, but there it is. This funk influence on me comes from Carlos

Alomar, who has been playing with Bowie for a few years now, along with Talking Heads, who seem to favour a thin and scratchy tone. My Telecaster is constantly set to the bridge pickup with the tone knob dialled all the way up to the high-pitched world of maximum treble. Heavy sounds were kind of out and the crisp and thin tones were the way forward. I expect this was in order to be as far away from the heavy-metal sound as possible.

I will be witnessing Carlos Alomar in action very soon: I have got tickets to see Bowie at Bingley Hall, Stafford. To celebrate this, I am making a stencil with the words 'Welcome David' and I am going to spraypaint them on a white T-shirt and wear it at the gig! My God, what was I thinking? What a divi I was. In my defence, I was only twenty, and a very naive twenty at that. When Macul sees my efforts at the following Thursday's practice, he is quick to take the piss out of my T-shirt, which he dubs the usual 'cherry on'. It is a little embarrassing; OK, it's a lot embarrassing. It's a fair cop.

Macul is also going to the Bowie gig – not with me, though. Bowie is set to play three nights: 24, 25 and 26 June. I am going on Sunday the 25th. Me and BiBessant.t from over the road will be driving down the M6 to Bingley Hall. I had missed Bowie's Liverpool show at the stadium a few years earlier, so it's time to make up for that. When we get there, the queue is massive.

Bill is not too impressed and says, 'Why don't we just go up to the front?'

It's an audacious and simple plan, as the best plans usually are. I agree, and as bold as brass that is exactly what we do. I am no hardcase by any stretch of the imagination, so hopefully no irritated Bowie platform-boot boy is going to kick off. We walk slowly right down to the very front of the line with a display of cocky commitment, as though we have every right to do it. We amble past the rest of the swarming masses without a challenge. Standing at the front of the queue is amazing. Maybe my 'Welcome David' T-shirt is acting like an access-all-areas pass? When the door opens, we are ahead of the rush and we easily get a place about ten foot from the front, centre stage.

The crowd's apprehension is building. Seeing Bowie shows are a rare event that doesn't come far north very often. Just before Bowie comes on, the Funkadelic star Bootsy Collins appears high up on the right. He is on a balcony that seems to be set aside for guests. You can't miss him. Bootsy is dressed in full cosmic-funkster glam. He is shining brightly in a green sequinned jumpsuit, like he has just beamed down from the Mothership, his trademark star sunglasses perched on his nose above a smile as wide as the Mersey Tunnel. All are turning around to wave, and a shout starts up: 'Bootsy! Bootsy!'

Suddenly the lights dim, and we all remember why we are here. A slow dripping synth pulse, deeper than the Mariana Trench. It vibrates us back to the reality of what we are about to witness. The stage lights flicker into life and there he is: Bowie playing a keyboard, the keyboard tune of 'Warszawa' from my current favourite Bowie record, *Low*. Bowie moves like a cat across the stage; every movement is precise and elegant. The clothes he is wearing are some sort of sailor suit, his trousers sporting multiple pleats. These become a fashion pretty soon after Bowie's tour. Trousers with a plethora of pleats at the waistband start to pop up all over the city, worn by effete hairdressers and thin white dukes. These are usually paired with the classic bum-freezer jacket, a kind of cut short suit jacket. I avoid all this. With little money and the shape of a lumpy bricklayer, it doesn't seem right for me to besmirch such clothes.

I am chuffed Bowie has started the set with a track off the *Low* album. I have recently been playing that record pretty much nonstop back in the parlour, while I'm waiting for Macul to show up. It is not the easiest Bowie album to listen to. This more than likely added to the anxiety of the regular waiting period that always accompanied these practice sessions.

Back in the parlour, we are at the guitars again and I am taping everything we play on my new acquisition, a Bang & Olufsen cassette recorder. I got this cheap off Maz. We need to record everything because it all sort of just happens; not much planning goes into these sessions and usually the first thing I come up with is generally the best. It would be easily forgotten unless we had it on tape.

I am going to buy an acoustic guitar. Because Bowie plays a twelve-string, I head down that road. I don't spend much time researching anything about them and I'm back at Rushworth in Liverpool. They have a Fender hanging on the wall with the other acoustics. Using the simple logic of, 'Well, my Telecaster is a Fender,' I get the Fender twelve-string. It even comes with a case. I don't try it out in the shop; I'm way too self-conscious for that. I hand over my savings of £90. I get it home and immediately break a string while trying to tune it up. Luckily, on the advice of the shopkeeper, I bought a spare set of strings when I got the guitar. I am threading the thinner of the two G strings into the guitar's machine head mechanism. I am not very confident at tackling the job and the sharp end of the metal string pushes into the brand-new varnish on the headstock and gouges an ugly and randomly shaped scratch; I have hardly played a note on the sodding thing. I am well cheesed off and all my attempts to polish the scratch away fail. I have to learn to live with it. If I thought the Telecaster was hard to tune, this is on another level entirely. It takes me hours to get it sounding right, or as close to in tune as I can get. Tuners were available back then, but they were very expensive and complicated: lots of controls and weird spinning strobe light displays that would have looked more at home at NASA.

Macul and I have been playing together for a few months now and have the bones of a few songs, although I have never heard him sing a note. I never question this and am happy for us to craft the instrumental elements of the songs, more like sequences of chords really. Chord changes we think sound good, following one to another. Sometimes I would get a few chords together while he wasn't there and phone him up and play them to him down the phone. 'Do It Clean' is one such song. I phoned Macul up at his mum's house and played the chords down the line. He thought it was great. At the next rehearsal, we hammer it out for hours. There is still no sign of any singing or lyrics. The new acoustic has given me a lot of inspiration and I have the chords for the song that will eventually be our first single, 'The Pictures

on My Wall'. It is loosely inspired by Iggy Pop's 'The Passenger' and the circular chord movement of that song.

It's 13 July 1978, a normal night at Eric's. There is a band on in the main room, but it is a weekday and not much attention is being paid to them. I decide to wander in and only a few others are watching the stage. The band's bass player seems to be leading the songs with melodic lines not normally played on the bass. The drummer is accurately displaying a mastery of the drums. Out are the corny rock 'n' roll fills that most other bands use to denote the verse from the chorus. He can convey that message with pure power, beating the shit out of the kit.

To his left is a black, flying saucer-shaped disc about the size of a dinner plate. Is it a Frisbee? No! It is a synthesised drum trigger called a Synare. These electronic drums are favoured by the disco scene and are generally used to make a high pinging sound, like on the recent Rose Royce hit 'Love Don't Live Here Anymore'. In between the songs, the drummer is hitting the Synare while he is twiddling a few knobs to change the tone. When it is hit, it makes a truncated whoosh sound. This drummer is using it to punctuate the drum pattern with an electronic white noise clacking tchuck tchuck, a sound not too dissimilar to a closed hi-hat in the style of Kraftwerk. The drums are kicking off now and the Frisbee is in the sequence of hits. The bass is soon to join in.

The bassist's instrument is slung ridiculously low as he is strafing the tiny crowd with a sonic Gatling gun. The repetitive and hypnotic bass run is thickened with a droning open string: it's a style all of his own. The guitarist is very neatly dressed in a shirt with sleeves rolled up; he has a job to do. His pressed sixth-form school trousers seem out of place here. He plays intermittent stabs and sequences of notes. I feel he has a slight Black Sabbath growl and the simplicity makes it all the more interesting.

The singer is a lanky lad, thin with a very ordinary haircut. He is wearing a pretty bad shiny shirt that someone at a disco might wear. It all looks a bit Eastern Bloc and that's exactly how the song sounds too. His voice is low – very low. As the band build to a crescendo, the singer jerks into a weird dance, flailing his arms about like he is trying to ward off invisible demons that are attacking him. It is really something to behold. It could have been a comedic sight but for the intensity and seriousness that he and the other members of the band are displaying. The song finishes and I rush out to the bar area. I am excited and tell the others who are sat there expressing zero fucks about what is occurring in the main room. They are on the little raised area of seats by the bar, chatting. They have a few half-empty lager bottles about the table.

Over the sound of the drummer's Synare tune-up, I am shouting and gesturing to Les, Paul, Macul and Julian to come in.

'Quick, you have got to come in, this lot are amazing.'

They slowly amble into the room where a brand-new Joy Division is playing. Just last year, only a few months ago, they were called Warsaw and were pretty crappy. An average punk group, still with an angry shouting singer centre stage, but something has happened; how could this be? They have metamorphosed into an amazing outfit with a Cold War (as you already know, my favourite war) coolness that is original and truly its own thing.

The music is perfect for the current climate. The UK and the USA are always at loggerheads with the Soviet Union. Submarines, packing Polaris nuclear missiles, are constantly on high alert. They are creeping around the Arctic Circle ready to obliterate Moscow and the east. The Soviets are also lurking under the ice with their ballistic missiles trained on London and Washington and all points west. There is fear and a real possibility of nuclear war. No amount of 'Ban the Bomb' badges pinned to students' lapels or beardy marches can make a difference.

In some weird way, the darkness of the late seventies atmosphere is impregnated into the songs of Joy Division. They manage to look like fascists and communists at the same time. (I am not suggesting they are either of these, by the way, before I get a lawsuit slapped on my ass; they just struck me like that.) To my mind, this is real Cold War music, a perfect soundtrack to our imminent doom if the Russkies decide to get all shirty with the West and, as they say in Liverpool, kick off big time. Joy Division are instantly my new favourite band and fit in nicely with my passion for the Manchester scene. Nothing like this has been seen before. All is now changed. This really is the death of punk in my eyes.

20.

Rock 1 plus Bossa Nova

'30 Seconds Over Tokyo' – Pere Ubu

Winter 1978. The Thursday meetups with Macul at my house are going well. We have a few good musical ideas, the bare bones of songs. We have that funky tune called 'Funky Whelps', 'The Rocky One', one called 'Mister', 'I Bagsy Yours' and 'Ashes to Ashes'. There has still been no singing from Macul, so no final titles or any lyrics. They are going to all remain instrumentals for all I know. I have been writing poems and song lyrics myself. One short piece I have been messing about with is called 'Happy Death Men'. It was inspired by a photo in the *Radio Times* of some soldiers in neat lines at a passing-out parade, all beaming smiles having completed their basic training. Very juvenile; I don't think Shakespeare has anything to worry about.

Something big is around the corner and we are blissfully unaware of good things lurking just out of sight. We are all at Eric's again on Saturday 11 November, 1978. It's one of those nights when we go just because that's what we do; it's not for the bands, but because we always go to Eric's no matter what. Tonight, all the bands are from a Manchester indie label called Rabid Records. They tend to put out records with a sort of comedy element. (That seems a bit silly now, but at the time it was sort of fun in a student humour way.) The bands on this particular night are Gyro, who had a single called 'Central Detention Centre'; Ed Banger and the Nosebleeds with their single 'Kinnel Tommy' and Gordon the Moron, who had shot to a kind of fame because of the chorus of Jilted John's top-five single, 'Going Steady', which features the chorus 'Gordon is a moron'. These bands are not my scene, though I did help Jilted John have a hit as I bought his track.

Julian and the rest of the Teardrop Explodes are at the club. Julian, who is jumping about like Tigger on speed, is telling us that they are playing at Eric's on Wednesday. It's a private party for the teacher training college that he is attending. But like all these parties, it will be fairly loose and anyone who wants to come can. The show is set to be on the 15th, in just four days.

News travels fast in Liverpool. Julian and Paul are well aware that Macul and I have a sort of band thing going on.

'You and Macul have got something going; why don't you support us?' says Julian.

It's an interesting idea, as we have no real songs or knowledge of how a band works. Despite the fact that I've never heard Macul sing a note, we do not hesitate and say, 'OK, we will do it.'

The excitement soon fades as it dawns on us that we consist of only two guitars and a drum machine. Someone suggests that we will need a bass guitarist. My old schoolmate Les Pattinson pipes up, 'I'll play the bass.' He's never owned or even, as far as I know, held such a thing as a bass, let alone played one. He does, however, fancy Tina Weymouth, the bass player from Talking Heads. Consequently, Les had watched her a lot when they played at Eric's. (I had missed this gig when I was too spotty to show my face in public.) I guess this was good enough.

'OK, you're in.'

'Now, where do we get a bass guitar from?'

Luckily, an Eric's regular – a punk kid called Robbie – had been earwigging our conversation and said, 'All right, Les, I have a bass for sale and a little amp; you can have them both for thirty quid.'

The punk-rock gods are looking down on us today. Crisis averted and problem solved. It seems they have a plan for us. Or at least everything seems to be aligned.

We arrange to go to Robbie's on the next day, Sunday, and have a look at the bass, though we are not sure what we will be looking for as neither of us knows the slightest thing about bass guitars. Sunday arrives and Les picks me up in his car and we head to Bootle. Behind a large pub called the Mons, we find Robbie's terraced house. The deal is done with no haggling; Les is now the owner of a bass. Normally bass guitars have four strings. This one only had three; one would need replacing. I think Les would have bought it even if it had been in two pieces. He is a dab hand at woodwork and has been building and repairing boats since he left school. It would have presented little problem to him and his tools. Les is not fazed in the slightest. I think he likes the fact that it has only got three strings; it feels a bit more punk rock to play a three-string bass.

By Monday afternoon, we have also sorted somewhere to practise: we meet up on my lunch and walk the short distance around to see the people at the MVCU art centre. They give us access to a rather miserable cellar on Tuesday. The floor is uneven and consists of mud with puddles all over the place. When the tide comes slurping up the Mersey estuary, the water level gets a little deeper. We perch the amplifier as high as we can on an old chair, out of the way of the water. Water and electricity don't get on very well, as you more than likely know already.

I don't have any recollection of Macul being with us in this dank and dismal cellar. I need to clarify this, so I call Les up in Melbourne, where he now lives, and I get his side of the story:

Me: 'Hi, Les. Do you remember our first rehearsal for the Teardrops' party at Eric's? I can't remember Macul being there. Do you?'

Les: 'All right, Will. Yes, that's right, he never showed up. Don't you remember? It was just me and you in the cellar and we ran through the basic idea you had. I came up with the bass, we both liked it and that was that.'

He adds, 'We weren't there very long.'

Incredibly, Macul never actually turned up to this, our first rehearsal. Even up to the time we went on stage, we still never really knew if he could sing or not. I don't recall this worrying me or Les at the time.

That day in the squelchy cellar, Les keeps it simple and lays down a solid bed that we assume Macul and I can weave in and around and sit melodies over the top. This bass foundation is what has been lacking in the backroom practices. Les has an instinctive and unwavering grasp on what a bass should be doing. Somehow, he is instantly solid as a rock.

With no instruction on how to play the bass, Les created his very own style, which still baffles me to this day. He was using a heavy pick and plucking the strings in an upward motion. I think most would choose to strike the string downward. It seems to me this is an incredibly difficult flicking movement. He made the whole process of playing much harder for himself. I was too wrapped up in my own self-doubt, fears and worries to notice at the time, or I would have suggested that he strum downwards. I'm so glad I didn't spot Les's technique, as he would never have sounded like Les. I only picked up on his unusual way of playing years later, when he had been doing it that way for ages. He was a master by then and it was too late to change. I have tried to play the bass guitar Les style. The wrist gets tired very quickly. He had randomly stumbled upon a technique that gives him a unique sound no one can reproduce.

After an hour or so, we decide to abandon the rehearsal in the swampy depths of the MVCU cellar. We feel like we could maybe get away with it at the party and I'm a little less worried. The gig is on tomorrow. Even though we are scared, it's good to have a mate as solid and reliable as Les on my side. He's always good back up. If we fall, we all fall together.

Finally, the day of the gig arrives. Straight from work, I head over to the club. We are at what we soon learn is called a sound-check. (I'm joking; we all knew what a soundcheck was. We used to get into the club early sometimes and see various bands engaging in the soundcheck. We had even sat in a couple of times when the Fall were doing their pre-gig checks.)

It is now 7.30 p.m. The club is filling up and many of the regulars are filing in. Among them are Jayne Casey and her band Big in Japan. This is adding to the pressure I'm feeling; I would hate to look a knobhead in front of that lot. Julian's mates from the teachers' college begin to show up. Not many know we are also going to be on the bill, as we have no name. Macul and I have never really discussed what to call ourselves.

We are ready to go on. We have checked all the equipment. My trusty FAL amplifier red light is lit and ready to go. Les has borrowed a bass amp and we are all set. Julian bounds on to the stage like a 1970s Radio 1 DJ. 'Hello. This is Echo and the Bunnymen.'

I'm thinking, *What was that? Echo and the Funnymen? Where the hell did he get that from? Sounds really shit. We are not going to be called that, that's for sure!*

It transpires that Julian had randomly read this band name off a half-arsed list that Macul's flatmate – the posh kid known as Smelly Ellie – had come up with. He had a list of ridiculous names, the way that a student with a 'wacky' sense of humour and a taste for the surreal would name a group. I never saw the list, but I find out about it later. The names included Glycerol and the Fan Extractors – awful! The Daz Men – shite. Mona Lisa and the Grease Guns – are you kidding? The least repugnant of the bunch and, of course, the one that got chosen, was Echo and the Bunnymen. I was never keen on the idea, fearing that Macul would be seen as Echo and us chumps in the band – me and Les – as his minions, the Bunnymen. No thanks. I hated bands with those sorts of names: Huey Lewis and the News, Elvis Costello and the Attractions, Eddie and the Hot Rods; all naff and not my cup of tea. This was not what I was starting a band for, to be just one of the backing band. I felt at this point the group was my creation, my baby, my band. It was apparent that everyone, including Julian, knew about the bloody list of names except me. I don't get to name my own band!

Our first gig at Eric's. (Top: The back of Bill Drummond's head.)

Back to the stage. I have more immediate worries to deal with. We get in position. I look out into the small crowd of friends, enemies and pissed up student teachers. All eyes are on us on the stage, some just staring. I notice Les is glowering at some lads at the front who are chatting among themselves; I refuse to be intimidated. I have marked the speed setting or, if you want to be all musical, the tempo on the drum machine. This could be a bit random; it is very sensitive. To get the exact beats per minute every time you adjust this dial is almost impossible. I get the beat going and fade up. The drum pattern is a little slow, so I give the silver tempo control a tweak and the speed is fractionally increased. The drum machine button is firmly set on 'Rock 1'. There are only a few settings that we have found useful: 'Rock 1' and 'Rock 2'. Sometimes a combination of two settings would be OK. It was possible to add 'Bossa Nova' or 'Samba' to these rock settings by depressing two buttons at once. On it goes and around and around a few times I nod to Les, who starts the bass riff: dum da duum dum da duum da da da dum da duum. The drum box is blissfully nerve free; he just keeps on keeping on, the only true pro in the band.

I look down at the guitar. I am feeling incredibly selfconscious and scared I'm going to mess it up. The adrenaline has me a nervous wreck. I look out into the gathered crowd again. The club is rife with jealousy and a few sneering faces are spotted. This is a very Liverpool thing, even a very English thing; most are wishing you to fail. This helps me. I steel myself and think, *You lot can fuck right off.* Rivalry helps you progress. The influences you have are as much from things you hate as things you love. The ones you love are signposts to the way forward; the ones you hate are warning signs that you don't want to go down that road and be or sound like them.

I need to concentrate on the guitar. I'm not a guitarist that can just feel his way around the neck. I have only been playing for a few months and I'm still in no way proficient. I am looking down at the guitar. This also helps with the nerves. I concentrate on the high E string on the instrument. Les, the drum box and I circle around a few times, my little primitive spiky guitar notes riding over the top of the bass. (After years of looking down at the guitar, it becomes a trademark stance of mine that becomes known as shoegazing.) My fear is intense, but the spell is broken when Macul, wearing an anorak belonging to Paul Simpson, approaches the microphone. He digs in a pocket, produces a little notebook and is looking at the lyrics he has written. At last, Macul breaks his silence. His voice is dark and menacing. He launches into an amazing, angry, poetic rant about evolution – or the lack of it:

'You talk to me about evolution / All you want to do is swing like a monkey.'

This is the first time I have ever heard him sing anything. Wow! It's brilliant, not conventional boy-meets-girl kind of stuff. It's a lot deeper and he seems to be having a massive go at humanity for being a bit shit and not progressing up to his level of genius. A tad arrogant but we are a team and I'm with him all the way.

I chance a glance at the crowd. I see lots of familiar faces. At the front is Big Bill Drummond, the guitarist with Big in Japan. Bill will become a pivotal part of our story, but for now he's just another face in the crowd. All assembled seem to be digging it – or, at the very least, they are thinking, *This is curious. Guitars plus a robotic drummer.* I start to relax and almost enjoy what is occurring. The comforting hypnotic tick of the drum machine plus the unwavering and simple bass riff driven home by Les give my sparse and slightly random spikes of the guitar a good bed to jump up and down on. Macul is now in full vitriolic flow. We are all of one purpose; it feels great. Me? I'm sticking to the crisp treble pickup on the Telecaster, reverb on maximum. I'm riding the white horses of a surf-guitar wave. As I become more confident, occasionally I decide to break away from the basic high E string riff. It seems the exuberance that is swelling up in me has given me more courage. I am realising we are actually doing this, live on stage with people looking at us – and not booing. I am taken and I'm pushed along on pure adrenaline. Now I am daring to attempt some risky darting up and down the frets. It's not as frightening as I imagined and most of the notes I am hitting are even in tune with the bass. We are all now glaring at the small crowd, probably more from fear than design – but it comes across as aloof, slightly weird and a bit scary.

Quite a few of the people watching are in bands themselves and are way more accomplished musicians than us. I see that as their downfall; we are not held by the constraints of traditional rock music. We don't know all the clichéd changes and guitar runs that they pepper their songs with. I am soon to realise our basic skill level helps us stand out from the rest. Along with the constant electronic ticking of the drum machine, it's all a kind of new approach for a guitar band. Les is at the tiller and holding a very steady course. How the hell is he doing this? Four days ago, he had never touched a bass. I keep going with the little riff. We manage to make this unbelievably minimal effort last for around the twelve-minute mark, after which we start to sense that we have accomplished what we set out to do. Macul has exhausted the lyrical content of his notebook and slips it back in his pocket, then glances my way; I instantly understand what he is trying to convey. He's said all he wants to say and is out of lyrics and it's time to end now. Reluctantly, we wind it down, slowly fading to a stop. The Mini Pops drum machine still ticks on for a short time, running until I turn the little silver volume knob down to silence and we all walk off the stage.

The small crowd seem to love it and we get a good cheer. Even the reluctant arseholes hoping for us to fail are clapping now, if a little resentfully. We go back to the dressing room; the Eric's royalty and our friends in the Teardrops are telling us, 'That was great.' Jayne Casey comes into the cramped and messy dressing room. She is gushing about how cool it was, how she loves the name and how we are amazing. I am a little taken aback at how good it all feels. This euphoria could have been the relief of getting through the one song set without any major disasters. Macul is buzzing and wants to do it all over again. Les is smiling like a Cheshire Cat that's got the cream; I am like a dog with two dicks. We are all happy and can't wait to repeat this experience somewhere. It feels good to be accepted and it is a comforting feeling, like being in a gang or the Boy Scouts or something. We have a common purpose – and that's what it feels like. I am not alone any more. We feel like we can take on anything now. The accolades feel good. We think what we have just done is the single most important artistic statement ever conceived by anyone, and to me – and for the rest of my life – it really was.

We are now a band; I am even warming to the name as it seems to be getting universal approval from all in the room. We can always call the drum machine Echo and then we are all in the Bunnymen and everything is on an equal footing again. I am no longer just the kid that looks a bit like a secret member of the Ramones, perhaps the hidden away brother; Willy Ramone, the spotty one they keep in the attic of CBGBs. This is the birth of the Bunnymen.

21.

The Invisible Becomes Visible

'Three Imaginary Boys' – The Cure

The year 1979. Mrs Thatcher had been elected to the position of prime minister; she would rule with a handbag of steel and sell off just about every industry the country had built up and owned. No wonder Liverpool was a militant hotbed. Her then Chancellor Sir Geoffrey Howe would suggest a few years later that Liverpool, plagued by industrial action, should be abandoned to a 'managed decline'. What a cheeky arsehole. It was a gloomy time for the city. Thankfully my love of listening and creating music kept my pecker up.

The following days after the gig, things seem to have changed – or is it me that has changed? I am gaining confidence and I am 'coming out of my shell' as some of the waitresses at Binns have remarked. I have a new self-assurance, that's for sure. The regulars from Eric's who normally walk past now stop and acknowledge me. The new acceptance I am getting feels good. It is what I need: a bit of hope after the closure of the department store restaurant and its replacement with the downmarket café. Now my job that had some sort of future has overnight flipped into a job with none. This is subconsciously making me focus on the good stuff that is happening. One of the advantages of having played at the club, even if it was just for twelve short minutes, is that I have entered another level of the Eric's hierarchy. I am becoming accepted, part of Eric's furniture.

Doreen on the door would wave us in with no fee to pay. It was a sort of magic; the invisible had become visible. It suddenly clicked; I recognised her from when I used to go to the Liverpool Stadium shows. Doreen had been the girl behind the bar selling beer, tea and the big cheese and ham rolls known as Nudgers. Roger Eagle and Doreen had been at the epicentre of the musical underground in the city for at least a decade.

I had no serious thoughts of what would come next for my budding ensemble. It was enough to have just become a real thing. A few weeks passed and we were practising at my dad's house. Three of us are making a right racket in a cramped parlour; it wasn't ideal. Mr Harrison, who was next door, wasn't too impressed either and would bang on the wall. We needed to find somewhere else.

Our friends the Teardrop Explodes had a real practice space. It was in a basement close to where Julian Cope had a flat. Julian had become friendly with a local kid called Yorkie – real name Dave Palmer. He had offered his mum Gladys's basement as a rehearsal place. The Teardrops put a word in for us to use it too. We moved our meagre equipment in, and we all shared what we had. The basement was pretty sparse and cold, but big enough to get all the equipment in for two bands, with space to spare. Yorkie's mum looked like a typical Liverpool middle-aged woman: floral dresses, large, clear-framed glasses and a tight, curly-haired permanent wave. Not much fazed her; she had seen it all. She had a sarcastic sense of humour and was very funny. She would mother us and the Teardrops. She was always making us tea; her speciality was honey roast ham. I had never heard of such a delicacy but was quite happy to scoff down the sandwiches she made. If we got too loud, she would shout down the stairs, mordantly scolding us, 'Can't you play that fucking song any louder? Turn those bleeding drums down.' We would piss ourselves laughing like school kids. Then we would turn everything down a tiny amount. Inevitably the volume would creep back up and off she would go again: 'I've told you lot turn it down,' and so it went on.

We have been asked to play at a Rock Against Racism gig at Eric's, supporting local group Tontrix. It is starting to feel like we were a real band. It's our first paying gig. We are getting paid expenses, a massive £13 enabling Les to fill up his car. The gig day inevitably arrives. We have five songs, enough for a live set: 'I Bagsy Yours' ('bagsy' is a Liverpool word meaning claim; this track a little later became 'Monkeys'); 'Ashes to Ashes' (this one became 'Stars Are Stars'); 'Happy Death Men'; 'Going Up'; and 'Read It in Books'. Macul brought this last track from his short-lived period in the band A Shallow Madness. It seems to be heavily influenced by the Fall's song, 'Stepping Out'. That is fine by me; I am not without the sin of trying to emulate the abrasive scratch of the Fall's first guitarist, Martin Bramah. I would say at this time the Fall are the greatest common influence of all three of us. We love them and travel over to Manchester to see their shows.

Our second gig . . .

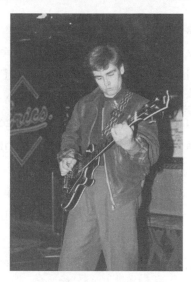

Les Pattinson and his three-string bass.

The Rock Against Racism gig goes well-ish. The set is a little stilted here and there. I have to mess about with the drum machine in between songs, mainly altering the tempo settings. These short gaps are a pain, not least because of the pressure of us wanting to keep it smooth and get on with it. At future gigs and on more than one occasion, I would press the start button on the drum machine, and nothing would happen. I would surreptitiously cry out to the others under my breath in a growing panic, 'Hold on! Nothing's working.' I would then be fiddling around the back of the bloody thing, replacing the shitty connections. Meanwhile, Macul would be glaring at me as though I'd pissed in his pint.

With hardly any cash, we had very cheap equipment back then. The jack-to-jack leads we were using were either made by me – with substandard components and my limited skills – or the cheapest, poor-quality ones bought from the various music shops about town. These cheapo cables and connections were bound to fail now and then. As we went on stage, always in the back of my mind was a nagging fear that it might all collapse at any moment. This anxiety over the equipment didn't help the already intensified nerves. Technical hiccups could create long gaps between tunes. A tiny section of silence could feel excruciating. The stage is a strange and elastic time zone. A gap of a few seconds stretches out, becoming like hours. Alternatively, as I would find out later, when the gig is going well, hours can shrink into seconds, thundering through the songs. Before you know it, you are on the last few chords of the final tune. Don't ask me how that works. Now that Stephen Hawking has died, I guess we will never know. When you are trying to portray yourself as a tight rocking unit, however, and all around you is failing, it is hell. You are standing exposed – cold and lonely, no sound to hide behind – with hordes of grisly punks gawping at you, saliva glands fully loaded and at the ready to launch buckets of phlegm in your direction. Luckily, we only ever encountered spitting at a few gigs. At one show, the viscosity of the fluorescent green gob that hit me right between the pickups was of such high quality that it instantly deadened the strings. It sounded like I was playing through an eiderdown, my Telecaster silenced completely until I scraped the sticky gloop off the guitar. I do hope that individual got his mummy to rub some Vicks VapoRub on his chest. It's not nice to be poorly, is it?

To my way of thinking, these idiots were falling into the trap of the newspaper's crafty and cynical demonisation of punk. Punk was a pretty harmless youth culture movement. I think the newspapers at the time enjoyed propagating the vile practice of spitting themselves. The more they reported that punks were always spitting at bands, the more the dickheads bought into it and started spitting at bands. The divs that came late to punk thought that's what punks did:

'Er, I'm a punk, punks spit, I'll do that too.' Splat. As the headline in the *Mirror* had said, 'The Filth and the Fury'.

As for Eric's patrons, spitting was never a big thing. I personally never saw much of it, anyway. Spitting and the moronic dance the pogo was seldom a big feature of Eric's nights. The pogo was a simple dance with only one step . . . and that is it: bounce up and down on the spot like a demented jack in the box. Very odd behaviour. Most who danced at Eric's did a kind of knee bend and then straighten up sort of thing, which was a really bad white-trash version of what we imagined was the dance you did to Jamaican dub records. (Not me though; I was far too self-conscious for any of that lark. OK, I'll come clean . . . maybe I did the odd bit if I was lubed up enough. Very embarrassing now, but there you go. You get the truth from me no matter how much it hurts.)

While I'm on about dancing in Eric's, I should mention a character called Chaz, a true hippie with long hair, still wearing loon pants that at one time I assume would have been purple (as you more than likely know, the favourite colour of the hippie). The pants were sadly washed out to an insipid pink. He wore one of those embroidered tunics you still see to this day at festivals. On his feet, long dirty toenails peeked out from the obligatory sandals. I would often spot him turning a corner or sitting on a church wall, trudging about the streets, smiling and floating along in a hashish haze. All around him, the busy city went on and he seemed to be on a different plane. He was living on the periphery of our world, walking in the twilight of tramps and hedgerow fairies. It was like he had fallen through a gap of our reality, slightly dishevelled and looking a little lost in this post Summer of Love grime.

Sometimes Chaz would turn up at Eric's. He'd dance and spin around, a big smile on his face. Reaching into his colourful hippie shoulder bag, he would begin casting imaginary seeds about the sweaty, bottle-strewn floor of the club. Chaz was oblivious to anything but the music. He was a gentle soul, sowing his imaginary seeds; it was a nice thing to watch.

Les Pattinson and I were fascinated by him. We loved to watch him dance, slightly in awe of the freedom and happiness he exuded. We christened him 'the happy gardener'. On occasion, we would chat with him. Where did he come from? Why was a hippie floating about in Eric's dancing to the Clash's version of 'Police and Thieves'? Strange, as punk was a very hippie-unfriendly scene – why was Chaz here? So many questions. We never shed any light on the enigma of Chaz. We got no info out of him. The last time I saw him, he was sitting cross-legged on the top of a red telephone box at the bottom of Bold Street. Perched like a pixie on a fly agaric mushroom, he was watching shoppers file past. No one was taking a blind bit of notice of him; maybe they didn't want to attract this weirdo's attention. Or maybe he wasn't there at all, and it was only me and Les who could see him. We may have slipped through a vortex into the astral plane which he inhabited.

Over the coming weeks, the feeling that the band was real was solidifying. We only had one full-set show behind us, but I was arrogantly thinking we were the dog's bollocks (dog's business, more like). We had done something that was quite involved, and even though there were some slight problems, we had come through it OK. The confidence this brought was a kind of cement that would keep us stronger together. An all for one, one for all kind of deal. We were feeling very pleased with ourselves. We sensed that something new was starting. Punk was over but we never really spoke about it. It came in without warning and it fizzled out without saying goodbye. We still considered ourselves comrades of punks. Yet we did feel different or better than the majority of punk bands. All that posturing and gurning at cameras was not for us. The scene was developing; 'post-punk' had not become a tag yet. Things were moving fast and other bands that had been inspired by punk were coming up for air in the background. It had seeped into us, what bands to like and what not to like. We instinctively knew what was good or cool. We never had to discuss it; it was obvious to us. Unwritten rule number one was never sell out. Difficult to do when the whole point of being in a band is to sell out. Our third gig was just around the corner.

Nestled high on Hope Street, at the top end of the city, sits the Catholic Cathedral, like a beautiful stained-glass and Portland stone-clad Apollo 11 command module. Just across the street is the Everyman Theatre. This place was a very important part of the creative environment back then; not the theatre as such, but the bar in the basement of the theatre. It was called the Everyman Bistro or, as is the custom in Liverpool, shortened to 'the Ev' or simply 'the Bistro'. A regular hangout, it was open until midnight. The Ev had an underground pub atmosphere, with subdued lighting and white-painted brick walls hung with exhibitions of works by local artists. The large tables gave it a welcoming touch. You could join a table of people you didn't know, but after a few pints would be on first-name terms; it was a very communal vibe. If you went alone to the Ev, you were bound to see people you knew from Eric's. The low ceiling gave it a cosy feel.

This is where all the heads from many scenes would congregate after the pubs kicked them out. In those days, Liverpool was not the destination for nightlife it is now. It was still a dark and grimy place. Pubs shut at ten on a weekday, clubs shut at two at the weekend, and that was about it. Places to go and hang out other than pubs were few and far between. And beware the novice wanderer stepping into the wrong pub; wearing the sort of clothes we did could be dangerous. The Ev was safe, always awash with pretentious hipsters like me. The Ev's bohemian cellar was crammed wall-to-wall with budding artists, actors, poets and hordes of baggy-trousered musicians, the hippest toes of which were wrapped in stout brogues. The rustic tables were occupied by dozens of fashionably Soviet badged philosophers, a few even wearing the international sign of the deep thinker, the French beret. What is more – so you would be in no doubt you were in the presence of first-rate clever clogs – some would be billowing clouds of choking smoke from those rather unwholesome-smelling French ciggies. In short, all the hip people on the Liverpool scene would be in attendance.

The Ev's three open-plan rooms are linked with a walkway at the opposite end to the bar area. Someone has the idea of putting gigs on for local bands in what is known as the third room. We are asked to play. Without a second's thought – after all, we are now seasoned professionals – we say, 'Yes, we'll do it.' What could possibly go wrong?

A couple of practice sessions down in Yorkie's basement, with the permed Gladys upstairs looking after all our teapot needs, and we are ready to rock.

The Ev gig is midweek (if I remember correctly; I can't find a date or a mention of the gig anywhere, which is probably a good thing). We set up everything and did a soundcheck. We have our five or so songs and we're ready to go. The time is ticking on and there is quite a crowd gathering. After our triumphant arrival on the scene, many of our friends and rivals are in attendance. The tension is mounting. When we can't stand it any more, we decide it's time to go on. This schoolboy error is a measure of our naivety. We all plug our instruments in, checking that they are still reasonably in tune. I start the drum box. Reassuringly, I can see the pulsing light; the drum box is ticking away happily. I slowly begin to increase the volume; nothing . . . not a bleep. The dial is up to maximum . . . still nothing. Les starts to get a bit twitchy and is looking my way. The controls all look correct; what the fuck is going on? No sound is coming forth. Macul stands nervously, giving me the look of daggers. It seemed to us that just about every hipster in the greater Merseyside area is staring at us with the satisfaction of watching these bright new upstarts fail. We still don't know anything about live gigs. We have no clue that the bloody PA is not turned on and the fader channel for the drum machine is down and silent. We should pretend we are just checking something and leave the stage, find the bloke that came with the PA system and let him sort it out. But we are green behind the gills and haven't a clue, so we just plod on regardless. The geezer that is meant to be mixing the sound is still in the Philharmonic pub up the street. So here we go and start with a new track, 'Going Up'.

Someone from the Ev realises we have started and runs the few hundred yards up to the Philharmonic pub and tells the sound guy to leg it back up to the Everyman. Back at the Ev, we are still going; the crowd are as green as us and think, *This must be what they want to sound like.* The sound man lunges into the room, jumps behind the small mixing desk as we are struggling to get through the song. The vocals are at least coming through the stage speakers. Macul is spared the total humiliation of singing and nothing coming out of the speakers. It's a complete mess and a shambolic start.

The sound man pushes up the faders for the drum machine and it gets worse; we are not in time with the drum machine as it is been clattering along unheard in the background. When it joins us, it throws everyone off and it's all confusion. Somehow, we struggle through the song and manage to end it. We get through the next song, 'Read It in Books'. We are starting to feel not exactly comfortable but maybe a little less embarrassed. Bravado and confidence are starting to return.

But fate hasn't finished with us yet. Things are about to go from bad to worse. Halfway through the next song, 'Villiers Terrace', I am compensating for my lack of skill on the guitar and I'm putting my energy into hitting the thing as hard as possible. The strings can't take this punishment and the steel string gives way and pings broken. *So what?* you may think. *Just put your other guitar on and get the road crew to change the string.* Problem is we have no crew; we don't even know what a crew is or what it does. I have no backup guitar and no spare strings. We are stood there like lemons. The tension on the five remaining strings is relaxed; this makes the whole guitar go out of tune, and I doubt the crowd would appreciate me tuning up for ages.

I think someone else must have tuned the guitar for me in the first place.

We have to abandon the gig. It's all extremely embarrassing: our third gig a disaster. And all in front of the wall-to-wall hipsters that frequented the Ev. We crawl away into the first room, find a table and have a beer. We have only done three gigs and already we have been excited, petrified, proud, euphoric, anxious, relieved, panic-stricken and now embarrassed and humiliated. It's a roller-coaster ride, this showbiz malarky; that's for sure.

22.

Tea at the MVCU

'Kirkby Workers Dream Fades' – The Teardrop Explodes

At the MVCU, there is talk of a compilation record being put together featuring some of the new bands emerging from the ashes of the Liverpool punk scene. The MVCU has a small studio with a TEAC four-track tape machine and a Revox for mastering on. This little studio is run by a bloke called Mike (Noddy) Knowler.

Noddy Knowler at the MVCU four-track studio.

He is assisted by Roy White; Roy's band Fun will also be on the compilation. Roy is a perfect Bowie clone, right down to the powder-blue bum-freezer jacket and well-rouged, impossibly high cheekbones. He helps with setting up the mics. We know Noddy and Roy vaguely, from hanging around the carrot cake at the MVCU's café. (We used to hang out at there all the time, so I'm sure we got asked to be on the record while we were sat in there having a cup of tea.)

A chap called Colin Wilkinson is running the Open Eye Gallery. He intends to start a record label called Open Eye Records, beginning with this compilation album using the demos of up-and-coming Liverpool bands. We don't jump at the chance. We are a little sceptical as to whose company we would be in. We pretty much think all the other bands in Liverpool are crap except for our mates the Teardrops, though Macul thinks they are crap too.

After a bit of deliberation, it is agreed that we will be coming into the studio. We will record the track we had recently played at our debut at Eric's. On the day of the recording, we are all setting up the gear in the little recording room. Paul Simpson has brought his organ and is going to play a simple three-note line, but first nips out to get something. The advantage of only having a drum machine to deal with and not a full drum kit is that it gets plugged in and that's it; no endless arranging of microphones and balancing the various drums for hours. It only takes about half an hour until we are ready. This presents us with a slight problem: Paul is not back from his wanderings. We have no idea where he has gone. Paul must have thought he had more time, not realising how quickly we would be ready to go.

In the studio, time is precious, so we have to press on regardless. The free-form arrangement of the twelve-minute track from the first Eric's gig has had some serious cosmetic surgery. We have created a chorus to slot into the song. Julian pops in for a visit and is hanging around in the café. With no sign of Paul, he steps in and plays the simple three-note organ part. The drum machine is set off and fed back to us via headphones. We count in and begin a few trial run throughs. We have got the new arrangement down pretty good. Noddy works his record-ing engineer juju like a shaman of sound and squeezes our back-ing track on to one track of the tape, leaving three of the four tracks for vocals and overdubs.

Noddy has the idea of adding a snare drum to augment the drum machine's pedestrian trudge. Roy White is the best of everyone there on drums and he steps in. He adds a short drum intro and snare pattern throughout the track. Noddy is now left with two tracks to play with for the vocals. The time has come for Macul to step up to the microphone. He insists on a darkened recording room. Though he might not have been singing at the rehearsals, it becomes quickly apparent that he has been working on the words and the melodies in his head. The vocal goes down very quickly. Noddy has chan-nelled the voice through the Revox tape machine; this is a technique to create an echo effect. The Revox is put into the record setting and the playback head can be fed back into the input to create a slap-back echo effect. This technique was very popular in the fifties rock 'n' roll era. John Lennon loved a bit of slap back on his vocal, so it's good enough for us too. The effect is adding an unusual dimension to the track; it is ancient and modern all at the same time. I am a fan of New York electro punks Suicide and it reminds me a little of their sound. After all our hard work, it is time to mix the song. This only takes a few run throughs; there is not a lot of mixing necessary with only four tracks to play with. All is done, cassettes are made and we pack up and go home. Presumably Paul then arrives at the studio.

The Teardrop Explodes record their first single for Bill Drummond and Dave Balfe's new label, Zoo Records, some of which is done at the MVCU's four-track. Paul gives me a copy; it is so cool, very impressive. I love the cover's red background with a stylised graphic of a piano. It looks unlike anything that the punk scene has thrown up. The A-side of the record, 'Sleeping Gas', is not overtly trying to be commercial. It is groovy and a little weird, more prog rock than punk rock, like an English Pere Ubu or some lost Canterbury-scene nugget. Julian's posh, perfectly enunciated vocal is not a million miles from the tones of the Soft Machine's frontman Kevin Ayers, Julian's melange of surrealistic psychedelic lyrics sitting on top of a strange bass riff. It has a slight jazz feel; 'Camera Camera' and 'Kirkby Worker Dream Fades' on the flip side are under the influence of Paul Simpson and are quite at home residing in the experimental world.

Paul Simpson.

We meet up for more nights at Eric's. What will become legendary bands come and go throughout 1978 and into 1979. Many influences are seeping into me as a guitarist and creator of music.

Pere Ubu's singer David Thomas stands like Orson Welles in a dishevelled, tour-weary black suit; a grubby shirt with a black tie complete the look. He stands teetering right at the front of the stage. In his left hand, he holds a foot-long, rusty pig-iron spike. In his right hand is a heavy lump hammer to beat time to their recent album's title track, 'The Modern Dance'. He rains blows upon the iron, causing flecks of rust to sprinkle on to the stage like dead glitter. As he wallops the spike, it swings in a forward motion towards the front row of punters, very nearly hitting me in the face. I remain transfixed; this is something quite extraordinary and it's worth the risk to witness. The keyboard player is a long-haired professor who looks like he has been rescued from an underground lab in Area 51. He is manipulating a homemade synthesiser, all knobs and plywood. It emits whooshes and squeaks, spitting white noise at the crowd; I find it fascinating. The bass player looks out of place. His hair is in a perfect quiff; he wears a showbiz shirt, its large collar resting over his tuxedo's lapel. He has the look like a Las Vegas mafioso enforcer. He could be lying low inbetween hits, or maybe hiding in plain sight, blending in with this gaggle of weirdos. (They are one of my all-time favourite bands. I recommend you immediately buy *The Modern Dance*.)

A few days later it's the Gang of Four's turn. Their incendiary guitarist Andy Gill (sadly now late of this Earth) is revved up like a chainsaw, the throttle's safety is flicked off and he is released to randomly administer violent hacks at his guitar, viciously flaying the strings in a frenzied attack. I watch in awe as he is pummelling seven shades of shite out of the poor Stratocaster. The Strat seems to be enjoying it. Well, it sounds like screams of delight to me. He coldly stares the crowd down like he's cock o' the north, and he probably is. He's wearing a black plastic anorak; maybe he was expecting it to be a spit fest? It isn't.

The next gig is Generation X. Les Pattinson, Paul Simpson and I like the sixties, groovy Carnaby Street pop-art imagery of Billy Idol and his mates. Their styling takes a lot from the Who's early mod clobber. The gigs keep coming. Next is Wayne County and the Electric Chairs. They are a regular feature at the club, and I have seen them several times; it is always a great night. They start as usual with the track 'Night Time'. We all know this from the sixties garage band the Strangeloves, who are featured on the *Nuggets* compilation LPs. The bass kicks it off and goes on for quite some time, building the tension, until Wayne (now Jayne) flounces on to the low stage, lifts his skirt and shows his fishnet-covered pant-ies: saucy boy/girl! On it goes, the conveyor belt of brilliant groups. A few days later, the all-girl group the Slits are on. They are irreverent and wild. Bill Drummond tells me that on the way into the club they pushed him down the stairs. He's a big lad and survived to proudly tell the tale. The Slits have their own ragamuffin style and sound. They have lots of fun larking around on the stage. They are our punky pin-up girls; it's impossible not to fall in love with them.

The next notable gig is Adam and the Ants. This is Adam pre-pirate-dandy chic; it's all leather trousers and bondage imagery. The Ants turn up with uber punk mistress Jordan in tow. She is managing the band and watches from the side of the stage like a protective sentinel. No one is going to mess with these gimps on her watch. The gigs go on and the bands keep coming. In the budding post-punk electro world, Orchestral Manoeuvres in the Dark have their TEAC four-track known as Winston centre stage, providing a backing track to Paul Humphreys's catchy organ drones while we struggle to stifle giggles at Andy McCluskey's strut-and-shimmy bass-playing shenanigans. They are not quite as mad as Richard Jobson from the Skids, though; his high-kicking antics are like the least erotic can-can performance ever. But 'Into the Valley' is a cracking tune. I am also there to witness the early doors Human League. There are only two or three of them on stage accompanied by their Revox tape recorder providing back up. They play a cover of 'You've Lost that Lovin' Feelin'', the Righteous Brothers hit. Joining in on vocals, the keyboard player is standing there proudly with a beard. Beards on a punk or even an electro-post-punkster are an abomination. He makes a good effort of molesting the hell out of the synthesiser, so the beard is forgiven. Coming to the rescue is Phil Oakey's famous asymmetric hairdo; this is counterbalancing the un-coolness of the beard and the equilibrium of the universe is maintained.

In February 1979, Joy Division are back; this time, everyone is watching. They also come back in August. Mid-set, Ian Curtis's eyes roll back into his head, he falls to the stage and has an epileptic fit. He's taken off to the dressing room to recover, while the band play on. I seem to remember that Hooky took over on singing duties for a couple of songs. After about ten minutes or so, Ian incredibly returns to the stage to finish the set. Also, that year I see the Cure, the Associates, Jonathan Richman, the Fall, the Specials, Madness, Wire, the Pop Group, and many more. It goes on and on, so many bands it would become boring to list them all. With no entrance fee to pay and Doreen letting us in, why wouldn't we go every night it was open? We were there, whether we liked the band or not.

★   ★   ★

It is April 1979, the twelfth to be precise. It's my birthday. I am twenty-one today. There is nothing planned and it's just another day. I never expected or wanted a fuss. My other big birthday – my eighteenth – had come and gone without notice, just how I liked it, another day, a non event. I am at home listening to records in the back parlour.

Early evening, Maz knocks at our door.

He has some news. 'All right, Will. Your mum is over at our house. She wants to see you.'

I'm shocked. I haven't seen her since I was thirteen years old and I'm not that keen to see her now; I don't know why. I expect I feel guilty and now I have to confront this. Any affection for her died a good while back. I had hardly thought about her since she left and had not attempted to see her or get in touch. Up until then, nor had she. I didn't even know her phone number or if she had a phone. Eight years is a long time at that time in your life; the teen years are what mould you. After she had left, it marked the end of the horrendous antagonistic atmosphere in the house. It had become such a relief that I think it outweighed any feelings of missing her. I didn't dislike her in any way; I just think my brain was too undeveloped to understand. In no way do I blame her for bailing out when she did. I think she should have done it sooner. I expect years of my dad treating her like shit must have rubbed off on me and my young and impressionable mind. It just never seemed like a big deal to me.

Maz knows it's a bit uncomfortable for me. He says, 'You should go over and at least say hello.'

I don't want to, but I head over to the Mazenkos'. She is sat with Sylvia, Maz's mum, having a cup of tea. It's all a little strange and awkward, to say the least. There are no tears or hugs like you get on these long-lost relative shows that are all over the telly now. Back then, at least in my world, no one hugged like they do now. I am standing in front of her. I'm painfully shy; and this is compounded by the awkwardness of this situation. I show no emotion. She is smiling, causing deep dimples in her cheeks. In a much stronger Liverpool accent than mine, she says, 'All right, lad.' This is so obviously more important to her than it is to me. I am confronted by this woman, my mum. I feel I don't know who she is. All the years of her bringing me up mean nothing to me now.

''Ere ya are, William. I've got you a present. Happy birthday.'

She hands me a long, thin, black velvet-covered jewellery case.

I open it up and look at the gold bracelet nestled in the velvet and silk-lined box. Square embossed links, not my kind of thing at all. I'm finding it hard to look like I appreciate it. This adds to my feelings of guilt and dislocation from her. She is now just some woman that I don't know and it's apparent. It could be anyone sat there. She has no clue what I am about, and I have no clue about her. I am itching to get out of there.

Only now, years later and a parent myself, do I think I should have been more loving or emotional, though I'm not sure what that means, or how I would have done that at the time. Big displays of emotion are not my forte. I am more than likely on the spectrum, a little bit detached. I do have a habit of saying the wrong things to people and can be blunt. I am often taken the wrong way. I think I have changed now and I'm better with people around me.

The visit was pretty short, and I didn't see her again until years into the future, when, in my thirties, my wife Paula persuaded me to make contact. She was concerned that our daughters should see their grandma. Paula came from a large family, and everyone was around the house all the time: cousins, aunties and uncles, etc. I had never known family life like this. Avoiding family members seemed to be the Sergeant way. It was strange to see this happiness; they welcomed me into the heart of the family.

The odd relationship with my mum wasn't a conscious plan. I never decided that I was not going to see her for some reason. It was just what it was like back then. I felt like I was on my own – I really can't explain it any other way. The troubled house was subconsciously affecting me, and I was not even aware of it at the time. With my mum gone, Dad at work or the pub and me left to my own devices, I felt much better in the house. I regret it, but it was so hard to pretend at the time that I missed her or the aggro. Let me be clear here: the trouble was not her doing, it was all my dad's strange, cold persona that was the problem. He was obviously unhappy with the marriage and, instead of seeking a divorce, he just cut her off completely.

This strange episode was put behind me and on I moved like it never happened.

It's a big night, Saturday 21 April, 1979. The level of excitement is reaching fever pitch. For a few weeks now, the Eric's community has been counting down the days to the event of the century: Iggy Pop is coming to play at the club.

Les Pattinson lives in Aughton, the next village to Melling, and kindly calls past my house, picks me up in his car and we head off into town. As soon as we get to the entrance of Eric's, it's obvious something really special is on at the club. Crowds of kids are gathered outside, the numbers of which are way beyond anything we have seen before. Iggy has already played a matinee for the underage kids and a few hundred are still outside trying to sneak in past Doreen's vigilant gaze. We are lucky and get spotted by Doreen. She calls us over to squeeze through the throng and we are in.

We head down the short stairway into the club. It hits us, a solid wall of humidity. I taste the moist brine of sweat in the air. Les and I look on the sea of people. Fucking hell, it's hot. I have my thick leather biker jacket on (wise choice); I'm thinking, *Where the hell can I stash it?* The club is easily the most crowded I have ever seen. I think the capacity is around the three hundred mark, but tonight there must be double that number. The spring evening chill on the outside is instantly transformed into the ambience of a mangrove swamp deep in the steaming everglades. The heat is broiling up the stairs towards the exit; it is incredible. Even the heat is finding it too hot in there and is desperately trying to escape. The collective swelter of bodies is creating a microclimate; a cloud of human vapour sits above the heads of the squashed punters. This rising mist hits the cold brickwork of the ceiling, instantly condenses and all around is the constant drip of salty rain drizzling on to the heavily lacquered spiky-haired punks. The hair that was only an hour or so ago proudly standing erect and threatening the elderly of our town is now drooping, flaccid and sad.

It is time. Iggy hits the stage. His band features the bass player Glen Matlock, formerly of the Sex Pistols, allegedly kicked out for liking the Beatles. Iggy should be playing the gig in a much bigger venue, but none of the other venues in town would have him. Iggy was insistent on playing a show in Liverpool and the small club was the only place willing to welcome Mr Pop. Iggy – shirt off, his well-documented sculptured torso already glistening with sweat – kicks off with 'Kill City'. The crowd erupts and throbs as best it can while being desiccated by the temperature. This is his second show in a few hours but it's not showing; the energy level is out of this world. He clambers into the crowd and body surfs around under the low ceiling. Eventually he gets deposited back on the stage. Iggy's set goes by like a rocket, and the big finish is the Stooges' classic 'I Wanna Be Your Dog'.

After the gig, a whisper goes around that Iggy is staying at the Holiday Inn on Paradise Street. Quite a few of the regulars, including me, go up there and stand in the hotel bar, rather gawkily hanging around, looking at Iggy having a beer, thinking we are in his company. Of course, we are not, but he doesn't seem to mind us and makes small talk with the fans and various Eric's stalwarts that have followed him over to the hotel.

It's a weird thing to have done but that's fandom; it's a kind of madness. It can turn you into a ligger very easily. I now hate going backstage to say hi to bands, even if I must or am expected to. I try to make it brief. This is not because of the Iggy ligging session but because I have now experienced the other side of this weird and stilted situation, and been gawked at while trying to have a bit of food or quiet time after a gig.

23.

Quartermass and the Hit

154 – Wire

Early 1979. The winter is subsiding, and the weather is turning from a freezing cold winter to a freezing cold spring. We are greeted with the news that Sid Vicious has been found dead of an overdose in New York. Sid was out on bail after he was charged with allegedly killing his girlfriend, Nancy Spungen. It's all rather grim and grubby news and the end of an era. In other grim and grubby news, the leader of the Liberal Party, Jeremy Thorpe, is tried for the attempted murder of a gay lover; he gets off but is finished as a party leader.

The good news is that the Teardrops have released their first single on Bill Drummond and Dave Balfe's Zoo label. Because they are Zoo Records, Bill and Dave adopt 'cage' as part of the catalogue number. The Teardrop Explodes single is CAGE 003. It has been selling well and Bill and Dave have a few quid in the coffers to look for the next release. Bill is being badgered by Julian Cope, who is pushing the idea that Zoo should put out a single by us. I think Julian may have been having a little bit of a guilt trip for kicking Macul out of the precursor to the Teardrop Explodes. I think he wanted to give us a little push and get us going to ease his conscience. That might be me reading more into the situation; I could easily be wrong on that one.

I expect it went something like this.

Julian says to Bill Drummond, 'Hey, Bill, why don't you put our mates' band Echo and the Bunnymen out as your next single?'

Bill replies, 'Who?'

Julian says, 'You know – Macul, Will and Les? You know them, they're always at Eric's?'

Bill is finding it hard to remember us.

Julian continues. 'They supported us at that party we played a couple of weeks ago. You were watching them stood at the front.' Julian explains, 'They have a drum machine and they are going to be on that *Street to Street* album that Noddy from the MVCU is putting together.'

Bill is getting slightly intrigued, I am assuming by the idea of a guitar band with a drum machine.

It clicks with Bill at last. 'Oh yes. They went on for ages with one riff,' says Bill.

'That's them,' Julian replies.

272

'Have they got any proper songs?' Bill asks.

'Yes, they have a few now, I think,' Julian responds.

A few days later, Dave Balfe is visiting Bill Drummond's house and the idea is mooted.

'Let's see if the Bunnymen would like to be on Zoo.'

Dave Balfe fries up . . .

By chance, just around the corner from Bill's house lives Dave's Teardrop Explodes bandmates, Gary Dwyer and Mick Finkler. They have moved into a new flat above a greengrocer's shop on Liverpool's Penny Lane – yes, that Penny Lane, the place made famous by the Beatles, who witter on about barbershops, bankers and firemen. By incredibly good fortune, Macul has also moved into this flat; his time at Smelly Ellie's hovel has come to an end. Bill and Dave pop round to the Penny Lane flat and ask Macul about recording on Zoo.

The next time Les and I see Macul, he tells us the news. All three of us are well aware that Bill and Dave have started a label. I have bought Bill and Dave's first Zoo release by Big in

Japan, CAGE 001. Bill and Dave's next single is from Those Naughty Lumps and is called 'Iggy Pop's Jacket', CAGE 002. The song is a bit silly. It is about the singer from the Naughty Lumps (Pete Hart) touching Iggy Pop's jacket. The fact that someone would write a song about something so dull proves that Iggy Pop is revered as a god in Liverpool. I've had Slade's second-hand cider spat in my face, but I don't feel the need to make a song and dance about it – until now, that is.

A few days later, Bill is working at the MVCU café. Bill more than likely got to hear the recording we had made with Noddy at the controls in the MVCU four-track studio. He comes over to our corner table and asks the whole band if we are into the idea of a single release on Zoo. We do not bite his hand off but decide to cautiously consider this idea. We have already talked about it, of course, but we are a very suspicious bunch, even at this early stage. We are not that desperate to go with the first thing that comes along. It feels like we will be sharing our coolness, so we have to make sure we are not compromising our artistic integrity, or some such bollocks.

We have also been approached by Pete Fulwell to make a single for him. He is starting up a label of his own and calling it Eternal. Pete is Roger Eagle's business partner and is instrumental in the running of Eric's. We have only done three gigs and we already have two labels wanting to make a record with us. This is the way it appears to go with us through the early months: things just fall into our laps with very little effort on our part.

The three of us talk for the next week or so. Only one subject is on the agenda: whose label to go with? We always meet up in various cafés around town; the Armadillo on Mathew Street is the favourite; we all congregate there. We decide Bill and Dave's Zoo label is the best option. We make this decision purely because they have already had a record out, and sort of know the ropes. We are wandering around town when we spot Pete Fulwell on the corner of Whitechapel and Richmond Street.

'Oh shit. There's Pete – he'll want an answer,' I say.

This might be awkward. We hadn't been avoiding Pete, but we were also not rushing to tell him our decision either.

'All right, lads.' The very approachable Pete beams a smile at us. 'Have you decided who you are going with, Eternal or Zoo?'

I say nervously, 'Sorry, Pete. We are going to go with Bill and Zoo.' Pete looks pretty disappointed; the beaming smile has subsided slightly. I follow this with, 'It's just because they have already had a record out and are a little bit more experienced.'

He accepts it with good grace and wishes us and Zoo good luck. 'OK, see you down at the club,' he says.

Off he goes, around the corner, up Richmond Street and on into Williamson Square.

I felt a bit sad and guilty; we all like Pete a lot. He is not as scary as Roger, who towers above everyone; Roger is well over six feet tall and generally scowls through a magnificent wall of moustache hair that Stalin would have given his left testicle for. It is very sad and like giving a girl the elbow – not that I would have much experience at that. In fact, zero.

I could say I am a little scared that we have made the wrong decision, but I'm not; it's just a bit of a laugh at this stage. If we get a record out, it legitimises us as a band, it makes it all real and it's kind of a cool thing to do. It could get reviewed in the *New Musical Express*; that would be great. BBC Radio 1's John Peel might play it on his show; that would be unbelievable.

We'd had a small mention in *Sounds* music paper already. It was written by a lad called Andy Courtney, who used to come to Eric's now and then. I think he knew Macul. At the time, on the first few pages of *Sounds* were printed all the pop single and LP chart positions, the top forty and all that. They also listed what they called the 'writer's charts' — the various staff writers' favourites. These were generally the more obscure bands that were not likely to make the top forty. Andy was well aware of the (yet to be named post-punk) scene happening around the club. He had noticed there was a fast-expanding flock of bands born of punk, but now mutating into something else. In his chart, he had Jayne Casey's new band, Pink Military Stand Alone; their entry was 'Don't Bomb China'. He also included the Teardrop Explodes with 'Straight Rain'. For some inexplicable reason, Andy had put Echo and the Bunnymen in his chart with 'World Shut Your Mouth', preceded by the words 'private tape'. We had no song called 'World Shut Your Mouth' and, as far as I am aware, no cassette was given to him. We had done no demos or tapes of any sort at the time that Andy had us in his chart. The idea tapes recorded in my dad's parlour would not have been played to him as they were very rough. It seemed like he had just made the whole thing up because:

a) he wanted to help us out and get some attention (he was friendly with Macul, after all);

b) he wanted to let people know he was early on to this scene that was evolving in Liverpool;

c) he wanted to help propagate a scene that needed a push;

d) he had nothing better to write about that week.

We did later use the tag as a working title for a new tune, but I can't remember which song it became. A couple of years on, Julian would appropriate this 'World Shut Your Mouth' title for his own. We thought it was a bit uncool to do this at the time. It is a good title; shame to waste it, I suppose.

After we agree to record the single with Zoo, Bill and Dave organise the recording session at August Studios.

Back at my dad's house, we had sorted out a set structure of the chord sequence for 'Pictures on My Wall', which will be the A side. There are no lead guitar lines and it's just a strum fest. We decide to also record Macul's tune 'Read It in Books', as this is pretty well arranged and ready to go.

On a wet day in spring, we drag our sparse equipment along a little cobbled lane called Benson Street. We hump it up a steep flight of stairs and into the recording room of August Studios. It's a big step up from the MVCU's four-track: August has an eight-track machine and the hessian sacking that studio walls are padded with the world over.

I have brought my new Fender twelve-string acoustic guitar and Macul also has his acoustic. Les is patched into a bass amp (not sure where we got this; might have been in the studio). Just like at the MVCU, we are all given headphones. The drum machine is plugged in and connected through to the control room. After several lengthy attempts, we get somewhere near tuned up; Bill and Dave have helped with this by utilising the studio's organ – Bill or Dave playing the corresponding notes, and us trying to match the guitar up. It was awful and took ages.

At last, we get set up and in comes the engineer, a cheerful chap with curly hair named Martin Mitchell. Macul is sitting down. I am standing up. Martin positions the microphones on both of the acoustic guitars. He patches the drum machine into the mix and sends it to the headphones all three of us are wearing. After a few false starts – more than likely my fault – and some timing issues, we get the backing track down. The two acoustic guitars played in unison give an insistent and interesting wash to the track. Les's simple one-note bass is left to ring out through the verses and works well as it stands out among the busily strummed guitars. The drum machine is ticking away in the background. I have dialled the settings to Rock 1. I also have added bossa nova by pressing – you guessed it – the Bossa Nova setting button at the same time. This gives the beat the addition of a percussive clave sound and a bit of reverb; it becomes all subterranean and eerie, reminding me a little bit of Pink Floyd's epic 'Echoes' off the *Meddle* album, one of my favourite Pink Floyd tracks. I don't mention this, as any association with a progressive rock sound would be an abhorrence to my bandmates. We repeat the recording process for the next backing track of 'Read It in Books'. I swap my acoustic for the Telecaster. The sound is very thin from my FAL amp, but that's what we are into. Macul doubles the sound again with his acoustic; this thickens the rhythm up quite a lot.

I wouldn't have known anything really about sounds, or how to get them anyway. This was more than likely the way I always set up the controls on the amp. I had this weird notion back then that everything needed to be bright in tonal quality, with any amp distortion to be avoided. I now know distortion in its many forms is the guitarist's friend.

On 'Pictures on My Wall', we have a massive four tracks left to play with. Martin the engineer has an idea. A tom-tom drum that is lying about the studio has caught his eye. He records a hit of the drum, placed on the first beat of the bar of the verse. His trick is to record the drum at double the speed of the track. When it's played back at the correct speed, the sound is stretched, and now the register is much lower. Add a shed load of reverb and this gives the drum an otherworldly thunder-crash sound. I am well-versed in this technique as I have been messing about with tape recorders for years. But it never struck me to do it on a drum. When you are in a studio, things just happen like that. It isn't planned; ideas present themselves out of nowhere. It has been suggested by the late great George Martin that the recording studio is as much an instrument as the guitars or bass; I can only agree.

Macul double-tracks the vocals. His aggressive and earnest delivery is perfect. On 'Read It in Books', a snare drum is added to the beat. I think Dave Balfe does this; he has the best timing. Paul Simpson, who has popped round for a visit, is drafted in to sing just one word: 'Rainbows'.

Paul Simpson in rather fetching plastic trousers.

The weird little organ we had used to tune up with is a Philips Philicorda (pretty rare now). It is part of the studio's collection of odd instruments. I grab it and suggest we use it to play the simple three-note motif in the verse. I quickly put it down on the tape before anyone can object.

We had toyed with having a keyboard player. It was sort of expected at the time and would open up many possibilities. We had the odd organ part played for us. Paul Simpson and a friend of ours from Eric's, Andy Eastwood, had stood in on a couple of our early gigs and played the simple three-note keyboard part on the track that became 'Monkeys'. To me, the organ was OK-ish but synthesisers seemed to be at odds with guitar bands. You were either a synth keyboard band or a guitar band. Because of the influence of Television, I was against synthesisers at the time. We were thinking we'd need a guitarist and occasional keyboard player. With no get-out plan, we had asked a fellow Eric's regular and Ramones fan, Jamie Farrell, to play the guitar. This was so Macul could concentrate on the singing and ditch his guitar. Macul has a very distinctive choppy and rhythmic style that is hard to replicate. Jamie was finding it at odds with his style; he was more out-and-out rock.

After a couple of practices at my dad's house, we realised that it was not going to work with the new addition. Jamie's style just didn't fit with us. We were sort of against his rock sensibility. Our experimental post-punk roots were showing. Jamie's time with us wasn't an audition as such; this was another measure of our naivety – we just assumed that he would be able to do what was needed as he was a guitarist. We weren't after Keith Richards on the guitar or Keith Emerson on the keyboard; we just needed a few choppy chords and the odd organ note here and there. After a few attempts, we felt awkward and didn't know what to do. We had a chat about Jamie. We all decided that we should go forward without another guitarist/keyboard player. I like Macul's playing; it is unique and our sound would have become more mainstream without it.

Jamie was a hard knock and we were a little bit scared he would stick one on us if we booted him out of the band.

OK, who's going to tell him?

I'm nervously grinning and my stomach is churning with fear.

'Get lost, I'm not telling him,' I say. 'He puts the shits up me.'

We look to Macul, who pipes up with one of his catch-phrases, 'Think again,' followed by, 'I'm sodding not doing it, no chance.'

My face is held in a forced smile.

'It's up to you then, Les. You get on with him the best,' I say.

Macul agrees. 'Yes, he likes you. Les, you do it.'

It was true that Les and Jamie had mutual respect. Les was strong: his job at the boatyard had built muscles in places me and Macul didn't even have places. He was no wimp when it came to any sort of aggro. He and Paul Simpson had dealt with some ruffians on the train on his way home from Eric's a few weeks earlier. Paul's punk style often attracted bad scally attention, plus Les with his bright white hair . . . back then, are you kidding? They were bound to be a target. Some idiots had been taking the piss out of them, calling them pouffes, queers, etc. – all the usual stuff. One of the thugs crossed the line and pulled Les's punk-customised, cut-off plastic worker's jacket over his head. They soon realised they had bitten off more than they could chew. Paul was no slouch in a barney and was packing.

In his hand, a weapon – an emergency corkscrew – and he was not afraid to use it. Les soon had one of these fools in a head-lock. In went Paul with a textbook boot to the bollocks and it's 'Goodnight, Vienna', as they say. Les and Paul quickly bundled them off the train and on to the platform.

So I have no doubt that, if Jamie kicks off, Les will be able to deal with it.

Les steps up. Out of loyal friendship to Jamie, he says, 'OK, I'll tell him.'

Les goes over to Jamie's flat to give him the bad news. As it turns out, there was no need to worry. According to Jamie, they both just laughed about it all and he's cool. We all meet up later in the Masonic pub on Berry Street and there are no hard feel-ings; sometimes things just don't work out. Jamie quickly moves on and starts a short-lived band called the Opium Eaters with Holly Johnson, Paul Rutherford and Gary Dwyer on drums. We are all still friends to this day. We weirdly share a love of gothic architecture.

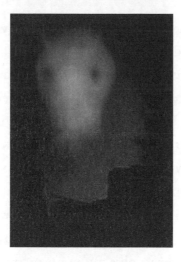

Back at August Studios, the single is completed all in one day. The next thing to do is the cover art.

Our name has been giving Dave Balfe psychotic ideas. He has been imagining a bunny rabbit crossed with a demon. His mind is spinning as he remembers the final scene of the 1958 sci-fi horror series *Quatermass and the Pit* that has been on the telly recently, which he quite freely admits, 'Shit him up as a kid.'

The premise of the series revolved around an ancient alien spaceship that is unearthed by workmen while tunnelling deep underground during construction of a tube station in London called Hobbs End. The ship is found to be chocker block with dead and crispy giant alien grasshoppers. At the end of the series, a devil rises above the London skyline, backlit in a cloud of haze. The demon looks down on the cowering pitiful humans. This is the bit that stuck in Dave's mind. Dave twists this image to his own devices, splices this memory with a bunny rabbit and calls it a bunny monster. (I recently re-watched the film and the little horns and shape of the head are very familiar to what became our logo. It is all making sense now. I always wondered why the bunny monster had horns.)

Dave's friend from art school, Kevin Ward, completes the design with scribbled graphics and scratchy lettering.

A few days later, I bump into Dave and Kevin on Whitechapel Street. They are on the way to the brand-new Zoo office. Dave shows me the artwork in the street, eager to get my approval. I'm not that keen; no consultation has been made with any of us about the cover. I like the devil/bunny god creature that sprawls across the cover in red. I'm not that fussed by the scratchy and messy writing all over it, plus my name is spelt incorrectly. I am persuaded to let it go as we need to get a move on. The single is getting pressed and they need to get the artwork to the printers. The covers are being printed separately to the records and will have to be married up by hand.

It only takes a couple of weeks and the records are now at the Zoo office. I can't wait to see the product of our toil. I am on my lunch hour and have escaped the heat of Binns café-kitchen. I walk over the damp and glistening street, dodging the black cabs and buses thundering down Whitechapel. The brand-new Zoo HQ is on the first-floor, number 1 Chicago Buildings. Chicago Buildings – wow, it sounds so romantic, like somewhere Al Capone might have hung out. But nope, it's not. I head up the utilitarian, tiled stairwell and through the dowdy, olive-green door. It looks like an intimidating institution where electroshock therapy might be administered, or the unremarkable headquarters of MI6, the minions within coordinating their grubby trade of espionage. No, forget all that; this is the central hub of a brand-new scene. From here Echo and the Bunnymen will take on the world. I am starting to think that we are important; the arrogance is growing in me. (Today they call it self-belief and it's seen as a good thing. You can buy books on the subject to make yourself into a right cocky fucker.) I enter the Zoo office in this imposing Victorian brick and stone construction. I am here to help by shoving the shiny new singles in the printed sleeves. The sleeves have been glued the wrong way around. The opening for the record, the lip, is on the front and not, as is normal, on the back. Also, we have a scratched inscription on the record. We have instructed the person who cut the record to write 'The Revenge of Voodoo Billy' on the runout groove.

This might need some explanation. In Gary Dwyer and Macul's flat was a small, hairy coconut carved into an ornamental monkey. Gary Dwyer was freaked out by it and had christened the critter Voodoo Billy. We thought it would be funny to get the guy doing the cut to add this on the runout.

Back at the office, Bill and Dave pack up the records to be sent off to all the magazines at the time: *Sounds*, *Melody Maker*, *New Musical Express* and even *Smash Hits*. They also send a copy to John Peel at the BBC.

The release day comes. It's Macul's birthday, the fifth of May, and the record is due to be reviewed that week in the music press. We wait to see our name in the paper, just hoping for a mention. But this is crazy; 'The Pictures on My Wall' has been given the honour of single of the week in all the papers and even in the rather teenybopper rag *Smash Hits*. We can't believe it. It's nuts; yet again, things happen for us. After these reviews, Dave and Bill rock up to record shops around the land with a handful of singles. The shops are snapping them up. In the coming days, we are listening to John Peel and he plays 'The Pictures on My Wall'. Inwardly, I can't believe it; I am almost in some sort of religious ecstasy! Outwardly, you would never know; my emotions of joy never seem to reach the surface of my miserable face. But John fucking Peel has played our record on his show on the bloody BBC! Things get even more frenzied when, after playing the song, Peel says, 'That was the mighty Echo and the Bunnymen.'

The next day, Bill has a rubber stamp made with the words 'The Mighty Echo and the Bunnymen' on it. We stamp everything in sight, all our letters, all the record mailers – they all get the stamp treatment. Rough Trade in London, the main independent record label distributors, get in touch. They want four hundred singles for their first order. These are big figures for a brand-new unknown band from the far-flung reaches of the galaxy . . . well, Liverpool anyway. After all that Beatles and the Merseybeat overindulgence, Liverpool had been pretty much forgotten by the music establishment until Deaf School had appeared in the mid-1970s.

Me and Bill Drummond outside the Zoo office.

The week goes on and Bill is getting offers of gigs. The record is still in demand and has fairly quickly sold out, and they have to re-press. I am drafted in on all my lunch breaks to help bag up the singles. I also place them in brown card mailers and add the addresses of the army of new Bunnymen fans. This is a little disconcerting and I am worried about who is buying the single. What are they? Who are they? Are they divs? What if the most uncool record collectors in the land are buying the single? I want to vet every record sale, like the RSPCA check out if a puppy is going to a good home. This is ridiculous, of course, so I just carry on bagging the singles with Bill and Dave. It is a fun time and it feels great. I think we are possibly the coolest band in the land.

24.

YMCA

'Love and Romance' – The Slits

Alongside the first few gigs and the seven-inch record that we had recorded for Zoo, I am making recordings on my reel-to-reel just for the fun of it. I also still have the sort of semi-fictitious band 'Industrial/Domestic' going with Paul Simpson. The idea is experimental; we don't have songs as such.

I never thought that my music career would be anything other than a cool thing to do. And I certainly had not thought that Echo and the Bunnymen could make any money or have any success. My only desire at that time was that it would be seen as something new, worthy or worthwhile in an artistic way. I never thought anything about the future or what it might bring me. There was no idea that the Bunnymen would become a band that would be able to play gigs all over the world.

One night I am at Eric's and I see Macul.

Just for a laugh, I tell him, 'I'm going to pack in the Bunnymen and go off with Paul to do Industrial/Domestic full time.'

I suppose my twisted sense of humour was a little off course that day. I never meant it. I was just a wind-up merchant and thought it would be funny to see what he would do. He freaked out, calling me all the names under the sun.

I'm laughing, taking some perverse satisfaction that it has upset him so much.

I see the joke has gone far enough.

I say, 'It's OK. I'm only joking, you div.'

To me it was funny, but I could see Macul wasn't seeing it like that. I expect the fragility of the band was suddenly exposed to him. I could easily have just packed it in at any time and done something else, just for the hell of it.

The music that I liked was so out there and difficult that there would always be a battle with the commercial side of music. I expect it all stemmed from a love of the Velvet Underground. Some of their tunes are the most melodic in the world, 'Pale Blue Eyes', for example. Some are pretty challenging, as in the discordant viola drone of 'Venus in Furs' or free-form freakout that takes up most of 'European Son'. There was never a question that they would sell vast quantities. This was what was attracting me to bands like the Velvets and the Residents; it feels like you belong to them and them to you. It's a secret society. It's art purely for art's sake. Anyone can write a catchy tune; after all, it generally follows an obvious and well-tried prescription. My view of the Bunnymen was that we should be cool and not play the game. Artists that became too successful were a real turn off to me. Even Bowie had started to irritate me as too many people were getting in on the action.

I had been following the San Francisco band the Residents for a while by then. The art ensemble were still anonymous and in 1974 had recorded an album called *Not Available*, which they had said would not be available until they had forgotten they had made it.

Well, they had not forgotten about the record, but in 1978 they released it anyway, all because their next release *Eskimo* was delayed, and the record company Ralph Records wanted to get something out quick. I think this that was bollocks and just a ploy by the Residents, wrapping the album up in a legend. You have to realise that creating legends was all part of their art. This approach was a big influence on my way of thinking about music and bands. The legend is often better than reality. The record business calls it hype, or basically bollocks, and lies to create a band's own legend. If you lie enough times, it becomes the truth. The Residents were experts at this, and I was learning fast.

Not Available turned out to be as shadowy as the Residents themselves. Distant, slightly out-of-tune piano notes limp across empty wooden church halls. Unusual chord progressions sweep into jabbering voices that are stumbling over poetic verses. The vocals come across as disturbed and frightened. At times, it feels more like they have woven paranormal activity into the grooves somehow. I loved it, and it became my favourite Residents record so far.

* * *

The Residents' concept of obscurity gets me thinking about the long-playing record as a piece of art. I could make an LP of which there is only one copy. I will create everything: the cover, the recording, even the pressing of the vinyl. My mind is now racing ahead at the thought of this concept. Some dub records are coming out of a low-fi cottage industry in Kingston, Jamaica. Each record is pressed by an individual – no real automation.

I delight in the idea that a human has been involved in creating the object. The record physically pulled by hand, pressing the machine's stamper on to the hot vinyl and then watching it splurge out of the edges as the metal imprints the silver microscopic valleys of sound, the physical tracks held within. It is an amazing process. The indentations on the record stampers are actually grown on the cut groove of acetate wax by electro-static plating. A process similar to getting knives, forks, cheap jewellery and motorcycle parts plated. These DIY dub records arrive on our shores in heavy cardboard covers that house thick slabs of vinyl. The plastic is often pockmarked and the labels slightly off centre. Paul Simpson even has one with a piece of straw fused into the runout groove; it still plays the music, so who cares? The rough nature of these pressings adds to the charm, in the same way a Robert Rauschenberg piece or early Dada movement collage was constructed with unrefined and tatty elements; this adds tremendously to the reality of the pieces. My mind is musing about all this. I could go over to Kingston and get my record pressed in the same way. It would be a one-off work of art.

It soon dawns on me that this is an impossible thing for me to do. I can't afford a fare to Jamaica Street, Liverpool, never mind the Caribbean. Back to the drawing board.

Then it hits me: I could make cassettes. That would be OK. I could make the cover and record the tracks and then give them away to people I think might like them. I set about recording tunes that are way too out there for the Bunnymen. I limit it to seven cassettes, all with slightly different content and different covers, of course. The music is heavily influenced by the Residents, Brian Eno, Tangerine Dream and my silent partner, the decrepit industrial landscape I travel through on the way to work on the train from Kirkby station. Yes, I'm a big boy now and the fear of skins has subsided; the short walk to Kirkby station holds little threat any more. I call this series of recordings *Weird as Fish*. I want it to achieve legendary status: the ultimate rarity for any collector.

At Chicago Buildings, Bill is getting more offers of gigs. Even Granada TV have been on the phone. They have a spot at the end of the north-west's news show *Granada Reports*. We are to be on the local cultural news section of the show called 'What's On?' They want us to play the single 'The Pictures on My Wall'.

Back at my house, I have to get this drum machine thing working properly. It strikes me that it would be good if the drum machine could be going before I count everyone in. My inventor's mind kicks in: I have a plan. Out comes the soldering iron, an old footswitch and some guitar cables. I attempt to create a way of routing the signal through my hi-fi amp. This way I can listen to the beat as it plays via a set of headphones. Only I will be able to hear the drum machine's heartbeat pulsing in my ears. I can send the signal to the input of the PA after I have counted in Les and Macul. One, two, three, four, then clunk! I would stomp down my boot on to the pedal. This would release the signal to the mixer. It seems to work OK, and I'm set to try it out at the next gig: Granada Studios.

In this next section the names have been changed to protect the innocent, namely me.

One of the people working on the show is an attractive but scary and loud peroxide-blonde Scouse woman that we have often seen at Eric's. Now it all gets a little tricky. I want to tell the story but don't want to piss off anyone so let's call her Miss Zerox. She has a band, let's call them Zerox the Fox. They are into the same kind of theatrical shite that Toyah Wilcox or Hazel O'Connor were into. You know the sort of thing, all flanged guitars, operatic howling, stupid sci-fi clothes and movements, crimped hair accomplishing gravity-defying structural integrity with the aid of buckets of Elnett. These bands are all well wide of the cool mark. Miss Zerox has recently put the fear of God up me.

Not long after the first few gigs, it seems that my reputation as being a good songwriter has been growing and we are the talk of the town. I'm in my dad's house when there's a knock on the door. I open the door to find Miss Zerox standing there. She pushes her way into the parlour. I am in shock, not knowing what the hell she is after. I have never talked to her at the club and we all think her band is a joke.

In a thick Scouse accent, she says, 'D'ya wanna write some songs with me?'

I am embarrassed and can't believe this is happening. *Shit! How am I going to get out of this?* I frantically think.

I am doing this whole band thing to be one of the cool kids. Having anything to do with Miss Zerox and her synth-rock pantomime would surely be the kiss of death. I'm scrabbling around for something to say, something to put her off. Oh God, I'm starting to really panic now. How the hell did she know where I live anyway?

I say, 'Nah, er . . . it's not my thing, er . . . we are too busy with the Bunnymen.' I'm saying anything now. 'And anyway, Macul wouldn't like it.' That is desperation talking right there.

She is standing in the room and I am sitting on a chair quaking in my winklepickers. Suddenly she flings her legs across my thighs and straddles me. Now I'm really scared. What the hell is she doing? I had a couple of snogging sessions at terrible parties back in the early seventies around my village, while girls moaned in the background for Motown records and we lads insisted on playing the full twenty-two minutes of 'Supper's Ready' by Peter Gabriel's Genesis. But that's about as far as any exploits into the sexual arena have gone for me. I'm petrified and shaking like a starlet in a Hollywood movie executive's hotel room as the door slowly clangs shut and the lights are dimmed. She sees my discomfort and is putting the pressure on even more.

Oh Jesus, have mercy on my soul.

She leans into my petrified face.

Oh shit. She's gonna attempt a kiss.

I am freaking out as she goes for the lips and I do the old 'turn my head just at the right moment' trick, like a kid trying to avoid the hairy-chinned advances of a cooing auntie. Not that this had ever happened in our family, but I'd seen this sort of thing on the telly. The kiss awkwardly touches base on the side of my face, smearing red lipstick across my mush, though you would hardly tell as my cheeks are blushing several shades brighter than her gob's waxy sheen. She sees the fear in my innocent and virginal green eyes. Thankfully, this look tells her this is not going to work out, so she decides to call it a day on this grotesque scene. She dismounts me like she's getting off a disappointing donkey ride on a grey day at the seaside. She looks at my face; I'm grinning with terror. Miss Zerox rather unhappily spits back at me:

'It's all right, lad. Don't worry, I'm not going to fuck ya.'

Like that was an option?

I am relieved but the message has not reached my heart yet and it's still pumping fear though my veins like a high-pressure hose. She heads for the front door; weirdly the taxi is still waiting as she trots her clicking kitten heels back to the cab. As she gets in, she turns and shouts back at me:

'If you change your mind, let me know won't ya, lad?'

I nod my beetroot-red face; I'm still in shock. This really was cherry on. I was only twenty and I had no experience of women at all. Tricky tackle, these feisty scouse birds.

The day comes for our TV appearance. We head down the East Lancashire Road to Granada Studios in the centre of Manchester. When we arrive, I am horrified to confirm my worst fears: Miss Zerox is one of the people working on the show. I am not ashamed to say I'm petrified of her. I spend the day making myself busy and trying to avoid her. I have nothing to fear now she is on the way up in the TV world.

In the Granada TV studio, the audience consists of wall-to-wall grannies getting nicely warm from the studio lights – I can't think of any other reason they would be there anyway. As the show closes, we are set to start the song. I am freaking out; 'Fear is the mind killer.' I think the pressure has got to me, and I mess up the intro. As I count the others in, my foot slips and misses the all-important footswitch to release the drum machine signal. We could carry on without drums, but I quickly decide we have to start again. I'm bellowing across the stage: 'Fucking hell! Hold it! Nothing's working!'

The headphones I am wearing are giving me that false perception of volume. I think I am quietly letting the cameraman know I have made a mistake, but I am in fact shouting it at the top of my voice all over the acoustically perfect confines of the studio.

'Stop! Stop! I've fucked the fucking thing up! Stop!'

The grannies in the audience are not too pleased and are tut-tutting and whispering about these awful scouser boys:

'It's that Sexy Pistols and that Bill Grundy filth all over again, Doris.'

Some are giggling; I want to be swallowed up by the floor. The show is recorded live, so this means no editing is done. The show is put together as it is flowing along and not long before it goes on air.

The floor manager is on the scene very quickly. Les and Macul are fuming and are well pissed off with me and my amateur-hour drum-machine problems. There are still a few sniggers from the audience and that isn't helping. It's all very embarrassing. The floor manager has got the videotape rewound and I get the go-ahead to start the song; this time I get it right. My face is bright red, and I am distraught. I slink back in the shadows; I'm looking down at my shoes and I have rarely looked up since. I can't wait for the song to be over.

The next day, after the pressure of Granada Studios, I'm glad to be back in Liverpool and at work in Binns. The single on Zoo is still in demand and the TV appearance was edited, so my fuck up is now history and has not harmed our march forward in any way.

Around this time, we did an interview with *Sounds* magazine. For some fevered reason, I thought it would be a good idea to cut my fringe the night before. I was quite used to cutting my own hair; this was a sort of punk thing to do at the time. It was a random hack rather than a Vidal Sassoon precision operation. Not all of us could afford the up-and-coming trend of unisex hair salons that were popping up all over the city, though at the birth of punk I did go to the Melling barbershop one time with a picture of Paul Simonon from the Clash and say to the barber, 'I want it like that, please.'

'What's that, lad?' he chuckled. 'No, you want a short back and sides, kid, or a feather cut, our kid,' he said.

It took a bit of persuading for the Melling barber to head out of his comfort zone and get experimental.

'It's basically a slightly longer haircut than the one the skin-heads have,' I explained.

So, with a shrug of his dandruff-covered shoulders, he gave it a go. The resulting haircut was not too bad. It was even quite spiky for a few days until the relentless heavy growth of my fringe was too substantial. I tracked down the ancient industrial-strength hairspray my mum had abandoned to the darkest reaches of her dressing table, all those years ago. The punky spike doesn't last long and it's soon history. In the next year or so, I decide to head down the sixties bowl-haircut route. If it is good enough for Brian Jones (my favourite Stone), several of the Byrds and Sky Saxon, it's good enough for me.

Soon the fringe was flopping in front of my eyes and it was starting to annoy me but it also gave me cover while on stage. It was like I was not really there. I felt like I was looking on, sort of peeping through a curtain. This new high-chopped fringe was very successful in keeping my hair out of my eyes but, as for looking cool, not so successful. I was self-conscious enough as it was without making myself look like the village idiot. My far from precise hacking attempt at a fringe only gave me a medi-eval appearance. For some reason this look had never caught on. Not since Hieronymus Bosch was a lad, anyway.

I had to roll with the punches. With my leather jacket on, I accepted that I looked like a feudal Ramone, and headed off for the *Sounds* photoshoot. This took place at the bandstand at

Newsham Park, just outside our practice place in Yorkie's basement. By the way, we always called it practice back then, and not rehearsals. We all awkwardly posed for a few pics. I love a bandstand and have often thought of doing low-fi gigs on bandstands around the country. Turn up with a generator and a few bits of gear, play and see what happens.

When the piece came out, dodgy haircut and piss-taking from Macul and Les aside, it was great seeing myself in the music press, even if it was *Sounds*, the second coolest of the three papers. *NME* was top of the cool tree, *Sounds* was second and *Melody Maker* came third. But to be in any of them was a thrill, and we would read them over and over again. It really made me believe we were the centre of the musical universe.

Our first appearance in the music press (*Sounds*).

Bill and Dave at the Zoo office have had a call from a couple of arty girls from Manchester. They have asked us to do a gig at a night they are starting called 'Tingle Tangle', from the German word *Tingeltangel*, meaning sideshow or cheap cabaret. Edvard

Munch, the grumpy Norwegian painter most famous for *The Scream*, depicted a seedy *Tingeltangel*. A dancing girl in a red dress kicks up her leg in a can-can move and flashes her knickers, while some old bald dudes cop an eyeful. It's a far cry from the neurotic anxiety of *The Scream*, but even Munch had to have a little fun sometimes down at the boozer.

Because 'The Pictures on My Wall' had been received so well, Dave and Bill asked us to be the band's managers. It seemed to make sense, so we said yes. They were already managing the Teardrop Explodes, though the management role fell on Bill's shoulders more than Dave's as he had become a full-time keyboard player of the Teardrops. After Peel had played the record, we were getting a lot more interest from venues and promoters. We never sought this out; one good thing just led to another good thing. Good stuff just started to materialise.

Les had recently invested £350 of his own cash in a 1968 Ford Transit van to transport the band about. By doing this, Les, it must be recognised, helped set us apart from the rest of the bands. We were able to travel anywhere and all we needed was fuel for the van. Les would pick us up and ferry us around. His part in the rise of the band was crucial, not least that he is a brilliant bass player but one with a van . . . that's rock 'n' roll gold dust. As we never had any money, getting to gigs would have been difficult or out of the question.

We set off the thirty miles down the East Lancashire Road to the Tingle Tangle gig in Manchester along with several label mates from Zoo – Paul Simpson, Julian Cope, Bill and Dave – and one of our mates from Eric's, Bernie Connor. Bernie wears a pork-pie hat and an army-style parka complete with the Who logo daubed in emulsion paint on the back. He has recently become a mod, but we don't hold that against him. The mod revival is just starting to gain traction with the Jam at the forefront. The van has no seats in the back and Les has nicked a few of his mum's sun loungers and deckchairs, which causes lots of jollity as these seats tip and sway on all the corners. I opt for the front seat as co-pilot.

There was no way I was going in the back. I would have vomited all the way down the M62 if I had been tossed around. I never was a very good passenger and was often throwing up on journeys as a kid. One particular time when I was in the scout group (1st Melling 34th Ormskirk), we were all bundled into the cargo area of an open-back removals lorry. I vomited all the eighty miles to Grasmere in the Lake District. If foolish car drivers got too close, they were being rewarded with my puke all over their bonnets.

Because of these past exploits, I cement my place as riding shotgun next to Les, often with the *A–Z* map in my hands trying to navigate the city centres, while holding back the spew that's beginning to bubble up from my guts.

The Tingle Tangle show is in the basement of an Italian restaurant called Gaetano's. Like all cool underground scenes, it's off the beaten track. The entrance is down a grubby street at the back of Oxford Road. We get the equipment out of the van in a typically rainy Manchester.

As the licensing laws only allow alcohol to be served with food, part of the ticket price weirdly includes a delicious plate of pallid sausage and chips. The pale fleshy sheen of the anaemic porky fingers does not put us off and all in the club scoff them down with gusto.

We have opened the doors early and the first band on are a local group, the Beat Silhouettes. The set is very short. We still have a couple of hours to wait until our time to flip the drum machine's switch and kick off. Bill and Paul Simpson quickly decide to step up to have a kind of jam. Paul uses Les's newly bought Fender Mustang bass. The factory paint job is finished with some funny go-faster stripes that cut across the guitar's paintwork like it's a sports car or a pair of trainers. This guitar is another nod to the high esteem in which Les holds Talking Heads bass player Tina Weymouth, who also plays the short-scale Fender Mustang bass. Bill is playing his own Gibson 330. Macul has been borrowing this guitar and will also be using it for our set a little later. But now it's time for the first and last performance of Danger Quentin, There's a Dog Behind You. No worse a name than Echo and the Bunnymen, I suppose.

This gets reviewed by *Sounds* as . . . 'a few minutes of lunacy'.

The sausage and chips go down a lot better.

When it comes to our set, the gig goes pretty well. There are the usual drum-machine problems. When it is working, the headphone system is OK except for the fact that once the band has started, I can't hear anything other than the drum machine blasting through my ears. This rhythmic racket blocks out the rest of the band. Bill sees I'm struggling and steps up after the song starts, removes the headphones and rests them around my neck. This becomes his main duty for the rest of the night: he is on standby to remove the headphones after every count in. This system might still need a little work.

Our next gig is about a week later. We are back at Eric's, supporting our heroes, the Fall. We get on well with them; they are a friendly bunch, even Mark E. Smith, who calls everyone 'Cocker'. Easier than remembering all our names, I suppose. They are well aware that we come to see them on occasion and appreciate our loyalty. We are hanging around during the soundcheck and Mark E. haunts the stage.

'Yeah! Yeah! Industrial Estate!'

Martin Bamah slices out wafer-thin shrill tones from his Stratocaster. We sit in the back of the club, shrouded in shadows, and watch in reverence.

The gigs are getting offered quite regularly now. We head across England on the M62 towards the east and into Yorkshire. We continue to Leeds to a venue called the F Club. I think the F stands for Fan. We are supporting the Tourists, Annie Lennox and Dave Stewart's band. We are not fans and see them as old farts. They seem to be much too competent for our liking and still use the rock clichés we hate, but it's a gig and Bill knows we need to do gigs to get more confident.

When we arrive, a Mini is blocking the load-in entrance. We are unable to get our equipment in. Shit! We are already running late as we had to wait for Macul to wash his hair. It is possible to bounce a small car like a Mini out of the way, even when the handbrake is on. We all gather around. By lifting in unison and dropping the car, we can shift the car. We bounce it down the road and re-park it well out of the way of the load in.

After the Tourists have done their soundcheck, Annie Lennox leaves to get her car. Yes, you've guessed it: it's the Mini we have dragged down the road. She comes storming back in, screaming at us. 'What the hell? Who has been moving my fucking car?' I think she believes it was us because of the popular myth that all scousers are all well versed in the dark art of car thievery. This defamation is proliferated by the press and is utter bollocks. We have no more thieves than anywhere else.

A screaming argument ensues between us and the Tourists. We are not about to tell her we bounced the car down the road. The gig atmosphere is conclusively ruined. We do our short set and can't wait to get out of there. Scottish women can be scary at the best of times but Annie Lennox in full kill-the-Sassenachs mode is best avoided.

After the gig, we remove our equipment from the stage and Les goes to get the van. He is ages and we are starting to worry: where the hell is he? Eventually, he returns with the news: some arsehole has nicked his van. Is this karma? Luckily all our equipment is still in the club, but our plan to get the fuck out of there as quick as we can has been scuppered and we have to stick around. With no dressing room, we have to watch the sodding Tourists do their set; we really are getting punished now. The vibe is toxic between our gang and the Tourists. We get a lift home with the PA company. It's been an eventful gig.

Cops find the van a few days later. Les gets it back and we are back on the road. We return to the M62. This time we have a gig in York. (Oddly, I can't find this on any of those online lists that people with too much time on their hands do so idiot musicians like me can pretend we have a good memory.) We are booked as the main band at this weird little café/tearoom kind of deal. The place has a very dark wooden Victorian village hall feel about it. When we turn up, a local band that is supposed to be supporting us turns out to be a gang of skinheads called Cyanide. I'm not sure exactly what has happened, but we are now supporting Cyanide. I think some threat of being battered might have smoothed the way for this change of billing.

We have recently acquired a small cymbal and a stand from somewhere. At this gig in front of Cyanide's skinhead fans, Macul has to play this cymbal on 'Stars Are Stars'. At a given point, we drop out and let a chord ring. This leaves a hole in the sound that Les fills with two harmonic notes on the bass. It's all to try and make the constant tick-tock of the drum machine a little more interesting and it works – sort of – although I'm not sure whether the skinheads agree.

We knew the limitations of the drum machine. Such devices were not as sophisticated as they are now – they are infinitely programmable with thousands of sounds and styles – and the Mini Pops Junior was very primitive. It was already becoming a bit of a pain to keep the rhythm interesting, with no way to add fills or builds in the construction of our music.

I find it hard to believe now that Macul would agree to play the cymbal, but there you go, it happened. Well, at least for a few of these early gigs anyway.

Our next gig is in Manchester at the Russell Club, also temporarily called the Factory. The Fall has asked us to support them. The set goes down pretty well and we are pleased with ourselves. We head over to the bar. John Peel is there; he is a big Fall fan too and we chat to him a little. Macul's topic is Liverpool Football Club, and Peel is a well-known LFC supporter.

Our schmoozing seemed to keep us on his mind. Very soon after, John Walters, the John Peel show's producer, got on the blower to Bill at the Zoo office. He asked us to do a Peel session.

It's hard now to express how important Peel sessions were at the time. Listening to his show was as much a part of punk as Johnny Rotten sneering at you down the lens of a TV camera – when he was allowed on the telly, that is. Invitations to do a Peel session at Maida Vale Studios in north London were much coveted. We didn't just listen to the Peel show. We recorded them on cassettes and played them over and over in the van. Everyone would be talking about his show.

'Hey Will, did you hear the Slits on Peel last night?'

'Yes, great wasn't it? I recorded it from my tranny.'

'God, did you hear Wire last week? Brill.'

It's 2 August 1979. The next gig will prove to be the most important gig of our careers. It is a kind of indoor festival in the YMCA near London's Tottenham Court Road. The venue is a huge underground room that goes by the rather snazzy title of the Prince of Wales Conference Centre. It sounds nice and is nice. It has the look of an underground car park more than anything else. Pillars are dotted about; the sound in the room is crisp and the carpeted floor soaks up any extraneous echoes that would usually be flying around in a concrete box such as this. This is easily our biggest gig so far and I am more than a little nervous.

The bill consists of us and the Teardrops from Liverpool and Joy Division from Manchester. Top of the bill is Essential Logic, a new band formed by the sax player of X-Ray Spex. They are a little too jazz-rock tinged for us and do all that high-pitched, squeaky saxophone crap, stuff that is only good for dislodging earwax from lugholes or annoying dogs. In my view, Joy Division should be the headline act.

Outside, the brutalist skin of the YMCA building sours into the London sky. The August evening sunshine bathes the city's hubbub with golden light, sending beams glinting off the shiny, beetle-like shells of black taxi cabs as they stand frustrated and motionless in traffic. Vans, delivery trucks and the omnipresent red Routemaster buses are on parade. All are lined up the length of Tottenham Court Road.

On the pavement, there is a figure ambling through the throngs of people making their way home after work. It is the great record executive from New York's Sire Records, Seymour Stein, who happens to be visiting the UK branch of his label in Covent Garden. Sire's man over here is Paul McNally. Paul has played him our single. Seymour has worked in the record business for donkey's years and has an ear for a good tune and an eye for an interesting band. His label Sire Records is one of the coolest on the planet, with the Ramones and Talking Heads on the roster.

This New Yorker always seems to be in the right place at the right time, and the fates are seeking us out again. As we are setting up our gear on the inside, a matter of yards away on the outside, trotting down the Tottenham Court Road, Seymour's eye is drawn to a poster in the window of the YMCA: Final Solution presents new bands from Liverpool and Manchester at the YMCA.

That night at the YMCA, we are the first on the bill. I don my Telecaster and headphones, Les quick as a flash straps on his Mustang bass. Macul approaches the microphone and shyly speaks, 'We are the Bunnymen, as you obviously know.'

Seymour is stood among the crowd at the back. To him, we

are an unknown quantity. He may have heard our single but other than that he knows nothing.

We are just about to kick off when Macul says, 'Hang on. I haven't got a plec.' He means plectrum.

I pass him one of mine and say, 'Oh, 'ere yar are.' I then asked Les if he is ready. He gives me a nod and says, 'Yes.'

The drum machine is switched on. In my headphones, the steady pulse of the beat starts. This is it, no turning back now. I begin to count in: 'One, two, three, four' and stomp the home-made footswitch on the next beat; to my relief, it works perfectly. We open with a new instrumental track that I've had kicking around for a while. I think Les came up with the title of 'Mister' – I have no idea why. Just like God, Les works in mysterious ways.

'Mister' never gets any further than a few runouts at these early gigs. It's considered as filler for our short set and we never take this song seriously (though now I listen to the tape of the gig, I think we must have spent quite a bit of time on the arrangement). No demo is ever made of the song and it vanishes over time.

Next is 'Going Up', followed by 'Read It in Books' then on to 'Stars Are Stars'. Macul is a virtuoso on the occasional cymbal.

At the end of the song, he asks sardonically, 'Did that move you at all?'

The set is flying by very fast now. On we go through to 'Monkeys'. The next song, another new one (they're all new ones, you knob), is 'All That Jazz'. Someone takes a wrong turn on the song. I know it wasn't me, but I'm pointing no fingers. On the stage, the morbid fear is rising through my veins again. As the track goes on, it gets very shambolic. We are looking at each other for help but there is no cavalry coming. The drum machine blindly stomps along, clacking its way against our disorientated detour from the arrangement. We muddle through, and eventually reach the end and kill the last chord. Glad that one is over. The wall-to-wall London hipsters do not seem to notice and it's quickly on to the next song, 'The Pictures on My Wall'. This gets a slight ripple of recognition through the crowd and goes off without a hitch. On to 'Do It Clean', with the riff I had recently played down the phone to Macul. This will develop over the years and become one of the staples of our live shows throughout the eighties. Then it's the rather psychedelic 'Happy Death Men'. We finish on 'Villiers Terrace'. A quick 'thank you' from Macul and that's it: all over in thirty minutes.

At the back of the auditorium, Seymour is struck by the songs and is transfixed by Macul's stage presence. He seeks out our management and has a word with Bill. Why Seymour decided on a whim to answer a rather vague poster's call and come on that day is a mystery. His band radar must have pinged and brought him to us.

After we get our gear safely stashed away, ready for the load out, we head out front to watch the Teardrop Explodes. They are on next but the band we are all waiting for is Joy Division. They are still fairly unknown at this stage; the level of fanatical cult worship has yet to materialise. The Teardrops join us and we are all standing together as the sensory assault of the Joy Div – as we are now calling them – begins. As always, they are transfixing. At the end, we all leave the gig with the comforting squeal of tinnitus rattling around our brains.

When we meet up with Bill later, he tells us, 'The bloke

from Sire Records was here, and he wants to sign you.' He looks at us slightly forlornly. 'There is only one catch.'

We all look at each other. Here we go. 'Go on then, what is it?'

'He will only sign you if you get a drummer.'

I think Bill is a little worried that we will tell him to fuck off. He has come to learn how awkward and precious we can be, especially me. He probably thinks I'm going to say something like: *We love the drum machine. We don't want a fucking drummer.*

We already know that the drum machine is limiting our growth. There are only so many times you can use the same beats. Plus, the muddle up in the middle of 'All That Jazz' could have been a lot less painful with a human to lead us back on to the righteous path. Drum rolls, subtle skips and fills along with cymbal crashes are all there to signal the changes in direction of the song. Real drums would definitely have helped us get back on track and we may never have got lost in the first place.

'That's great, we want a drummer anyway,' we all say with beaming smiles.

Yet again, we are in the right place at the right time. And more importantly, so is Seymour Stein.

After the gig, the van is loaded up and we head back to the M1. After the obligatory stop at Cannock truck-stop services for a late night fry up, Joy Division start to pass us in their much faster van. Les's pride and joy Transit is trying to keep level but can only muster fifty miles per hour under full steam. These future legends are riding in some luxury; they even have seats in their Transit and are reaching a mind-bending sixty miles per hour. Much flicking of V signs and honking horns are exchanged as they rocket past. We shout out, 'Wankers, tossers, Manc bastards' and various other terms of endearment.

As the two hundred miles are slurped up by the van's diesel chug, I am snoozing in the front of the van. I keep waking up and suddenly remembering what Bill told us a few hours earlier.

And I'm thinking, *Jesus Christ, Sire Records? That is ridiculous!*

Les's trusty van.

25.

Deckchairs Down the M1

'When I Live My Dream' – David Bowie

Just two weeks after the news that Sire Records wanted to sign us, we are on another exciting mission. The deckchairs are back in Les's van and we are off back down the motorway, this time to record the John Peel session.

'Peely', as we had started to call him, was ahead of the wave and indeed was often creating the wave that all of us post-punks were riding the crest of. He was always there at the coal face of the underground, championing all the latest subculture bands and the do-it-yourself attitude that came with them. The big labels were shitting themselves; the old school was now out. Peel was an important part of the picture for us if we were to be seen as – that all-important word favoured by the music press – 'relevant'. This was the aim of most bands, at least at the start: to be relevant. It's an ambiguous way of saying hip, that's all.

All the bands we had any time for had recorded a session for Peely. Peely was a pivotal part of the whole rise of punk, which is quite odd in itself as he was from the era before punk: a child of the sixties and no stranger to the brushed denim flared trouser, tie-dyed grandad vest and long hair. Somehow Peel managed to transcend this background of hippiedom; after all, he did tend to like the more esoteric bands from the sixties and seventies. He was an early fan of Tyrannosaurus Rex and Marc Bolan's hairy-fairy, flower-power folk. Syd's Pink Floyd had been on the show in 1967. The Edgar Broughton Band, Captain Beefheart . . . Peel was always ready to accept new and exciting scenes. Punk and all the related sub-genres were no exception. He just knew what was cool and would be cool forever.

On the long and boring trip down south, Les and I try to relieve the boredom by playing a game to see who could spot the most Michelin Men or Bibendum ornaments. The plastic symbols for Michelin tyres are bolted to the cabs of many of the trucks that thunder past us as we languish in the slow lane, barely reaching fifty miles an hour. We have a couple of piss stops and the odd sausage roll or cheese sandwich in our bellies. In our ears, filtering through the relentless growl of the Perkins diesel engine just beyond the van's bulkhead, a tinny cassette-taped soundtrack of very early Bowie, John Peel shows, the Doors back catalogue and *Marquee Moon* from Television help us on our way. Eventually, we approach the outskirts of London. We chug past the landmark pub, the Swiss Cottage.

It won't be long now, we are all thinking.

The excitement level peaks as we see the bustle of London before us, then it falls quite quickly as we join the congested London traffic. We are now crawling along, stopping at every red light and every pedestrian crossing, getting cut up constantly by white van drivers and taxis. This last section of the trip takes almost as much time as the two hundred miles we have just done down the motorway. Eventually, we turn on to Delaware Road and pull up outside the front door of Maida Vale Studios.

We make it inside and are met at reception by a uniformed security man. His kit is pristine even down to his shiny-peaked cap and boots. My post-punk uniform is not in any way pristine. It is comprised of a charity-shop crumpled shirt and pre-war grey jacket complete with pre-war dandruff-encrusted collar. This garment had never seen a dry cleaner. I'm not even sure such a thing as dry cleaning was invented when this thing was stitched together. Les is a bit neater, with white sixties-style trousers. He looks like a Jet and, as we all know, when you're a Jet, you're a Jet all the way, according to the opening lyrics of the classic musical *West Side Story*.

Les was basing his look on the Jets' white slacks, striped colourful casual shirts, suede desert boots or white sneakers. We loved *West Side Story* and Les had been known to get taken over by the exuberance of the Jets he was channelling with his look. While singing 'The Jets are in gear', he would run up the wall of the girls' toilets in Eric's and bounce off it. It would have been sheer folly to perform such acrobatics in the lads' bogs as the floor was always an inch deep in piss. Piss, white slacks and desert wellies don't make for a happy marriage, I'm sure you realise.

Macul is in his checked lumberjack shirt and shiny suit pants. The razor-sharp crease is still intact, so I'm assuming they must be of the Sta Prest variety. I don't think ironing is Macul's strength. Showing his white socks, the bottoms of the pants hover a couple of inches above his transparent plastic sandals. With his floppy mop of hair to top it off, it's a convincing look for a post-punk hero in waiting.

The BBC at Maida Vale has that comforting long-established vibe; its influential recordings reach all the way back to the dance band days of the thirties. I imagine that the engineers in

the studios are still wearing lab coats, like scientists experimenting in the concept of popular music, several pens in the top
pockets, with a shirt and tie neatly in place, a clipboard at the
ready. The walls are thickly painted in a wartime shade of BBC
grey. Originally built as a roller-skating palace and club, it had
been converted into studios in the 1930s. Inside the studio
complex, there is a maze of corridors. Hardwood floors lead to
thick doors that open on to hanger-size studio rooms. Some are
big enough for the largest orchestras. We are bringing the equipment in, stacked high on BBC trolleys. We inevitably get lost in
the passageways. The distant sound of Mozart manages to escape
the leaky 'soundproof' doors. From another studio seeps some
jazz band. They are rehearsing and the effervescent fizz of a
saxophone wafts in the air, notes of faded mumble just recognis-
able as music. We carry on up the corridor. We are greeted by
more muffled sounds of the easy-listening programme *Sing
Something Simple*.

This BBC Radio 2 show was a Sunday evening staple all
through my youth growing up in Melling. I associate this close
harmonic vocal sound with depression and dark times but also
with the cosy and slightly dusty nostalgic pleasure of hiding
away in a den made of seat cushions and army blankets as the
harmonies wafted out of the transistor radio and around the
house. I can vividly remember it being dark very early so it must
have been deepest winter, my mum getting the Sunday tea ready
in the tiny kitchen. Sunday tea was usually a salad of some sort;
tinned sardines were a regular component. And now, by some
fickle finger of fate, I am wandering around the polished,
parquet-floored studios where those Sunday night sounds had
originally emanated from. A lot of the songs were accompanied

by the slow breathy rasp of a French accordion. This sound still fills me with a weird mix of comfort and dread.

As we go further into the BBC labyrinth, we pass a room with an embossed black plate screwed to the heavy door. It reads the BBC Radiophonic Workshop. Wow! The mysterious Radiophonic Workshop. This is the BBC's legendary department dedicated to experimental soundtrack work. These sonic boffins are part of the shadowy world of the BBC. Behind these doors in 1963, the experimental pinup girl Delia Derbyshire had manipulated magnetic tape in this room and realised the *Doctor Who* theme tune by bashing a lampshade, slowing down the tape to tune the emanating pings, then splicing the thing in order and, Bob's your uncle, space rock! Her name is known now, but back then she was just part of the team.

Les and I can't resist a nose; we try the door. It is unlocked. We slowly open it and take a look into the very small studio. We are peeking into a room full of shelves; heavy benches are stacked with sound equipment, walls are clad in perforated hardboard, painted white and clinical. It strikes me this really is a workshop; the equipment is almost military in appearance. We could be in a secret listening station, ready to tune into the coded messages emanating from Soviet Russia. Electronic equipment with many dials and switches is housed in vented metal boxes. There are slatted grills there to let the heat escape out of the burning hot valves. Sound generators that look more like lab apparatus are stacked and patched with cables. There is a collection of very hefty, lumbering tape recorders, warmly analogue and clunky, with shiny Bakelite knobs. This gear was built to last in the satisfying way things used to be. There is not that much in the way of musical instruments evident in the room, just the odd keyboard and a plastic box of percussive bits and bobs most studios have. It is fascinating, however, to see the special little studio where these experiments in sound have taken place. I am a big sci-fi fan and the legendary Radiophonic Workshop has always been at the cutting edge of sci-fi soundscapes.

The studio we are heading for is MV4. I am half-expecting John Peel to be sitting in the control room; he isn't. The sessions are recorded on to one-inch-wide magnetic tape reels; this gives us sixteen tracks to play with. It is more than enough. It will be quickly mixed down and then played back on Peely's show. Ours is due for broadcast on 22 August 1979, just a week later. We have a designated producer. He aims to finish the session as soon as possible, hopefully by 8 p.m. and then the team can get down to the local pub, the Warwick Castle, just around the corner. Everything is done efficiently: quickly the engineer sets up the microphones. He's used to working this way and knows the positions of the mics for optimal sound. We set off and do a few takes of each of the tracks and pick the best of the bunch, then move on to the next song. This way we get down the backing tracks of four songs: 'Read It in Books', 'Stars Are Stars,' 'I Bagsy Yours' (aka 'Monkeys') and 'Villiers Terrace'.

We break for our dinner and head up in the lift to the BBC canteen. We are amazed at how cheap the food is. It's subsidised by the BBC; a few pence will buy you a fairly decent pie and chips. We are scoffing ourselves stupid before we head back to the studio. A few guitar overdubs and I play an amateur-hour two-finger piano riff on 'Villiers Terrace'. It all gets done and dusted with not much time to refine the sound. Next, we get to the vocals. After a few takes the producer, Trevor Dann, takes Macul to one side and says in effect: 'Don't give up your day job.'

Mr Dann is delusionary. As if Macul is ever going to have a day job; it's a full-time post keeping his hair in order. (Macul still mentions Mr Dann's advice to this day, whenever the opportunity arises.) We finish the session before the boozers are closed and this makes the engineers very happy. As they head off to the pub, we load up and head back down the motorway. We arrive in Liverpool very early in the morning; there is no time for sleep. I have to be at work. In the morning, off I go to sleepily fry eggs and bacon for the morning crowd of shoppers.

Ten days later, we are off to the Chester Art Centre to do a gig with our mates, the Teardrop Explodes. We have a laugh getting there; everyone has piled into the van and fought for the deckchairs donated by Les's mum. Julian and Gary and the other Teardrops are sat back in the canvas seats pretending to be fishing. They hold imaginary rods and cast the lines into an imaginary river as we fly past, high on the banks overlooking the very real slow brown flow of the River Mersey. The water is so polluted that if you fell in – as some do on occasion, pissed up and wandering around the pier head – you would be rushed to Walton Hospital for stomach pumping after you were fished out. The last time a real fish had been seen in this goop, Adam was a lad.

We are looking down at Stanlow oil refinery's tall and thin chimney stacks, whiter than white steam billowing out of the stainless steel chimneys. The noxious gases invade the van's air vents with a sour chemical stench. It puts me in mind of Melling with the smells emanating from the BICC back in the sixties.

Paul and Macul watching The Teardrop Explodes soundcheck.

We press on and reach the old Roman town of Chester. We amble into the building and are taken aback. Some of the students involved with the Art Centre have painted a large, circular Zoo Records logo for the back of the stage, copying a badge that Bill and Dave got made. It looks fantastic and makes us feel like we are part of a movement. The gig goes off with the usual drum-machine hiccups and splutters but no major upsets – just the odd dirty look from Macul.

We are more resolved than ever that we need to get a drummer. This desire to become a four-piece is growing gig by gig now.

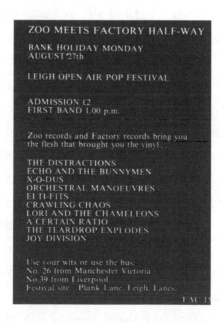

Our next gig is just two days later. It's a bank holiday weekend and we are to play on Monday. Months earlier, Tony
Wilson from Factory Records and Bill Drummond had been
conspiring to do an outdoor festival. Well, Tony Wilson had.
He called Bill up and suggested the idea: 'Bill, you bring your
bands and I'll bring mine.'

Tony had already booked the field, the PA and the staging, so
it was not like Bill had much of a choice or even reason to say
no. The field and the festival were to be called the Leigh Rock
Festival and held over the whole bank holiday weekend. Tony
Wilson had managed to hijack the bank holiday Monday to
showcase Factory Records. In typical Tony Wilson style, he had
made sure this Monday was the only day that mattered by giving
it a FAC number: FAC 15. (All Factory output, from posters to
Joy Division records to the Haçienda, was given a FAC number.)
To be fair, it was the only day that mattered.

Leigh is a small town roughly halfway between Liverpool and
Manchester along the busy A580 aka the East Lancashire Road.
They have called the event Zoo Meets Factory Halfway. All the
Factory bands and all the Zoo bands are to play on a piece of
National Coal Board waste ground, in between the coal mines,
slag heaps, odd bits of rubble, tyres and fly-tipped shite. This was
a glorious post-industrial wasteland and perfect for us post-
industrial bands. They had been expecting two thousand to pay
the £2 entrance fee. But it's a little out of the way, plus there's a
transport strike and, it being a bank holiday, not many buses are
flying up and down the East Lancashire Road. This has not
helped the situation. Not many kids have cars, so it might as well
be on the moon.

The site was lacking the usual festival facilities we are now accustomed to: holistic waffle houses, numerous bars, zen therapy zones, massage tents, legal highs and all manner of crap shops with all your overpriced festival needs. All this encased in a circle of ridiculously expensive glamping pods filled to the brim with upwardly mobile squares letting their hair down for a weekend. Plus, the obligatory twenty-four-hour rave tent to keep sleep away. This festival had a lone greasy-burger van manned by a lone greasy-burger bloke flipping paper-thin burgers to keep the freezing August weather at bay.

Coal was still a thing back then; all around this area were coalmines. The roads undulated with the bumps and dips of subsidence caused by the collapsing mine tunnels below. The brave miners were housed in the nearby villages of Tyldesley and Leigh. They still had an income, and the war with our new Glorious Leader Mrs Thatcher had yet to be declared.

Tony Wilson from Factory Records is hanging about with his flared trousers tucked into his rather naff, light-brown cowboy boots. His boys, Joy Division, are the headliners but the fame of this band is still yet to reach rabid proportions. We get through our set and settle down on the damp and scabby grass and gravel mix, along with about two hundred other grim northerners, to watch the other bands on the stage. Orchestral Manoeuvres in the Dark, last seen hopping around Eric's stage like an electro jack in the box, then it's the turn of Manchester's A Certain Ratio. They think it is a good idea to mix a devil-dark funk with the strange siren call of a WEM Copicat tape echo given free rein and left to get out of control. The feedback this delay unit generates is a squawking white-noise clatter and is really rather beautiful; another Manchester band are added to my list of faves. In fact, I am seen by the others to be so into the Manchester scene that Paul Simpson and a few of the gang christen me with a new nickname: 'Manchester'. It doesn't catch on and I remain Sarge or simply Will. (Not that I would have minded. The Manchester groups Buzzcocks, the Fall, Joy Division and A Certain Ratio are all on my list of all-time greats.)

The night brings the darkness slowly creeping over the landscape. Small groups of miners, black with coaldust, snap boxes still in hand, hop the barbed wire fence, a shortcut over the field as they head home. None of them stops for longer than a few seconds to look at the groups on the scaffolding stage. This is not a gate-crashing situation; their shift finished, food and a bath on the horizon. It's simply the quickest way home. The few primary-coloured flashing lights dotted about the stage are picked up now by the low mist that has arrived with the chill of twilight. The lights at our early afternoon set were only providing warmth. Now that it's dusk, the washes of light are much more prominent. This is not a Pink Floyd light show by any stretch of the imagination; but something about a lit stage in a dark field is still captivating.

The night air has a cold chill running through it now. The sparse punters have been raiding the edges of the field for old fenceposts, tyres, cardboard boxes, litter, hedgehogs and any other crap that will burn and provide a little warmth. Little fires are beginning to appear. It is a magical vision to see these small bonfires as Joy Division hit the stage.

Hooky is wearing a heavy overcoat slung over his shoulders. Stephen Morris's drums beat out the time for a few bars, then Hooky sweeps in low with thundering bass, as the tension builds into Bernard Sumner's incendiary guitar blasts. As the set continues, Ian Curtis is static at the mic, staring, distant and trance-like until suddenly some internal button is pushed and he flips his wig. Arms have become fleshy nunchaku flailing at unseen forces: he has launched into his trademark freaking out dance. Shivers collectively shoot up spines as fires twinkle in the damp night air.

I will never forget this. It is one of my favourite festivals. Yes, it was devoid of punters, and macrobiotic hummus, mindfulness tent, organic beer or stupid hats, but the atmosphere was magical.

Another week later and we are back down to London with the Teardrop Explodes in the Nashville Rooms, a large pub in Kensington. The week after we are in Gloucester; these are the final days of the drum machine spluttering its way through the gigs.

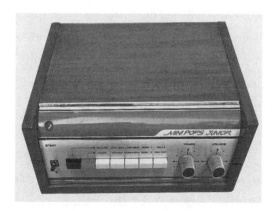

The next big event is the Leeds Futurama festival with a ton of other bands from the 'post-punk' scene. These include PiL, the Fall, Joy Division, OMD and shitloads of others. It is billed as the world's first science-fiction music festival, God knows why, other than some of the bands that are on the bill wish that they had been born as androids or genetically spliced up in a lab somewhere. Hawkwind is on the bill, so that could be construed as sort of sci-fi as they have the space-rock credentials and their LP covers generally involve some sort of spaceship.

The venue, the Queen's Hall in the heart of Leeds, is a cavernous cathedral. It is now a place of pilgrimage for the industrial post-punk generation. This building was once a tram shed; the floor has suggestions of old tramlines still embedded in the granite cobbles. Industrial ephemera are all around and it's perfect. All the trams are gone and now it's a freezing empty hangar, and completely unsuitable as a rock venue. Hard surfaces and a very high roof are perfect for causing any amplified sound to become a bouncing wash of incoherent reverb. This makes the whole business of playing to a beat almost impossible. The reflected music comes back at you in a confusing mess, sending you chasing the wrong beat. It is a nightmare and a mess. Our thirty-minute set is over in a blink of an eye (well, in thirty minutes if you want to be all technical about it). It's a relief. We make it back to the dressing room before the last bouncing beat of the set has finished reverberating off the brick walls. Les and I decide to go for a wander out front to have a look at the bands on offer. Nothing takes my fancy as all the bands that I like were on the previous day of this two-day event. We get lumbered with all the second division bands except for the Fall.

We are discussing finding a drummer in the Zoo office. Drummers are pretty hard to come by as everyone wants to be a guitarist or singer.

Dave Balfe says, 'My brother knows a drummer; he goes to school with him.'

Dave's younger brother Kiren attends some posh school called Downside, run by Benedictine monks, in Somerset.

The drummer is called Pete de Freitas. We all agree to give him a try. We have a couple of gigs at Eric's coming up in a few weeks with the Teardrop Explodes. Bill and Dave organise for Pete to come and see the Saturday gig, stay over and rehearse at Yorkie's basement the next day. This Eric's gig will be the last one we do with the drum machine.

In just under a year from our first step on to the stage at Eric's for our debut one-song gig, we have had two indie labels trying to sign us. We have had a single out on Zoo Records that was well-reviewed and given the accolade single of the week in all the music papers. We have been on the telly and had a song featured on the Liverpool *Street to Street* compilation album. We have been played by John Peel and recorded a session for him. We have been invited to several gigs with our heroes the Fall and been on the bill with some future legends.

Warner Brothers Music is making advances: they want to deal with our song publishing. For many bands, this sort of thing just doesn't happen; it's for most an uphill struggle, with demo tapes getting rejected and meeting after meeting with uninterested A & R departments. Even the Beatles were rejected many times until Parlophone took them on.

My naturally cynical nature hated that we have to get all these other people, outsiders, involved. I was young and rather stupid. It felt like they were intruding on our scene. I know now it was just another day at the office for them and if we had played too hard to get, they would simply have gone for the next band that came along. I know that to do anything and get anywhere we would need to have people like them on our side, but I never liked the idea of sharing what we had made; it was too precious to me. It felt like we were giving it away too easily. Bill Drummond told me that when he had mentioned to Tony Wilson that we were going to sign to Sire Records, he was dead against it and pleaded with Bill to try another way. He was keen to persuade Bill to go it alone, like he was doing with Joy Division and Factory Records.

Bill's attitude was, 'It's all right for you, Tony. You have a good job and a wage that can fund your label. We are all still on the dole and trying to get by on nothing.'

So, Bill and Dave had to get the big labels involved. This was never mentioned to me at the time or, as far as I'm aware, any of us. If I had known, I wonder if I would have tried to get Bill to stay indie. Indie was seen as very cool. It was a remnant of the homemade do-it-yourself attitude of punk, all stemming from the rejection of the big companies and the old way of doing things. It was a losing battle, of course, and a lot of it was just bullshit; the majors had it all sewn up, anyway. Some of the major labels even went to the extent of inventing imprints that they pretended were indie, just to appear cool to the fans. These imprints would be funded by them and would use their distribution networks to get the records into the shops.

So here we are. We could hardly play; we've done about ten gigs; the interest in the band is growing and we cannot stop it. The less effort we make to get a deal, the more deals are on the table. Great opportunities are being handed to us on a plate. If this keeps up, and we are not careful, there is a good chance we could turn into a gang of arrogant pricks.

Acknowledgements

I am especially grateful to Jennifer Otter Bickerdike for editing the book and for all her encouragement. Thank you to Les Pattinson, Ian McCulloch and Pete de Freitas for embarking on a stormy sea with no lifeboat.

Thanks for info, kind words and good vibes:

Doreen Allen, Dave Balfe, Dave Battersby, Billy Bessant, Tim Burgess, Pete Byrne, Andreas Campomar, William Corgan, Mark Davenport, Paul Davenport, Bill Drummond, Prof Colin Fallows, Jamie Farrell, Mick Finkler, Bobby Gillespie, Ian ('Peasy') Gordon, Terry Hall, Matthew Hamilton, Mick Houghton, Richard Hawley, Dave ('Noddy') Knowler, Courtney Love, Johnny Marr, Chris Martin, Dave ('Maz') Mazenko, Steve ('Maz') Mazenko, Ed O'Brien, David ('Yorkie') Palmer, Alan Roberts, Russ Sanders, Paul Simpson, Robert Smith, Kelley Stoltz, Chet Weise.

Will Sergeant

Will Sergeant is best known as the guitarist and founder of Echo and the Bunnymen. He has been the only constant member of the band.

Born in 1958, he grew up in the village of Melling in Lancashire on the outskirts of Liverpool. His initial pre-Bunnymen approach to the electric guitar included playing it with an electric shaver and his earliest experimental recordings were produced as a limited edition of seven in 1978. These early sonic experiments set the tone for his idiosyncratic approach to his instrument of choice and the ongoing development of a unique style which has earned him international acclaim as a guitarists' guitarist.

Throughout his career with Echo and the Bunnymen, he has also produced solo works as Glide and in 2013 formed Poltergeist with Les Pattinson to explore free-form extended compositions and improvisation. He has collaborated with Professor Colin Fallows on several international sound art projects since the 1980s. His work in the visual arts is informed by the view that the creation of art and music are parallel creative processes. In 2009, he began creating an ongoing series of paintings and suites of limited edition prints which have been exhibited and collected internationally.

A keen vinyl record collector, his eclectic musical influences are reflected in the programming of his occasional online radio series, Space Junk Radio, which features psychedelic music, the more adventurous bands born of the mid-1970s punk revolution, electronic music and experimental soundworks.

He is widowed with two grown-up children and lives in Lancashire where he enjoys nature, walking and motorcycling.

Photo Credits

Will Sergeant archive: ix, 4, 6, 9, 13, 15, 18, 22, 29, 34, 38, 55, 95, 99, 122, 129, 143, 157, 175, 215, 223, 243, 261, 273, 289, 293

Billy Bessant: 27

Kevin Luckett: 39

Dave Mazenko: 43

Archive PL/Alamy Stock Photo: 65

CBW/Alamy Stock Photo: 69

Michael Putland/Getty Images: 73 (Status Quo)

Records/Alamy Stock Photo: 73 (Slade)

CBW/Alamy Stock Photo: 479

Paul Simpson: 206

Mike Knowler: 212

Les Pattinson: 220, 227, 231, 258, 286, 312

Julie Marsh: 237

Mick Finkler: 246, 247, 279

Hammer Film Productions/Associated British Pathé/Ronald Grant Archive/Mary Evans: 282

Dave Eaton: 319, 320, 321

Greta Sergeant: 333